CHALLENGES FOR PHARMACEUTICAL POLICIES IN THE 21ST CENTURY

Proceedings from a workshop in Brussels, EIASM, January 18–19, 2001

PHARMACEUTICALS POLICY AND LAW

Pharmaceuticals Policy and Law

Volume 5

Earlier published in this series

Vol.1. J.L. Valverde and G. Fracchia (Eds), Focus on Pharmaceutical Research
Vol.2. J.L. Valverde (Ed), The Problem of Herbal Medicines Legal Status
Vol.3. J.L. Valverde (Ed), The European Regulation on Orphan Medicinal Products
Vol.4. J.L. Valverde (Ed), Information Society in Pharmaceuticals

Challenges for Pharmaceutical Policies in the 21st Century

Pharmaceuticals Policy and Law
Volume 5, 2002

Editor

Christine Huttin
EIASM, Brussels, Belgium

IOS Press
Ohmsha

Amsterdam • Washington, DC • Tokyo

ISBN 1 58603 287 9 (IOS Press)
ISBN 4 274 90551 9 C3047(Ohmsha)
Library of Congress Control Number: 2002113597

Publisher
IOS Press
Nieuwe Hemweg 6B
1013 BG Amsterdam
The Netherlands
fax: +31 20 620 3419
e-mail: order@iospress.nl

Distributor in the UK and Ireland
IOS Press/Lavis Marketing
73 Lime Walk
Headington
Oxford OX3 7AD
England
fax: +44 1865 75 0079

Distributor in the USA and Canada
IOS Press, Inc.
5795-G Burke Centre Parkway
Burke, VA 22015
USA
fax: +1 703 323 3668
e-mail: iosbooks@iospress.com

Distributor in Germany, Austria and Switzerland
IOS Press/LSL.de
Gerichtsweg 28
D-04103 Leipzig
Germany
fax: +49 341 995 4255

Distributor in Japan
Ohmsha, Ltd.
3-1 Kanda Nishiki-cho
Chiyoda-ku, Tokyo 101
Japan
fax: +81 3 3233 2426

Printed in the Netherlands

PHARMACEUTICALS POLICY AND LAW
Volume 5, 2002

CONTENTS

1. Introduction

Pharmaceuticals Policy and Law 5 (2002) 3–5
IOS Press

Challenges for pharmaceutical policies in the 21st century, proceedings from a workshop in Brussels, EIASM, January 18–19, 2001

Christine Huttin
EIASM, 13 Rue d'Egmont, 1000 Brussels, Belgium
Tel.: +32 2 511 91 16; Fax: +32 2 512 19 29; E-mail: huttinc@aol.com

1. Introduction

This special issue of the Journal Pharmaceuticals Policy and Law aims to present different contributions to a workshop held in Brussels in January 2001, on challenges for pharmaceutical policies in the 21st century. The central theme of the workshop was the impact of globalization, bringing together a representative set of academic researchers, policymakers, NGO[1] and industry stakeholders. Even if papers presented in this special issue do not address directly all the relevant issues, this selection helps to understand the complexity of interactions between the various stakeholders from different continents. The debate in Europe is sensitive, since most European health care systems are facing coming financing issues, with the growth of elderly (grey power) and "babyboomers" as representative elective force, increase of expensive medical technologies and enlargement towards central and Southern Europe, facing poverty, organised crime and high level of corruption in such a sector.

This workshop was the fifth of a series initiated in 1992 in collaboration with the European Institute for Advanced Studies in Management. The objective of such workshops is to bring together researchers and participants from industry and policy circles, interested in pharmaceutical policy and economics. It provides an interesting platform for researchers, industry and policymakers to canvas opinions and to reflect on the future of biopharmaceutical and life science. The first workshops addresses issues such as strategies for the pharmaceutical industry and patient interests, changing roles of public and private players, interfaces between European pharmaceutical policy, economics and corporate strategies, pharmaceutical and biotechnology innovation in the context of health care reforms (see www.eiasm.org/internationalproject/endep for more information on the previous workshops).

[1]NGO: Non Governmental Organizations.

At the beginning of the 21st century, numerous changes affect the pharmaceutical industry. The biological revolution provides more and more applications for medicines, raising legal, ethical, economic and marketing issues. It leads to vertiginous changes that are not addressed at the same pace by policymakers. In particular, pharmaceutical companies may launch 50 to 100 new drugs yearly, which is a 200 percent to 400 percent increase over the dozen new medications typically approved by the FDA [1]. It is foreseen that more knowledgeable patients and physicians might also increase their demand for new genetic-based drugs and diagnostics (e.g. gene testing is growing at a 20-percent [1]), by-passing the listed covered procedures and technologies from their insurance schemes. Moreover, new technologies such as nanotechnologies and pharmacogenomics will also provide continuous information on patients' health status, a revolution in drug diagnostic and delivery systems, and a trend towards customisation of medicines. Such a context of growth and patients needs or expectations lead governments to search for a large range of management strategies and policy tools that could help in particular to adjust drug budget management to uncertain and complex changes for medical coverage.

Another key challenge of the 21st century is the impact of the globalisation. This largely affects the all pharmaceutical and life science industry, through mergers and the emergence of biotech consolidators, changing the balance of key players in the field. Different business models emerge in the biopharmaceutical industry, with a large variety of players such as business tools companies supplying services to traditional stakeholders. Moreover, interconnections of players with the development of information technologies change the forms of knowledge management and may raise issues on accountability with regards to key strategic decisions, especially concerning Research and Development, approval and marketing issues of new drugs.

The Globalisation also seem to contribute to widen the gap, in terms of access to drugs, between developed and developing countries. Such impact already lead companies, governments and international organisations to take a number of initiatives such as decisions to cut HIV drug prices for African countries or Brazilian position to speed up manufacturing of generic drugs. The next paper from Juan Rovira entitled "pharmaceuticals, globalization and developing countries: recent development and challenges" provides some insights in some key issues for the interface between developing and developed countries, in particular North and South. Europeans have always promoted solidarity principles in their health care systems and this is especially reinforced with the strong leftwing parties in power in most western Europe. Such solidarity principle might therefore be discussed now, within a more global context, and this is in particular relevant in the area of pharmaceuticals and health care sectors.

The workshop was organised around four main themes: industry dynamics and company corporate policies, political approaches, pharmaceutical corporate marketing and distribution, demand for pharmaceuticals. Contrary to the four previous workshops, a roundtable was also organised during the workshop, aiming to raise some key issues and questions for setting a research agenda on globalisation and biopharmaceuticals. Such questions are already taken over by international organisations such as the World Bank, WHO or the United Nations; but the scope of these problems are such, that we hope this special issue may raise the awareness of more interested parties for searching solutions in the formulation of pharmaceutical policies facing growing conflicting objectives.

Reference

[1] C.R. Coile, Jr., Impact of the "New Science" of genomics, *Journal of Health Care Management* **46**(6) (November/December 2001), 365–368.

Pharmaceuticals Policy and Law 5 (2002) 7–10
IOS Press

Pharmaceuticals, globalization and developing countries: Recent developments and challenges

Joan Rovira

Developing countries face many problems in trying to ensure the accessibility of their populations to pharmaceuticals. The pharmaceutical market has traditionally been a global market. International organisations are trying to help developing countries in addressing the manifold problems posed by the need to make drugs accessible to developing countries' populations. In the following paragraphs the main problems and the most recent developments affecting that issue are reviewed and discussed.

1. The patent issue

R+D in new drugs is partly funded by the State through universities, research centres, and subsidies to industry. The pharmaceutical industry invests in R+D activities more closely related to the final product. Industry can recover its expenditure on R+D because the price of a (new) drug is usually higher that its marginal cost. This is possible due to patents, trademarks, subsidised administrative prices, etc. The increasing costs associated with the development of new drugs provides a strong incentive for innovators to sell their products world wide, so as to facilitate the recovery of the expenditure invested. For many years, the capacity to recover R+D costs in the sales made abroad was limited by the policies of less industrialised countries, that often provided limited or no patent protection at all to pharmaceutical innovations. These policies allowed national manufacturers to "free ride" the results of R+D, by taking advantage at no cost of the innovations developed elsewhere. Many countries did not offer any kind of patent protection to pharmaceutical products, or used to allow only process patent, a relatively weak type of IPR protection, which can be easily by-passed by manufacturers with a much lower investment than that borne by the innovator. National non research industries copied of course only successful innovations. With segmented markets and price control by many national regulators, innovative manufactures made some kind of price discrimination, which usually (but not always) meant charging higher prices in higher income countries. The result was that richer countries were paying a higher share of R+D. The TRIPS Agreement was the response of the research industry and of industrialised countries to that "free riding".

In April 1994 the Uruguay Round of the GATT (General Agreement on Tariffs and Trade) concluded after 10 years of negotiations; 123 countries signed the Trade Related Aspects of Intellectual Rights Including Trade in Counterfeit Goods (TRIPS), in Marrakech, Morocco, which became effective from January 1995. The Agreement was reinforced by the creation the same year of the WTO (World Trade Organisation), which included a TRIPS Board, responsible for administering the Agreement. The TRIPS Agreement (see Box 1, below) implied the generalisation of a minimum level of patent protection for pharmaceutical products, which included product patent. The TRIPS is not an international law in itself, but a set of agreed principles and rules that must be taken into account in the national IPR systems. Deadlines were established for all countries to set up or adjust their IPR systems in accordance with the TRIPS rules. Developing countries were allowed longer periods, up to 2006.

Globalisation of IPR tends to result in a single international price, due to the effect of parallel trade. But with a single price all parties loose, because there is a lower accessibility of poorer countries and individuals to drugs and there is also a lower total income for the industry, which may mean less R+D.

The TRIPS Agreement obviously reflected the interests of the multinational research industry and of the developed countries. Although some argued that it would also benefit the less developed countries by providing incentives to their industries to invest in R+D on their specific diseases, in fact, developing countries were generally aware that the likely impact on their industries would be a negative one, and that the prices, and consequently, the expenditure on drugs would rise for them. Developing countries accepted, however, TRIPS because it was a condition to join the global trade agreement, from which other benefits were expected. Moreover, some countries did probably not foresee the magnitude of the negative impact.

However, the negative effects of the TRIPS on the local industry and on pharmaceutical expenditures of developing countries became progressively apparent, while the expected trade benefits often did not seem to materialise. Some middle income countries, notably Brazil and South Africa, passed IPR legislation and adopted strategies based on an interpretation of the TRIPS agreement that conflicted with the interests and interpretations of the multinational research industry. The most debated issue is the capacity of the countries to grant compulsory licenses of patented drugs in case of public health emergencies. The conflict had world wide impact in the South African case, but there are other less known instances: in fact, some countries did not dare to make a full use to their advantage of the possibilities of the TRIPS for fear of reprisals or because of political pressures.

Solutions are not easy to agree and to implement. Differential pricing by multinational companies – e.g. a national price related to the country income – may be an appropriate theoretical solution, but it would require avoiding parallel trade, which is against the present trends towards international free trade. This approach may also be seen as an obstacle for developing countries to be able to develop their own industry. Allowing low income countries to grant compulsory licenses faces similar problems. And setting up large donation programs does not seem a sustainable option in the long term.

At the last meeting of the World Trade Organisation in Doha, a statement was issued that acknowledged the right of countries in making its own interpretation of what is a public health emergency, and of the consequent capacity to grant compulsory licenses. This statement has reinforced the position of developing countries, but a problem still remains in the case of countries that cannot effectively benefit from compulsory licensing because they do not have the industrial and technical capacity to locally manufacture the drugs they require. This issue must be addressed by the WTO in the near future.

However important they may be, the problems of accessibility of the poorer countries go beyond the issue of its contribution to R+D of existing drugs. Some of the remaining issues are briefly described below.

First, there is the problem of neglected diseases, that is, diseases which are very relevant in developing countries, but almost unknown in the developed world. In that case, the problem is the lack of a demand that leads an appropriate level of investment in R+D by for profit organisations.

Moreover, the cost of providing appropriate pharmaceutical treatments goes far beyond the availability and affordability of drugs, as the case of antiretroviral treatment has dramatically shown. Trained physicians, diagnostic and monitoring capacity, and other factors are essential for drugs to have their intended positive effects. Public health systems in developing countries are relatively weak, and around 80% of the cost of pharmaceuticals is directly paid by the patients.

Corruption and fraud are additional obstacles once drugs are available. They are responsible for drugs not reaching those in need at affordable prices. According to informal estimations of the share of counterfeited drugs in some African countries reach up to 50% of consumption.

The conflicts between industrial and health goals affects also national drug policies. Trying to develop a national industry may be a valid and legitimate goal, but it may also result in a drug supply of lower quality and at higher prices that those available in the international market.

Donations from the international community may ensure the accessibility to drugs that the countries would otherwise not be able to afford. However, financing the drug supply through donations does not ensure the sustainability of the programs and makes the countries dependent on the donors, which may impose their own priorities over those of the recipient countries. Moreover, donations are not delivered in appropriate conditions: inadequacy of donated drugs to country needs, too short or even past expiration dates, problems with drug information, like the language of the labelling and leaflets,

In conclusion, it seems evident that the problems of accessibility of a large part of the world population to safe and effective drugs go beyond the cost of the drugs. They require a global improvement of the economic situation of the countries, as well as a cultural and institutional development. It makes little sense to try to solve the drug accessibility issue if most basic needs – food, education, basic health care, etc. – are neglected.

BOX 1: Summary of the TRIPS Agreement

PARTS OF THE TRIPS AGREEMENT:

I. GENERAL MEASURES AND BASIC PRINCIPLES
II. STANDARDS PERTAINING TO THE EXISTENCE, SCOPE, AND EXERCISE OF INTELLECTUAL PROPERTY RIGHTS (IPR)
III. ENFORCEMENT OF NORMS FOR THE PROTECTION OF IPR
IV. APPROVAL AND MAINTENANCE OF IPR AND RELATED BETWEEN-PARTY PROCEDURES
V. CONFLICT PREVENTION AND RESOLUTION
VI. TEMPORARY AGREEMENTS
VII. INSTITUTIONAL ARRANGEMENTS. FINAL MEASURES

Matters covered by the TRIPS Agreement:

1. Copyright and related rights
2. Trademarks
3. Geographic indications
4. Industrial designs
5. Patents
6. Integrated circuit topographies
7. Confidentiality
8. Control of unfair competitive practices in licensing contracts

The TRIPS Agreement require

1. Patent protection for all susceptible areas (all fields of technology) provided they are new, involve an innovative step and are capable of industrial application.
2. Non discrimination based on place of invention
3. Non discrimination based on place of production
4. Minimum term of protection: 20 years
5. Reversal of burden of proof
6. Compulsory licensing allowed
7. Parallel trade

EXCLUSION CRITERIA FOR PATENTABILITY

1. Reasons of public and moral order (protection of life and environment)
2. Surgical, therapeutic, or diagnostic methods
3. Plants and animals (except for microorganisms) and essentially biological processes)

Pharmaceuticals Policy and Law 5 (2002) 11–24
IOS Press

The debate on the TRIPs Agreement and access to medicines in the WTO: Doha and beyond

Jean Charles Van Eeckhaute*
Administrator, DG Trade, European Commission

1. Introduction

Since its entry into force in 1995, the WTO Agreement on Trade-Related Intellectual Property Rights (hereinafter "the TRIPs Agreement") has been the subject of controversy. The main focus of this controversy has, without doubt, been the impact of its patent requirements on access to medicines, and in particular those needed to combat communicable diseases such as AIDS, tuberculosis or malaria in the developing world. Developing countries and non-governmental organisations had therefore criticised the TRIPs Agreement as being an obstacle to development and to the pursuit of public health policies. They had the impression that some TRIPs provisions such as those relating to the granting of compulsory licences were not sufficiently clear and constituted a hindrance to authorities when taking certain measures to protect public health.

The debate was highlighted in the widely publicised conflict between the pharmaceutical industry and the South African Government between 1998 and 2001. In this case, thirty nine pharmaceutical companies challenged the provisions of the Medicines and Related Substances Control Amendment Act with the South African High Court. This legislation, which aimed to balance patent protection against the need to provide medicines at an affordable price to South African patients, was challenged mainly on constitutional grounds. The TRIPs Agreement, in fact, played only a marginal role in the conflict. Finally, as a result of strong domestic and international pressure, the companies withdrew their case in April 2001 after a settlement was agreed.

From the outset, the EU has been at the forefront of the debate on the TRIPs Agreement and access to medicines. For the EU, this debate should not be considered in isolation. It is dealt with in the context of the wider action on combating poverty in developing countries and tackling pandemics such as AIDS. Price is indeed not the

*The views expressed are the author's own and do not necessarily bind the European Commission.

1389-2827/02/$8.00

only factor that impedes the access to medicines. Where price is concerned, patent protection is not the only determinant of the price level of medicines. Also, even if medicines were cheaper, many medicines would, for a variety of reasons, not reach the majority of those who need them most. That is why the EU's Programme for Action on Communicable Diseases[1] provides for a number of other measures and solutions for combating the most widespread communicable diseases by setting up an adequate health infrastructure, by increased R&D for adequate medicines and by addressing the relevant trade-related aspects.

The latter include not only the protection of intellectual property rights and the role of pharmaceutical companies in supplying medicines to developing countries at the lowest possible prices, but also the reduction, or where possible even the elimination, of tariffs by developing countries on such medicines and the prevention of their parallel trade. Some of these aspects require the active contribution of developing countries themselves with a view to ensuring that the cheapest possible medicines reach those who are in need.

2. The Doha Declaration on the TRIPs Agreement and Public Health

2.1. A new balance in the interpretation of the TRIPs Agreement

The Doha Declaration on the TRIPs Agreement and Public Health[2] (hereinafter "Declaration"), adopted at the Doha Ministerial meeting of the WTO in November 2001, marks an important milestone in the debate on intellectual property and medicines. This text clarifies the relationship between the TRIPs Agreement and public health policies of WTO Members and rebalances its interpretation. It now makes clear that the TRIPs Agreement should not stand in the way of government policies aimed at guaranteeing supply of affordable medicines to the neediest and confirms the flexibility of the TRIPs Agreement, in particular with regard to patents. It shows that the WTO Agreements, and in particular the TRIPs Agreement, are no static texts whose interpretation is cast in stone.

The Declaration was the result of an intensive preparation and negotiation process in the TRIPs Council. Throughout these negotiations the EU worked to bring together the almost irreconcilable positions of the opposing sides, in order to put forward a meaningful text for adoption by all WTO Members.

2.2. The substance of the Declaration

The main contributions of the Declaration are that:

[1] COM (2001) 96 of 21 February 2001.

[2] WTO reference: WT/MIN(01)/DEC/2, 20 November 2001.

- it relieves the apparent tension between intellectual property and the protection of public health;
- it confirms the flexibility of the TRIPs Agreement;
- it extends the transition period for least developed countries to implement the relevant part of the TRIPs Agreement.

Bridging the apparent tension between intellectual property and the protection of public health

The Declaration unambiguously states that "the TRIPs Agreement does not and should not prevent Members from taking measures to protect public health". This statement confirms the obvious principle that a Member's right to pursue public health objectives and policies is unaffected by the TRIPs Agreement.

Furthermore, it is affirmed that "the TRIPs Agreement can and should be interpreted and implemented in a manner supportive of a Member's right to protect public health". This means that, when implementing their IP regimes, Members can opt for a system that matches their public health objectives. Moreover, in case of disputes in the context of WTO dispute settlement procedures, the TRIPs Agreement must be interpreted in a way to support the Members' right to take measures to promote public health (see further). In other words, a Member of which the legislation, in particular in the area of patents, is being challenged by another Member because of alleged incompatibility with the TRIPs Agreement, can refer to the contents of this Declaration where the contested measures are driven by health policy objectives.

These preliminary clarifications are very important, especially in the light of Article 8(1) of the TRIPs Agreement. The latter provides that when Members implement the TRIPs Agreement, they may adopt measures necessary to protect public health as long as they are consistent with the provisions of this Agreement. This led to a discussion on whether intellectual property protection should override public health concerns. However, the issue is not whether or not intellectual property overrides public health or vice versa. Intellectual property and public health should be mutually supportive because without effective medicines, public health policies would be hampered. An effective public health policy requires new medicines, which will not be developed without the necessary R&D investments by the pharmaceutical industry. These investments will not be made, unless the innovators obtain adequate protection for a reasonable period of time. One should not forget that generic copies can only be made available to the extent that novel drugs have been developed and made public first.

One can not, at the same time, deny that patents do have an impact on the prices of medicines. Therefore, the Declaration expressly recognises the concerns about the effects of intellectual property protection on the price of medicines. [3]

---

[3] See its paragraph 2.

Confirmation of the flexibility of the TRIPs Agreement

Ministers have reaffirmed the right of any WTO Member to use, to the maximum, the flexibility in the provisions of the TRIPs Agreement. At the same time, they have confirmed that Members maintain their commitments in the TRIPs Agreement. This flexibility has been defined in terms of the overall interpretation of the TRIPs Agreement, compulsory licences and parallel imports.

Role of the objectives and principles of the TRIPs Agreement in interpreting the Agreement

The Declaration affirms that each provision of the TRIPs Agreement must be read or interpreted in particular in the light of the objectives and principles of the TRIPs Agreement. This is perhaps the most important provision of the Declaration. The principles and objectives of the TRIPs Agreement are laid down in its Articles 7 and 8, which refer, inter alia, to the need to take measures to protect public health and nutrition, the prevention of the abuse of intellectual property rights and the need to strike a proper balance of rights and obligations. The Declaration emphasis that Articles 7 and 8, which refer to public interest, play a central role in the interpretation of the TRIPs Agreement. Striking a proper balance between the interests of the right holders and those of the public, as well as between the rights and obligations of the right holders is an essential feature of intellectual property. Articles 7 and 8 provide essential guidance in setting that balance. In the context of WTO dispute settlement procedures, the panels and the Appellate Body must now use these provisions as primary interpretation tools when determining the TRIPs-compatibility of measures taken by a Member in view of protecting public health.

Although the Declaration was not, from a formal point of view, adopted as a binding interpretation of the TRIPs Agreement,[4] it is beyond doubt that it has legal value. First of all, it reflects the will of the entirety of the WTO Membership. Hence, it cannot from a political point of view, be disregarded. Secondly, from a legal angle, the Declaration is a "subsequent practice" in the application of the TRIPs Agreement which establishes the agreement of the parties regarding its interpretation. According to the rules of treaty interpretation, as laid down in the Vienna Convention on the Law of Treaties,[5] this means that the Declaration has to be taken into account when interpreting the relevant TRIPs-provisions when disputes arise over measures taken by Members on public health grounds. Were a panel or the Appellate Body to refuse to do so, this would have adverse political consequences on the WTO.

[4]See the procedure foreseen under Article IX of the WTO Agreement.

[5]Article 31(1) of the Vienna Convention: "A Treaty is to be interpreted in good faith, in accordance with the ordinary meaning to be given to the terms of the treaty in their context and in the light of its subject and purpose". Article 31(b) of the Convention reads that "There shall be taken into account, together with the context (...) b) any subsequent practice in the application of the treaty which establishes the agreement of the parties regarding its interpretation".

Compulsory licences

Compulsory licences[6] have always been a central issue in this debate. Many developing countries consider compulsory licensing as a way to be able to source cheaper generics. However, no case is known to date of developing WTO Members having issued compulsory licences in this context. Canada used to have a compulsory licensing policy for pharmaceuticals in the 1970s and the 80s, but it was abandoned in the early 90's. Certain developing countries have however successfully used the threat of resorting to such licence as a negotiating token in view of obtaining significant price cuts on essential drugs or voluntary licences. The EU has always recognised that WTO Members have the right to grant compulsory licences. However, it should only be used as a last resort solution. Systematic recourse to compulsory licensing (which, in view of the current situation is an unlikely prospect) would be detrimental to the patent system. The EU, therefore, does not encourage the use of compulsory licences. In the EU's view, voluntary licensing is a much better way forward.

With regard to compulsory licenses, the Declaration sets forth that "each WTO Member has the right to grant compulsory licenses and the freedom to determine the grounds upon which such licenses are granted". The TRIPs Agreement clearly allows Members to grant compulsory licenses, but is indeed silent on the grounds on which Members may base themselves when considering their granting, which means that the necessity to protect public health can be one of the grounds for granting such licence. This does not, however, dispose Members of respecting the terms and conditions of Article 31 TRIPs or of any other of the relevant provisions under the Agreement.

The TRIPs Agreement also provides for a "fast-track procedure" for granting compulsory licences in situations of national emergency or other circumstances of extreme urgency. In such cases Members can issue a compulsory licence without a voluntary licence being negotiated first. Therefore, the Declaration recognises that public health crises, such as those relating to HIV/AIDS and other pandemics, can represent a "national emergency" or "other circumstances of extreme urgency". This is without prejudice to a Member's right to define these concepts.

Exhaustion and parallel imports

Finally, it was confirmed that each WTO Member is free to establish its own regime of exhaustion of intellectual property rights without there being a challenge in the WTO dispute settlement system. This means, in other words, that Members are free to allow for parallel imports of patented goods that have been put on a third market by the patent holder or with his authorisation.

---

[6]Compulsory licences are licences granted by the government without authorisation from the patent holder. The TRIPs Agreement specifies that the right holder must always be granted a fair remuneration.

Extension of the transition period of Least Developed Members

Least-developed Members have been granted an additional transition period in the areas of patents and data protection for pharmaceuticals until 2016 (instead of 2006), whilst maintaining their right to an even further extension.[7,8] During this time, generic products can be manufactured in, imported to and/or exported from the territory of these countries without restrictions. The consent of the original patent holder would not be required. To the extent that patent holders have not applied for patent protection in a country or where the patents have expired, importation of generics into such a country is also always possible.

2.3. Conclusion

While it does not amend the rights and obligations laid down in the TRIPs Agreement, the Declaration usefully clarifies the flexibility of some of the relevant provisions and can be invoked by Members in dispute settlement procedures, thereby creating a safer legal environment for those Members seeking to benefit from the flexibilities of the Agreement.

All stakeholders should be happy with this balanced result which meets the long term interests of all, industry and consumers alike. The Declaration provides a delicate balance between the interests of those who had put the issue of the relationship between TRIPs and public health on the agenda of the TRIPs Council, and those whose major preoccupation was to safeguard the TRIPs Agreement.

The only regret from an EU point of view is that WTO Members did not give a favourable response to the suggestions made by the EU that, when medicines are exported to developing countries at discounted prices, Members should adopt measures to avoid exportation of these products from the markets for which they were intended. The EU is in the process of evaluating whether or not it needs to adopt special measures to avoid re-importation of such products.

3. The post-Doha work programme: Compulsory licences for countries without manufacturing capacity for pharmaceuticals

3.1. Tackling the needs of import-dependant countries

The Doha Declaration on the TRIPs Agreement and Public Health left one issue unresolved. It recognises that WTO Members with insufficient or no manufacturing capacities in the pharmaceutical sector could face difficulties in making effective use

[7] Under the TRIPs Agreement, least developed country Members have until at least 2006 to implement their commitments. An extension of this period can be obtained by motivated request to the TRIPs Council.

[8] Please note that a number of developing countries still benefit from a transition period until 1.1.2005 to provide for product patent protection for pharmaceuticals.

of compulsory licensing under the TRIPS Agreement, without presenting a solution though. The TRIPs Council is instructed to find an expeditious solution to this problem before the end of 2002.

This paragraph responds to one of the main concerns raised by developing countries. The basic argument underlying the present debate is that WTO Members with insufficient or no manufacturing capacities in the pharmaceutical sector could face difficulties in making effective use of compulsory licensing under the TRIPs Agreement with regard to patented pharmaceuticals. For many developing or least-developed country Members, the right granted by Article 31 of the TRIPs Agreement is indeed of no practical use because, in reality, there is no domestic manufacturer to which such licences can be granted.

It is not in dispute that Members can issue a compulsory licence for domestic production as well as for importation. However, concern has been expressed about the extent to which sources of supply are available. First, in case of compulsory licences for import, there is no guarantee whatsoever that one will find adequate sources of supply. Secondly, by virtue of the principle of territoriality of patent protection, these Members cannot grant a compulsory licence directly to a foreign manufacturer. At the same time, the TRIPS Agreement makes it very difficult, not to say impossible to rely on a compulsory licence granted by a third country. Article 31(f) TRIPs provides that only a non-predominant part of the product under CL can be exported. This means that it cannot work if there is no sufficient demand for that product in the country of manufacturing to absorb a predominant part of the production. The ratio legis of this provision lies in the territorial nature of patent rights and the need to avoid undermining the effects of patent protection.

As a result, countries with no or insufficient manufacturing capacity do not possess the kind of leverage that the ability to issue a compulsory licence can give, and may therefore find it more difficult to obtain substantial price cuts on essential medicines. What is at stake here is an issue of equal opportunities for all WTO Members to enjoy the rights granted by the TRIPs Agreement.

One should keep in mind that there are still many countries which do not yet provide for pharmaceutical patents, especially least-developed countries. In these countries, generic substitution remains an option for some time. Sources of supply may however dry up in future as all developing countries will have to grant product patent protection to pharmaceuticals as from 2005. In any event, the EC's view is that finding "an expeditious solution" to this problem means, in effect, that one should be found before the end of 2002.

3.2. The current discussion in the TRIPs Council

A first discussion among the WTO Members took place at the March 2002 session of the TRIPs Council.[7] In order to kick off the work at the TRIPs Council, the EU

[7] The TRIPs Council is the WTO body dealing with the implementation of the TRIPs Agreements. In general it meets four times a year for a 3 to 4 days session.

tabled a Communication under the form of an options paper, exploring two possible options for a solution (see further).[8] However, the TRIPs Council meeting did not make significant progress on this issue. This is rather unfortunate as the work will have to be finalised within a very short timescale. In fact, the EC's Communication was the only substantive written contribution put forward on this occasion. Other major contributions, by US and by Kenya on behalf of a group of developing countries were oral and informal, and remained rather vague. It is surprising that the developing countries, who have a major interest in this debate, did not come forward with a more elaborated position. It is now expected that more detailed proposals will be put on the table by the June 2002 session of the TRIPs Council.

3.3. Possible solutions on the table at the TRIPs Council

At this stage four main options have been put to the TRIPs Council's consideration.

i) An interpretation based on Article 30 of the TRIPs Agreement

In substance, this option would consist of interpreting the limited exceptions clause of Article 30 of the TRIPs Agreement in a way which would allow production for export, to certain countries and under certain conditions, of products needed to combat serious public health problems. To this end, WTO Members could adopt a declaration stating that a WTO Member may, in accordance with Article 30 of the TRIPs Agreement, provide that the manufacture, on its territory, of a patented product, without the authorisation of the right holder, is lawful when it is meant to supply another country which has granted a compulsory licence for the import and sale of the product concerned in its territory in order to deal with a serious public health problem.

The main advantages of that approach are that there is no need to amend the TRIPs Agreement and that it can be done within a reasonable timeframe. Its main disadvantage is that it requires an apparently unorthodox interpretation of Article 30, which meets with serious scepticism in certain circles. Therefore it has met with resistance from part of the Membership, and in particular most industrialised countries other than the EC (which has not taken position), which are concerned about the open-ended nature of such interpretation. Developing countries are very favourable to this approach, and would also see the exception apply to exports to countries where the product concerned is not patented (and which by consequence do not need to issue a compulsory licence). In view of these serious divergences, it may be extremely difficult and take much time before agreement could be reached on such a solution.

[8] IP/C/W/339, 4 March 2002.

ii) Amendment of Article 31 of the TRIPs Agreement

This option would consist of amending Article 31 of the TRIPs Agreement in order to carve out an exception, under certain conditions, to Article 31(f) (i.e. the principle that only a "non-predominant" part of the production under a compulsory licence can be exported"). Such an exception clause would state that Article 31(f) does not apply to compulsory licences granted for the purpose of supplying a poor country with a product needed to address serious public health problems. It would, in other words, create an exception to the principle stated in Article 31(f) of the TRIPs Agreement that compulsory licences "shall be authorised predominantly for the supply of the domestic market of the Member authorising such use". The TRIPs Agreement already provides for an exception to 31(f) to address cases related to competition law. In their statement at the March TRIPs Council, the developing countries proposed a simple deletion of Article 31(f). The EU can not accept this: while an exception could be negotiated, the basic principle of 31(f) should remain in force under the circumstances not covered by the exception.

The great advantage of this approach is that there would be a clear ground, in the TRIPs Agreement itself, to export, under a compulsory licence, products needed in view of addressing serious public health problems (whatever the patent situation of the product concerned in the Member in question). Another advantage is that it would apply to exports to countries with or without patents alike. Article 31(f) allows for exports under compulsory license without distinction of the patent status of the product concerned in the country of destination.

The main disadvantage of that approach would be that the procedure to amend TRIPs would be a complicated one.

iii) Dispute settlement moratorium

Members could also make a "gentlemen's agreement" that countries granting licences for export of medicines to certain countries under certain circumstances would not be subject to complaints from other Members. This option, aired by the US, was immediately rejected by Brazil, because it would, in its view, not be sustainable. It could be envisaged as a transitory solution pending amendment of article 31(f).

iv) A waiver of Article 31(f)

A "waiver" is a decision by the WTO Membership waiving one or more Members from a specific obligation under a WTO Agreement, such as for instance Article 31(f) TRIPs, under certain conditions and for a certain period of time. This could allow certain Members to export under a compulsory licence for a certain period of time. Waiver decisions[9] are rather heavy from a procedural point of view.[10] In substance it

[9] Article IX.2-4 of the WTO Agreement.

[10] Decisions must be taken by the Ministerial Conference (or, in the interval the GC) with a $\frac{3}{4}$ majority, following a report by the TRIPs Council. A waiver must be reviewed annually.

would boil down to the same as a dispute settlement moratorium, but the latter would be less cumbersome from a procedural point of view.

The question remains whether a waiver or a dispute settlement moratorium would be rally viable positions. In fact, they are difficult to defend. They would not recognise the existence of a right under TRIPs and would be seen as simply putting off the problem.

These solutions remain the favourites of the US and industry because they would leave the TRIPs Agreement unmodified and would have a temporary application. However, to be really meaningful, a moratorium or a waiver would have to extend well beyond the 2016 deadline for least developed countries to introduce pharma patents. The question is whether, politically, a moratorium or a waiver of 20 or 25 years could ever be put into question after such long period. For developing countries a waiver could be acceptable only as a transitory measure pending a definitive solution.

3.4. The EU point of view: Work in progress

At this stage, the EU has not expressed any preference with regard to options i) and ii). As regards options iii) and iv), the European Commission reckons that they would not offer a sustainable solution.

The EU Communication to the TRIPs Council[11] insisted on the fact that, whatever the solution finally agreed on, it will have to be carefully crafted in a way to ensure that the TRIPs Agreement is not undermined and that adequate safeguards are put in place to avoid abuses and trade diversion, to create sufficient transparency and to ensure co-operation with right holders.

First, the Communication emphasises that any solution would need to be carefully drafted and hedged around with conditions to prevent abuses and diversion of trade. This is of the utmost importance. Safeguards will be needed to ensure that production pursuant to any proposed exception is not diverted from its destination. Any abuse could open the door to massive circumvention of intellectual property rules, which would seriously impair the legal security of right holders and undermine the basic principles of the TRIPs Agreement.

Secondly, the Communication highlighted the need to make the system transparent, in order to allow other Members and the right holder to be informed, when a Member makes use of this mechanism.

Thirdly, it is important to ensure that the right holders of the products in question are given the opportunity to contribute to the solution. What matters is to ensure adequate and sustainable supply of reliable medicines to those in need, not to create a tool for industrial policy. Therefore, it will at all stages be crucial to ensure a sufficient participation from the patent holder, through his right to be heard and his right to make sustainable discounted pricing offers in view of avoiding to resort to

[11] See footnote 7.

these mechanisms. Effective results can indeed only be achieved, if the international pharmaceutical industry is on board and is willing to commit itself to supplying poor markets on a sustainable basis. Voluntary, long-term undertakings remain, in the EUfls view, the best way forward.

With these conditions, the EU does not aim at creating burdensome new obligations for WTO Members. The issue at stake is, both from a factual and from a legal-technical point of view extremely complex. There is no simple solution to complex problems. The need for an effective solution will have to be balanced with the need to deal with competing interests and to avoid abuses. Any abuse could open the door to massive circumvention of intellectual property rules or to illicit trade. This could seriously impair the legal security of right holders and, in the long term, be detrimental to the interests of those in need of essential medicines. WTO Members concerned will have to take the necessary measures within the context of their existing administrative procedures, notably in the area of customs, and provide for legal security and due process and to seek co-operation with right holders. A sustainable solution will not be found unless all stakeholders, including the industry, are fully involved.

Developing countries seem, at this stage, to contest the need for strict conditions. In their statement at the March TRIPs Council, they insisted on the fact that one should avoid taking a narrow approach in terms of scope, beneficiaries (any country without manufacturing capacities should be able to benefit; i.e. no limitation to least developed countries only), and conditions. This is a position the EU can not agree with. Finally, the developing countries also put heavy emphasis on the fact that the ultimate goal of this exercise should be to create a sufficient local manufacturing base, through transfer of technology. This aim does not seem realistic from an economic point of view. Regional approaches should be considered.

In view of the divergent opinions, and since no in depth debate has taken place yet, it is difficult to forecast which solution will ultimately emerge. At this stage, three options have met with serious resistance: the Article 30 approach (opposed by US, Canada, Japan and others) and the moratorium/waiver (opposed by developing countries). Therefore, they may have little chance to fly. It seems therefore that, the amendment of Article 31 may be to be the most appropriate solution to pursue. The final outcome will however depend on further negotiations between the Members, and no solution can be ruled out from the outset. The June TRIPs Council will allow us to have a better sense of the direction that the discussion will take.

4. General conclusions

As the process in the TRIPs Council is still ongoing, it is too early to draw definitive conclusions.[12] Nevertheless, we can already draw a few tentative ones:

[12] State of play 24 April 2002.

1) The Doha Declaration on the TRIPs Agreement and Public Health is well balanced. It safeguards the long term interest of all stakeholders. It is favourable to the interests of the R&D based pharmaceutical companies and it relieves pressure from the TRIPs Agreement: in the absence of any Declaration on public health, de facto non-compliance by several developing countries was a real risk. Likewise, it adequately responds to developing country concerns by adequately filling in the constructive flexibility of the TRIPs Agreement.
2) In a sense, the Declaration constitutes a first substantial expression of the spirit of the Doha Development Agenda, which places the needs and interests of developing and least developed countries at the heart of the further work programme of the WTO. It shows that the WTO is capable of finding appropriate solutions to developing country concerns. The EU has always been a strong advocate of this new approach and is fully committed to continue working towards these objectives.
3) The EU, through the European Commission, successfully played its role as bridge builder and facilitator in the WTO with a view to reconciling the almost irreconcilable positions of the extreme ends of the spectrum. This allowed it to play a key role in obtaining a substantial and well-balanced declaration on TRIPs and public health in Doha. What mattered for the EU was to ensure that a meaningful declaration was ultimately adopted by all WTO Members. This could not have been achieved by reinforcing one of both camps, but rather by keeping a position that would allow to keep negotiators around the table in order to continue to communicate and converge towards an agreement. Work now needs to continue on this basis. There is strong expectation for the EU to continue to play this role in the ongoing process in the TRIPs Council.
4) The Declaration also proves that the WTO is not only about making "classical" trade rules. The WTO membership has shown itself able to re-balance the TRIPs Agreement in favour of the developing countries even before the Doha Development Agenda was launched. The role of the TRIPs Council in this consensus-building was paramount. It was there that the discussion forming the basis of this Declaration took place. This discussion ultimately allowed the serious obstacles in the negotiators' way to be overcome.
5) Finally, whether the Declaration will have an immediate effect on prices of medicines in developing countries remains to be seen. One should keep the record straight: it can not be expected that any solution that emerges from the present discussion in the TRIPs Council will be a universal panacea for the problem of access to medicines. For the poorest populations, even the lowest possible price of generic medicines or medicines manufactured under a compulsory licence may remain unaffordable: even where they can produce at lower cost, manufacturers of generic medicines also need a return on investment. Reality shows that, for a variety of reasons, access to medicines in countries where pharmaceuticals can not be patented does not appear any better than in countries where they can. Therefore, the discussion within the TRIPs

Council should not overshadow other measures needed to improve access to medicines; nor should it divert attention from ongoing international efforts to make medicines available at affordable price. If other factors contributing to the price level of medicines are not tackled, and if no measures are taken to ensure that medicines effectively find their way to the patients, there is no reason to believe in a major change. This is a question of global responsibility, of international organisations, NGOs, industrialised countries, industry and developed countries alike. In this context, the EU is working on developing a tiered pricing concept to make essential medicines available and affordable for poor developing countries. Effective results can only be achieved though, if the international pharmaceutical industry is on board and is willing to commit itself to supplying these poor markets on a sustainable basis. This can be achieved through voluntary, long-term undertakings. In future, it should be the norm that the poorest countries have access to the drugs they need at the lowest possible price.

Annex

DECLARATION ON THE TRIPS AGREEMENT AND PUBLIC HEALTH
Adopted on 14 November 2001 (WT/MIN(01)/DEC/2)

1. We recognize the gravity of the public health problems afflicting many developing and least-developed countries, especially those resulting from HIV/AIDS, tuberculosis, malaria and other epidemics.
2. We stress the need for the WTO Agreement on Trade-Related Aspects of Intellectual Property Rights (TRIPS Agreement) to be part of the wider national and international action to address these problems.
3. We recognize that intellectual property protection is important for the development of new medicines. We also recognize the concerns about its effects on prices.
4. We agree that the TRIPS Agreement does not and should not prevent Members from taking measures to protect public health. Accordingly, while reiterating our commitment to the TRIPS Agreement, we affirm that the Agreement can and should be interpreted and implemented in a manner supportive of WTO Members' right to protect public health and, in particular, to promote access to medicines for all.
   In this connection, we reaffirm the right of WTO Members to use, to the full, the provisions in the TRIPS Agreement, which provide flexibility for this purpose.
5. Accordingly and in the light of paragraph 4 above, while maintaining our commitments in the TRIPS Agreement, we recognize that these flexibilities include:

(a) In applying the customary rules of interpretation of public international law, each provision of the TRIPS Agreement shall be read in the light of the object and purpose of the Agreement as expressed, in particular, in its objectives and principles.
(b) Each Member has the right to grant compulsory licences and the freedom to determine the grounds upon which such licences are granted.
(c) Each Member has the right to determine what constitutes a national emergency or other circumstances of extreme urgency, it being understood that public health crises, including those relating to HIV/AIDS, tuberculosis, malaria and other epidemics, can represent a national emergency or other circumstances of extreme urgency.
(d) The effect of the provisions in the TRIPS Agreement that are relevant to the exhaustion of intellectual property rights is to leave each Member free to establish its own regime for such exhaustion without challenge, subject to the MFN and national treatment provisions of Articles 3 and 4.

6. We recognize that WTO Members with insufficient or no manufacturing capacities in the pharmaceutical sector could face difficulties in making effective use of compulsory licensing under the TRIPS Agreement. We instruct the Council for TRIPS to find an expeditious solution to this problem and to report to the General Council before the end of 2002.
7. We reaffirm the commitment of developed-country Members to provide incentives to their enterprises and institutions to promote and encourage technology transfer to least-developed country Members pursuant to Article 66.2. We also agree that the least-developed country Members will not be obliged, with respect to pharmaceutical products, to implement or apply Sections 5 and 7 of Part II of the TRIPS Agreement or to enforce rights provided for under these Sections until 1 January 2016, without prejudice to the right of least-developed country Members to seek other extensions of the transition periods as provided for in Article 66.1 of the TRIPS Agreement. We instruct the Council for TRIPS to take the necessary action to give effect to this pursuant to Article 66.1 of the TRIPS Agreement.

2. Industry dynamics and managerial approaches

Pharmaceuticals Policy and Law 5 (2002) 27–40
IOS Press

Technological and strategic change in the Finnish pharmaceutical industry: The emergence of a cluster

Malin Brännback and Maija Renko
Turku School of Economics and Business Administration / Innomarket Rehtorinpellonkatu 3, FIN-20500 Turku, Finland
E-mail: malin.brannback@tukkk.fi; maija.renko@tukkk.fi

This paper focuses on the developments within the Finnish pharmaceutical industry during the past five years and the future prospects. We study the change in industry structure and the emergence of a Finnish Pharmacluster. The study of the Finnish pharmaceutical industry reflects the developments and changes in the technology base and business strategies in the international pharmaceutical industry. The paper suggests that the emergence of virtual operation modes is the result of the structural change process, driven by a technological paradigm shift, taken place within pharmaceuticals for the past two decades. Evidence is provided based on a one-year research project on the Finnish pharmaceutical industry.

Keywords: Pharmaceutical industry, strategic change, virtual organizations, Finnish Pharmacluster

1. Introduction

The pharmaceutical industry has during the past two decades been dramatically restructured. Biotechnology has emerged as a complement to traditional drug R&D and has formed a new R&D paradigm. Today the pharmaceutical industry is the leading industry in developing biotechnological applications. Turnover created by biotechnologically engineered products is growing rapidly at an annual rate of 25 percent [23]. Today, the development of biotechnological applications is divided between existing large companies (still the majority) and small, newly established companies [3,9,29], which may also be called new drug discovery companies (DDCs [1]).

Prior to the 1980s, drug discovery was primarily based on organic chemistry for the development of new chemical entities (NCEs). In the pharmaceutical R&D process, extensive amounts of chemical compounds were explored and incremental structural modifications were made on drug prototypes, all this organised around highly structured processes for carrying out mass screening programs. As a result of this paradigm, we only have 500 known targets today, although there are thousands of medicines on the market. With the sequencing of the human genome the number of targets is expected to reach potentially 3000–10,000 [16,27]. Since the 1980s biologics has evolved as the new dominant logic of drug R&D. The so-called molecular

[1] In this paper the abbreviation DDC refers to drug discovery companies, although in some other contexts it has been used to refer to drug delivery companies.

biology revolution, which started in the mid-70s has introduced drastic changes in the pharmaceutical R&D base. This revolution has opened new opportunities for the discovery and production of medicines. Simultaneously, it has brought along a radical shift in the knowledge base and in research procedures that have enabled the transition from more or less random screening to "discovery by design" [16,27].

Based on the general technology driven strategic changes described above, this paper focuses on the developments within the Finnish pharmaceutical industry during the past five years and the future prospects. We study the change in industry structure and the emergence of a Finnish Pharmacluster. In the early 1980s there were thirteen drug companies in Finland. Through mergers and acquisitions the number was reduced to two in ten years. From the mid-1990s small biotechnology companies and drug discovery companies (DDCs) have been established at an accelerating speed. The DDCs focus their business on drug discovery and development up to phase II clinical trials, after which partnerships are sought for with big pharma for phase III and commercialisation. The DDCs are small, employing approximately 10 persons and an annual turnover of EUR 1 million. The companies within the Finnish pharmaceutical industry call themselves the Finnish Pharmacluster. However, it is unclear whether the cluster meets the characteristics of a cluster as is the case of more established clusters, e.g. the Finnish forestry cluster. Previous research around this issue exists but it is based on secondary data. This study is based on both primary and secondary data.

The structure of the paper is the following. In the second section the strategic changes within the global pharmaceutical industry are described as well as the new forms of organisational structures emerging due to these changes. In section three the research method is described. The research results are then used for describing the Finnish pharmacluster in section four. Finally we conclude and offer suggestions for future prospects.

2. Strategic changes within the pharmaceutical industry

The changes seen within the pharmaceutical industry have essentially been driven by technological change, a decreasing number of new block-buster drugs, i.e. a decrease in R&D throughput, soaring health care expenditures due to an ageing population leading to tightening price regulations, globalisation of markets, and increasing competition. Firms have therefore – in seeking new sources of growth – been forced to restructure. A common recipe has thus been mergers and acquisitions in order to gain access to technological advancement or for the purpose of gaining market access. Mergers and acquisitions (M&A) have certainly proved their right with respect to gaining access to global markets and distribution channels. However, whether M&A have been successful in securing increased R&D productivity is largely doubted.

Quantitative evidence of the impact of firm size on R&D activity is mixed and limited [19]. For example, Henderson and Cockburn [19] suggest that there are significant returns to size in pharmaceutical research, but that only a small portion of these returns are derived from economies of scale. Jaffe [20] argues that the R&D of technological neighbours increase R&D productivity. Graves and Langowitz [17] again, have found evidence for decreasing returns to scale in R&D. Pavitt et al. [24] suggest that both very small firms and very large firms were proportionately more innovative than more moderate-sized firms. Controversially, mergers and acquisitions are often motivated by the desire to spread R&D costs over a wider base and to gain control of R&D in competitive firms [15], rather than to improve the firm's R&D performance. Production, distribution and promotion performance is often largely dependent upon sufficient firm size and scale economies. Size also gives access advantages to information from the benefits of experience and access to markets from mechanisms such as reputation and relations (the ability to work with regulatory authorities, for example) [32].

In the era of the old R&D paradigm, pharmaceutical R&D processes involved large laboratories and disciplined internal organisational procedures, which became the sources of competitive advantage generally in the form of economies of scale. As the industry evolved, these economies of scale along with additional organisational capabilities to manage the processes of pharmaceutical R&D and delivery acted as powerful barriers to entry in the industry [30]. A number of pharmaceutical companies in the past succeeded through imitation and generic competition after patent expirations, as well as through concentration on local markets and product niches. The molecular biology revolution has introduced major changes in the processes of discovery and in the organisation of research. The new situation requires novel technological and organisational capabilities for creation of sustainable competitive advantages. New technological opportunities have freed the entry of new firms – suppliers of specific technological solutions and intermediate products to larger companies – to this industry [16,27].

Established pharmaceutical companies have experienced complex processes of adaptation to new, academic-like organisation methods in their R&D. Overall, the importance of publicly generated scientific knowledge for industrial innovation has increased not only in the pharmaceutical but also in a number of other knowledge intensive industries. Research networks and virtual R&D organisations have been developed to enable collaboration between universities, public and private research centres and both established and new biotechnology and pharmaceutical firms. Although larger pharmaceutical companies continue to represent the inner core of innovators in this industry, the problems such as the shortage of targets, a rise in drugs going off-patent and projected decreases in annual sales lead to a strong M&A activity.

Despite the lack of empirical evidence, it is possible that M&A of companies proves to be a feasible strategy in the long run as the new "general purpose" research technologies of combinatorial chemistry, high throughput screening and genomics increase firm-specific economies of scope that relate to knowledge spillovers across projects and departments [16]. Moreover, the world wide emerging trend of science parks shows promise because academic and firm collaborations are key drivers of these formations. Science parks prove effective and efficient platforms for networking and shared knowledge creation. Hence, today's feasible strategies cover the formation of strategic alliances for enhancing R&D productivity as well as gaining access to global marketing and distribution channels necessary for the commercialisation of a new drug. These alliances have the potential for solving the major macro-level problem evident in the industry today; established companies need access to R&D resources of the smaller, specialised companies, while research units and biotechnology companies need access to commercialisation knowledge. In addition to strategic R&D alliances we have seen the formation of networks and clusters all aiming at developing virtual corporate constellations enhancing collaboration [4,22].

Pharmaceutical R&D today requires fusion of multiple technological disciplines of which a profound knowledge is required. The exponential growth in the amount of biological information available to pharmaceutical researchers makes today's pharmaceutical industry an industry with an extremely "high clock-speed" [6]. Pharmaceutical firms – especially the newly established technology companies, biopharmaceutical companies, and the so called toolbox companies – develop internally only few technological skills which are considered "core" and strategic and outsource the other ones [30]. The co-operative structures in the pharmaceutical industry do not restrict themselves to include only drug companies. R&D collaboration with the academic research community has long traditions and is expected to intensify. Pharmaceutical R&D in the 21st century requires creation of networks in which resources, knowledge and information circulate rapidly and at a low cost [7,10].

Authors have used various terms to describe what has been perceived as a new form of enterprise: modular corporation, agile enterprise, virtual organisation, virtual corporation, virtual company, virtual enterprise, and virtual factory are titles given to the "new" commercial activity [6,14]. Rather than being specific definitions of a new organisational model, Campbell [6] has suggested that these terms, if anything, are titles given to generic descriptions of organisational activity. In the same way as "virtual memory" has made it possible for computers to run much larger amounts of data than their physical memory would allow, "virtual organisation" enables companies exit their physical limits and extend their power to previously unreachable areas [5].

The term virtual corporation refers to an organisation consisting of dynamic co-operative relationships, which suggests that virtual corporation is a company that exists because it creates effects but does not exist as a company in fact. This understanding of virtual corporation is regarded as key to industry clusters and networks. In the heart of the virtual organisational structure lies the assumption that all the parties involved in the structure possess "best-in-class" core competencies [18]. The effectiveness of the virtual structure stems from the fact that by combining the competencies of the parties involved an exceptionally competent aggregate is formed.

To create extra value the competencies and skills of the companies involved in the virtual structure should not be overlapping but complementary. To our minds the notion of virtual organising is a conceptualisation of the structural change process, driven by the technological paradigm shift that has taken place within pharmaceuticals for the past two decades.

3. Research methods

To canvass the opinions of the decision-makers in the Finnish pharmaceutical industry on the current state and structures of the industry and on its future prospects, altogether 31 executive interviews were conducted. These theme interviews were carried out in the period from December 1999 to August 2000 among company executives and university representatives in the pharmaceutical industry and related fields in Finland. The interviewees were sent the interview themes a couple of days before the actual interview so that they could prepare their answers. The interviews were recorded and transcribed afterwards and the interview material was analysed by coding the transcribed material into various classes derived from the purpose of the study.

For the purposes of triangulation and because of the need for more structured data, a mail questionnaire was sent out to 100 individuals in the Finnish pharmaceutical industry in June 2000. The questionnaire was sent to representatives of all the Finnish established pharmaceutical companies, drug discovery companies, service companies, universities' pharmaceutical research and / or service organisations, technology companies, national agencies or associations, and a number of other – mainly venture capitalist – companies. The companies that the questionnaire was sent to included all the companies in the Finnish pharmaceutical industry at that time. The questionnaire was addressed to the company CEO or in the case of university units, the head of the department or unit. Out of the 100 questionnaires 51 were returned (Response rate 51%). The survey material was analysed by using a statistical computer program (SPSS). The analysis mainly included descriptive statistics and crosstabulations.

4. The Finnish Pharmacluster

4.1. *The status of the cluster*

The core products of the pharmaceutical industry are indisputably drugs, but the offerings of an increasing number of firms in the industry are either intermediate products or services offered to other industry members. When considered from a value creation point of view, a final pharmaceutical product that reaches the end consumer – the patient – has gone through multiple stages. Today the various discovery and development phases are increasingly performed in specialised companies unlike

Table 1
Biotechnology industry in Finland in 1999 (Finnish Bioindustries, www.finbio.net)

Sector	Number of companies	Annual turnover (EUR million)	Personnel
DDCs	16	16	220
Big pharma	3	640	4210
Diagnostics	29	300	2050
Biomaterial	8	20	90
Food and feed	17	260	1050
Industrial enzymes	3	68	270
Agro	7	14	130
Service companies	19	12	110
Others	8	12	70
Total	110	1342	8200
Total excl. big pharma	107	702	3990

in the past, when an integrated pharmaceutical company typically covered all the phases of development and marketing.

The current Finnish pharmaceutical industry is dramatically different from what it used to be little over a decade ago. The industry was from the WWII all the way to the 1990s primarily focused on serving the domestic market. Prior to 1995 when product patent was enforced, uniqueness was based on process patent. In the middle of the 1970's, the first steps towards developing original drugs – new chemical entities (NCEs) –were taken. Finnish Bioindustries currently lists 110 companies (incl. 3 big pharma companies) (see Table 1). The list includes DDCs (16), companies in the diagnostics (29), biomaterials (8), food and feed (17), industrial enzymes (3), agro (7), service sectors (19), and other related fields (8). By excluding the sectors of food and feed, industrial enzymes, and agro the industry totals 83 companies. If we exclude the three big pharmas the industry totals 80 companies with a total annual turnover of EUR 360 million (average per company EUR 4.5 million) and employing 2470 persons (http://www.finbio.net).

After the replacement of pharmaceutical process patent by product patent as Finland joined the EU in 1995, wealth of new companies have been established in the industry (Fig. 1). The reasons for this "boom" are multiple, but can mainly be summarised into two categories. Firstly, the global molecular biology revolution that has its roots in the scientific advances of the 1970's and 1980's contributed to the emergence of knowledge intensive, focused biotechnology companies in the pharmaceutical as well as in other life science industries. The long time scales typical for the pharmaceutical industry are illustrated by the time lags from the invention of novel technologies to their profitable commercial applications. For example, an increasing number of biotechnology companies world wide are today building sustainable businesses based on the maturing monoclonal antibody (Mab) technology. Mabs can be used to treat a variety of diseases from cancer to cardiovascular disease and because of their high specificity monoclonal antibodies may significantly reduce the side effects experienced with traditional therapies. Mabs are currently the fastest growing therapeutic drug class and they have been pivotal in many of the recent mergers or acquisitions in the industry [2].

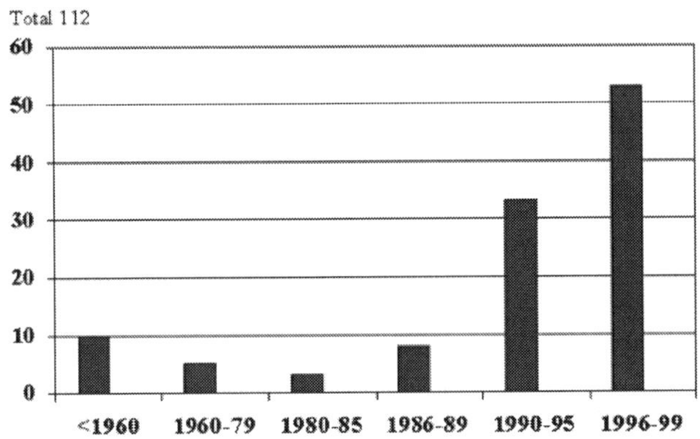

Fig. 1. Biotechnology industry in Finland, number of companies founded per year [12].

Secondly, the changes in the national macroeconomic environment and the restructuring of the established domestic pharmaceutical companies have contributed to the accelerating speed of new company establishment. The number of "big pharma" (although not "big" in international comparisons) companies in Finland, which in the early 1980s totalled thirteen, was reduced to two in ten year's time. As the remaining companies introduced more focused strategies than before they had to abandon some of the research areas from their wide portfolios. The researchers involved in these areas were practically obliged to leave the established companies if they wished to continue with those areas of research. This phenomenon of restructuring contributed to the emergence of numerous new start-ups. Simultaneously, the 1990's saw major alterations in the funding of university research. Over the past decade external funding of the universities (outside the governmental budget) has strongly increased, as the universities have developed their technology transfer mechanisms and rules for co-operation with private companies and EU counterparts. Especially the research intensive Finnish DDCs are dependent on research in universities; they participate actively in academic research projects and capitalise on them. The research co-operation between universities and companies in technical research grew significantly in the end of 1990's. The US and Finland have been found to be among the most effective nations in terms of university-industry collaboration [21]. Finally, the growth of the industry and establishment of start up companies has been boosted by the increasing availability of finance. Although the early stage development of innovations still largely depends on the availability of public funding, the private venture capital industry is an increasingly important source of finance. The Finnish private equity and venture capital industry was practically non-existent till the beginning of the 1990's, but today it is comparable to most other European countries. When the amount of investments made by private equity and venture capital companies is compared to the GNP, Finland ranks third in Europe, after the UK and the Netherlands [13]. All these changes in the macroenvironment have promoted the development illustrated by Fig. 1.

A special trait of the pharmaceutical industry in Finland is the limited number of executives and opinion leaders, which is a reflection of the small size of the country on the one hand and the past structure of the industry on the other. The industry remained fairly protected from foreign competition all the way to the 1990's and a limited number of domestic companies dominated markets. Practically all the industry peers today know each other and most of them have worked in the same companies before the end of the protectionistic era. This facilitates involvement in joint projects and enables knowledge spillovers within the industry.

"The Finnish Pharmacluster" is an informal discussion forum that was intiated in the end of the 1990's to promote co-operation within the industry. This "cluster" contains the agglomeration of companies and university organisations grouped around medicinal and pharmaceutical products as well as medicaments, including veterinary medicaments. In addition, companies offering new potential therapies for diseases belong to the cluster. (see www.tolppa.net/medinet.)

4.2. Strengths, weaknesses, opportunities and threats of the cluster

The strengths, weaknesses, opportunities, and threats of the Finnish pharmaceutical industry are in the following identified based on the survey we conducted. The points in Table 2 are derived straight from the answers of the companies in the Finnish pharmaceutical industry to the open question about their own respective strengths, weaknesses, opportunities, and threats today. The order of the attributes reflects how many of the companies referred to the specific attribute; attribute no 1 was mentioned more often than attribute no 2 etc.

In addition to technical know-how, also networking both between companies and between companies and universities can be considered as major strengths of the industry. The companies have also been successful in selecting and targeting specific market segments. Even small market segments in the pharmaceutical markets can be profitable customer bases for companies with a low level of fixed costs and products tailored especially to the needs of the specific segments. A strong patent position is essential for a company that wishes to trade with its intellectual property. Patents can be used as one indicator of the research activities of a company or a nation. Our survey revealed that the Finnish pharmaceutical companies, which participated the survey, expect their current research projects to lead to a considerable increase of 43% in the number of patents these companies hold by the year 2003.

As a large number of companies in the industry are today dependent on external investors and venture capitalists they are naturally worried about the deficiency of financial support. Another major weakness of the companies in the industry is the lack of marketing know-how and business skills. Additional weaknesses of the industry reflect most importantly the limited size of both the Finnish home markets and the companies themselves.

Companies in the industry expect the major future opportunities to arise as a result of advances in science and technology. This is in line with the current major strength

Table 2
SWOT analysis of the companies in the Finnish pharmaceutical industry

Strengths	Weaknesses
1. Focused technical / science expertise and know-how	1. Deficiency of financial support
2. Market leadership in selected segments	2. Lack of marketing know-how
3. Networking with other companies	3. Small company size
4. University – company co-operation	4. Not enough human resources
5. Experience of the employees	5. Young organisation
6. Strong patent position	6. Lack of business skills
	7. Small home market
Opportunities	**Threats**
1. Advances in technology and pharmaceutical science	1. Intense international competition
2. Collaboration with other companies	2. Lack of educated personnel
3. Internationalisation of both demand and company operations	3. Lack of funds
4. Increasing demand for company's products / services	4. Changes in legislation and authority performance hard to predict
5. Collaboration with universities	
6. Markets with unmet medical needs	

of the industry; superior technical know-how in the areas of focus. Companies also expect international collaborations and networking between companies and universities – both within Finland and with foreign partners – to provide them new business opportunities. Increasing demand of medicines and the unmet medical needs of the ageing population are naturally an important opportunity for all the companies in the medical field.

The concrete and threatening lack of funding was mentioned by many companies as a major future threat to their operations. The availability of funding is naturally dependent on the performance of the national economy on the whole. The most often mentioned threat, however, was the fear of intense competition on the markets and within therapeutic classes. This is probably a reflection of the lack of marketing and business skills that were mentioned as a weakness by many; scientific superiority alone does not guarantee success on international pharmaceutical markets, although it is a favourable starting point.

Our survey respondents were also asked to numerically evaluate the overall quality of various parts of the Finnish pharmaceutical industry. The survey results show that quality and performance of domestic industry actors in areas related to pharmaceutical science and research are considered remarkably better than quality and performance of domestic actors in the fields related to marketing, commercialisation, and production. Although an extensive pool of scientific and technical know how related to pharmaceutical R&D exists in the dynamic network of the Finnish pharmaceutical industry, the country-wide network does not include sufficient marketing and business knowledge.

4.3. Co-operation within the Finnish Pharmacluster

The emergence of network organisations as an operating mode in pharmaceutical R&D – and according to Chiesa and Manzini [7] especially on the R-side – is a natural consequence of changes in the operational environment of the pharmaceutical companies. Network organisations can be approached from two different angles; inter- and intra-organizational perspective. The intraorganisational network is a collection of individual people and sub-units of one organisation, whereas the inter-organisational network is a collection of independent individual companies [14]. Snow et al. [31] have identified three different typologies of inter-organisational networks: Internal networks, stable networks, and dynamic networks. Compared to the other two network organisation forms, dynamic networks are more temporary alliances of firms usually organised around a leading firm. Each collaborating unit is typically independent and co-operates on a specific project or opportunity. Member companies of a dynamic network are aware that collaboration in the network is fluid and restricted to a certain period of time. In many cases each new opportunity that arises to the network is approached through an aggregate that has a different, new kind of member configuration. The notion of dynamic network is synonymous to the "opportunity network" of Achrol [1], defined as "a set of firms specialising in various products, technologies, or services that assemble, disassemble, and reassemble in temporary alignments around particular projects or problems" [1, p. 62].

In network – i.e. virtual – organisations member firms contribute their competencies to the entity that does not need to have legal existence or location properties [8]. The competencies contributed to the network organisation can include both firm-specific competencies and profession-specific competencies [6,11]. However, the contribution of firm-specific competencies requires that the existing organisational structures remain in place because these competencies are hard to transfer between firms – they consist of specific knowledge and skills that are firmly embedded in the firm's architecture and work well within that domain. Thus, when firm-specific competencies are added up to create a network organisation the resulting organisation is likely to have the characteristics of a stable network. Firm specific competencies can evolve only over time in companies operating in stable environments. A dynamic network structure, on the other hand, requires profession-specific competencies to be in place in the member organisations. These competencies are easily transferable from one company to another and need no permanent organisation for their deployment.

The current structure of the Finnish pharmaceutical industry corresponds to the notions made about a dynamic network structure. The companies that form this network are knowledge intensive and their competitiveness is based on the profession-specific competencies of the individuals. Based on the empirical data, Fig. 2 has been formulated to reflect the players and their connections in the Finnish pharmaceutical industry today. Companies that belong to the groups presented in Fig. 2 form the dynamic network from which a number of companies come together whenever opportunities arise and form a virtual organisation to create value.

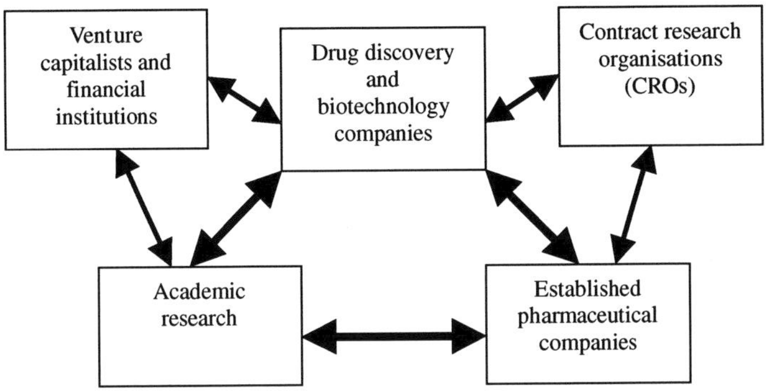

Fig. 2. Dynamic network in the Finnish pharmaceutical industry.

The evolving national pharmaceutical cluster is rather of vertical type than horizontal, because the co-operation between large and small Finnish pharmaceutical companies is not yet fully developed. For the pharmaceutical cluster to be successful, it is important that co-operation between companies, universities and authorities is further increased. Coopetition, which captures the tension between competition and co-operation, seems a viable form of procedure. However, an industry where competition is based on patents this idea of coopetition poses huge managerial challenges from a cognitive as well as an operational point of view [4].

5. Conclusions and implications

The current structure of the Finnish pharmaceutical industry illustrates the paradigm shift in the strategies employed by companies in the pharmaceutical industry. The past strict organisational barriers have been replaced by a more flexible operating mode that allows knowledge spillovers between industry actors. To our minds this development is a natural consequence of the paradigm shift in the tools and procedures employed for new drug development. The economies of scale have largely been replaced by profession specific competencies of individuals as a source of competitive advantage. Virtual organising and networking between companies and universities has emerged as a new model of organising for effective utilisation of ideas and knowledge.

The future of DDCs and also more established Finnish pharmaceutical companies looks promising provided that they will be successful in discovering compounds that provide major improvements over existing therapies. However, because of the limited resources of the newly established DDCs there is a growing concern that too many companies are being formed around only one or a couple of tools and technologies. What is more, if the one or two projects that smaller DDCs typically have at a time fail, they may be forced to sell their assets. Naturally these same concerns apply for biotechnology companies in all countries (see also [26]). Biotechnology has been burdened with tremendous expectations during its entire existence and in many cases the emerging biotechnology firms have failed to deliver. Some early enthusiasts went as far as predicting the downfall of big Pharma and with the numerous mergers and acquisitions it certainly looked to be true. However, it appears as if the emerging small biotechnology companies and big Pharma have found themselves in a situation where they need one another and can benefit from each other [4].

It is hard to see that rapid growth into an international integrated pharmaceutical company with an extensive distribution network would be a feasible strategy for any of today's Finnish pharmaceutical companies in the foreseeable future. Instead, Finnish companies can and should capitalise on high quality research in their specific areas of excellence. Outsourcing of R&D will be the key driver of success for the large pharmaceutical companies of the future and it is here that the Finnish companies will have their word to say. Successful development of the patented inventions through domestic and international collaboration networks is the key to the future success of the Finnish pharmaceutical industry.

Once a cluster begins to form, a self-reinforcing cycle promotes its growth, especially when local institutions are supportive and local competition is vigorous. As the cluster expands, so does its influence with government and with public and private institutions [25]. Cluster development that leads to frequent interactions and networking between companies can raise innovation and productivity in a number of ways. Companies benefit from sharing knowledge and reduce costs by jointly sourcing services. Interactions increase the efficiency of collaboration between organisations with complementary assets and skills. An existing network attracts further companies, investors, services, and suppliers into the cluster and a pool of skilled labour is born [28]. This kind of positive circle keeps on strengthening itself and the whole cluster, and the first signals of such a continuum being in place in the Finnish pharmaceutical industry are in view.

An apparent limitation of the approach of this paper is the restriction of empirical evidence and discussion to one country. Looking for evidence for the dynamic network structures from an area limited by country borders is a questionable approach in almost any industry today. Especially questionable it becomes when talking about a small country like Finland and about an industry that is as international in nature as today's pharmaceutical industry is. However, instead of emphasising the country borders as limits to the dynamic networks, the network that is today present in the Finnish pharmaceutical industry can be seen as an implication of the personal contacts between the industry peers. Interesting topics for future research can be derived from the approach of this paper. By expanding the scope from one country to other European countries it would be possible to conduct comparative studies on the industry level. This would provide further evidence on the strategic changes and new virtual and network organisations in the European pharmaceutical industry.

References

[1] R.S. Achrol, Changes in the theory of interorganizational relations in marketing: toward a network paradigm, *Journal of the Academy of Marketing Science* **25**(1) (1997), 56–71.

[2] K. Amdjadi, C.D. Herold, S.K. Patel and E.S. Razvi, *The Top 10 Merger & Acquisition Deals in the Biotechnology and Pharmaceutical Industries,* Drug & Market Development Publications, Westborough, the US, 2000.

[3] C. Arnst and J. Carey, Biotech Bodies, *Business Week,* July 27th, 1998, pp. 42–49.

[4] M. Brännback and H. Mäkinen, *The structure of the Finnish Pharmaceutical Industry – an evolving cluster,* Innomarket technical reports no. 6, 2000.

[5] J.A. Byrne, The virtual corporation, *Business Week,* February 8, 1993, pp. 36–40.

[6] A. Campbell, The agile enterprise: assessing the technology management issues, *International Journal of Technology Management* **15**(1/2) (1998), 82–95.

[7] V. Chiesa and R. Manzini, Managing virtual R&D organizations: lessons from the pharmaceutical industry, *International Journal of Technology Management* **13**(5/6) (1997), 471–485.

[8] W.W. Cooper and M.L. Muench, Virtual organizations: Practice and literature, *Journal of organizational computing and electronic commerce* **10**(3) (2000), 189–208.

[9] M. Corstjens, *Marketing Strategy in the Pharmaceutical Industry,* Chapman & Hall, London, 1991.

[10] C. David and J. Grindley, *When the ink dries on research alliances,* Scrip Magazine, April 1998, pp. 45–47.

[11] G. Fairthlough, Organizing for innovation: compartments, competencies and networks, *Long Range Planning* **27**(1) (1994), 88–97.

[12] Finnish Bioindustries, *Biotechnology: a promising high tech sector in Finland,* http://www.finbio.net, 2000.

[13] Finnish Venture Capital Association (FVCA), http://www.fvca.fi, 2000.

[14] U. Franke, The virtual web as a new entrepreneurial approach to network organizations, *Entrepreneurship & Regional Development* **11**(3) (July–September 1999), 203–230.

[15] C. Freeman and L. Soete, *The Economics of Industrial Innovation,* (3rd ed.), MIT Press, Cambridge, 1999.

[16] A. Gambardella, Orsenigo Luigi and Pammolli Fabio, *Global competitiveness in pharmaceuticals, a European perspective,* Report prepared for the Directorate General Enterprise of the European Commission, 2000.

[17] S.B. Graves and N.S. Langowitz, Innovative Productivity and Returns to Scale in the Pharmaceutical Industry, *Strategic Management Journal* **14**(8) (1993), 593–605.

[18] S.-O. Hansén and P. Zettinig, The spider in the network. From invention to innovation – virtuality as alternative for SMEs. Proceedings of the Annual Academic Workshop, "Connecting to Customers: Value, Volume, and One-to-One" January 16–18, 1999. Georgia State University, Center for Business and Industrial Marketing, 1999.

[19] R. Henderson and I. Cockburn, Scale, Scope, and Spillovers: the Determinants of Research Productivity in Drug Discovery, *RAND Journal of Economics* **27**(1) (1996), 32–59.

[20] A.B. Jaffe, Technological Opportunity and Spillovers of R & D: Evidence from Firms' Patents, Profits, and Market Value, *The American Economic Review* **76**(5) (1986), 984–1001.

[21] K. Kankaala and M. Lampola, *Tutkimustulosten kaupallistaminen Yhdysvalloissa – mekanismit ja säädökset,* Kansainvälisten verkostojen raportti 1/1998, TEKES, Sitran julkaisusarja nro 199, 1998.

[22] H. Mäkinen, *Klusteri vai Verkosto? Suomen Lääkealan Uuden Yritystoiminnan Rakenteesta,* (in Finnish: A Cluster or a Network? The new structure of the Finnish drug industry), Innomarket Technical Reports No. 4, 1999.

[23] T. Nakahara, Technology Strategy in a Borderless Economy, *International Journal of Technology Management* **17**(6) (1999), 711–724.

[24] K. Pavitt, M. Robson and J. Townsend, The Size Distribution of Innovating Firms in the UK: 1945–1983, *The Journal of Industrial Economics* **35**(3) (1987), 297–316.

[25] M.E. Porter, Clusters and the New Economics of Competition, *Harvard Business Review* **76**(6) (November–December 1998), 77–90.

[26] T. Rautiainen, *Biopharmaceutical Business in California,* Tekes Technology Review 81/99, 1999.

[27] C. Robbins-Roth, *From Alchemy to IPO The Business of Biotechnology,* Perseus Publishing, Cambridge, Massachusetts, 2000.

[28] Sainsbury (Lord), P. Cooke, C. Evans, M. Ferguson, G. Roberts and A. Wilson, *Biotechnology clusters,* August 1999. http://www.dti.gov.uk/biotechclusters/ 13.11.2000.

[29] J.G. Smith and V. Fleck, Strategies of New Biotechnology Firms, *Long Range Planning* **21**(3) (1988), 51–58.

[30] S. Suoniemi and M. Brännback, *Can Elephants and Mice Play? – Organisational and Market Implications of the Restructuring Process in the Drug Industry,* Innomarket Technical Report No. 2, 2000.

[31] C.C. Snow, R.E. Miles and H.J. Jr. Coleman, Managing 21st century network organizations, *Organizational Dynamics* **20**(3) (Winter 1992), 5–21.

[32] P.-L. Yeoh and K. Roth, An Empirical Analysis of Sustained Advantage in the US Pharmaceutical Industry: Impact of Firm Resources and Capabilities, *Strategic Management Journal* **20** (1999), 637–653.

Pharmaceuticals Policy and Law 5 (2002) 41–62
IOS Press

The key drivers and success factors for M&A strategies in the biotechnological and pharmaceutical industry[1]

Lars Schweizer*
Otto-Friedrich-University of Bamberg, Germany

This paper analyses the M&A and post-merger integration activities in the biotechnological and pharmaceutical industry resulting from a transformation process in both industries. To start with, the development of the pharmaceutical and biotechnology industry is analyzed from a more theoretical, literature-based point of view which leads to the conclusion that a strategic consolidation resulting in fewer but stronger, larger and more market capitalized companies is only a question of time. After that the M&A activities in both industries are described in numbers in a more specific, empirical way in order to support the first conclusion. This analysis is subdivided in three different layers: pharma-to-pharma, pharma-to-biotech and biotech-to-biotech deals and clearly shows a significant increase in M&A activities in each of these layers. In a next step-two of these layers are looked at more closely, changing the analytical focus from the industry perspective to the company perspective. In the final section, there is the confrontation of the theoretical and empirical considerations and findings. This reveals that the pressure from capital markets in terms of the need for a blockbuster as well as in market capitalization, the acquisition of knowledge and the building-up of a critical mass as far as capacities are concerned are the key divers for M&A activities. According to the specific situation different post-merger integration strategies (absorption, symbiotic or preservation approach) apply. The central factors that foster a successful post-merger integration – irrespective of what post-merger integration strategy is chosen – are the existence of a powerful integration manager, extensive personal communication and a cultural fit.

1. Introduction

Biotechnology is one of the most important technologies to have emerged over the past twenty years. Today this growing industry comprises a range of companies from research-focused start-ups to mid-size companies with manufacturing capabilities and even some large pharmaceutical companies. Biotechnology's novelty and scope inevitably causes considerable turbulence and changes within firms, and, particularly, in the relationships between firms relying on it. The rapid changes in the pharmaceutical industry occurring as a result of biotechnology's development provide the context in which this paper is placed.

[1]Paper presented at the Fifth Workshop on Challenges for Pharmaceutical policies in the 21st century January 18–19, 2001 Brussels, Belgium.

*Otto-Friedrich-University of Bamberg, Department of Business Administration, Human Resources & Organization, Feldkirchenstr. 21, D-96045 Bamberg, Germany. Tel.: +49 951 863 2656; Fax: +49 951 863 5570; E-mail: Lars.Schweizer@sowi.uni-bamberg.de.

The first central research question of this paper focuses on why takeovers between/among pharmaceutical and biotechnological companies occur. The second crucial research question is how the organizational integration of the acquired company takes place so that the intended synergies finally can be realized. In order to answer these two research questions the emergence of the biotechnology industry in close connection with the evolution of the pharmaceutical industry will be described shortly.

The structure of this paper can be divided up in three main lines of argumentation, each of them having different sub-lines. First, the development of the pharmaceutical and biotechnology industry is analyzed from a more theoretical, literature-based point of view from which conclusions about possible trends of M&A activities are drawn in a general way. Second, the M&A activities in the pharmaceutical and biotechnology industry which have occurred during the last years are described in numbers in a more specific, empirical way. This analysis can be subdivided in three different layers: M&A activities between pharmaceutical companies, being Layer 1, M&A activities between pharmaceutical and biotechnology companies, being Layer 2 and, finally, M&A activities between biotechnology companies referred to as Layer 3. Hence, the analytical focus lays clearly on the industry-level. Third, two of these layers are looked at more closely by depicting a single case in more detail and, by this, having the company-level as analytical focus. Fourth, in the final section, there will be the confrontation of the findings from the analysis of the industry- and company-level with the theoretical considerations made at the beginning of the paper. The research outline of this paper is again summed-up in the following Fig. 1.

2. New issues in the pharmaceutical and biotechnology industry – Some theoretical considerations

> "The early 1990s were a watershed in the evolution of the pharmaceutical industry. After years of relatively stable growth, high profits, and an enviable record of innovation, pharmaceutical firms found themselves struggling against a tide of hostile forces." [24, p. 51]

The development of the pharmaceutical industry

To start with, the challenges and the transformation process in the pharmaceutical industry have to be taken into account. Obviously, the pharmaceutical industry underwent radical changes over the last decades. As a result, a transformation process has started changing some characteristics in the industry in a complete manner. Competition in the pharmaceutical industry has historically been characterized by three factors. First, competitive advantage has been driven by blockbuster drugs, which were required to offset the cost of expensive hit-or-miss clinical trial programs. Second, most pharmaceutical companies have traditionally been vertically integrated from discovery through sales. Third, pharma companies have played a peripheral role as 'suppliers' in the health care system, providing marketing solutions to payers

Research outline

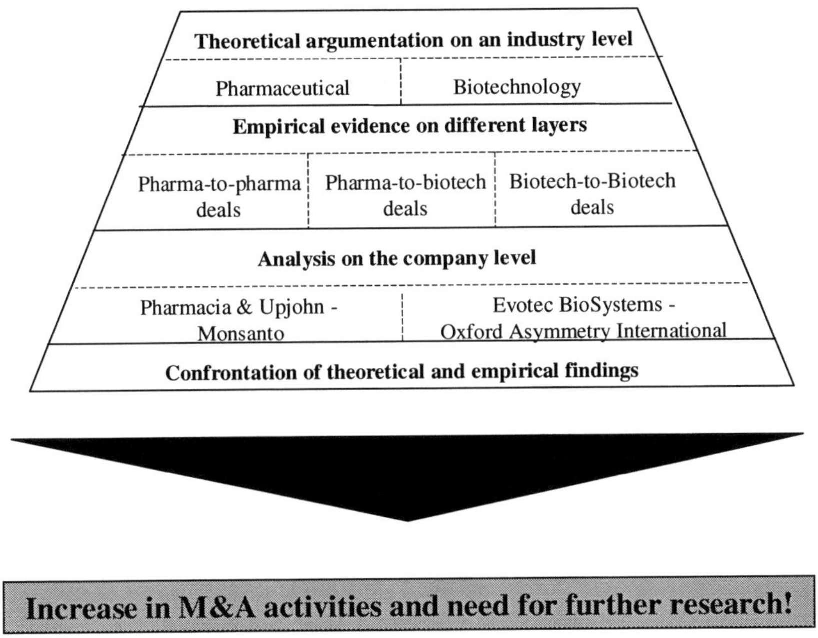

Fig. 1. Research outline.

and providers, but had no intention in driving primary consumer demand or becoming involved in care, diagnosis, or decision-making. Thus, in this environment success was based on a combination of serendipity and operational capabilities [4].

Nowadays, pharmaceutical companies face daunting stock market expectations and short-term operating pressures on earnings. Basically, they have to choose between two alternative strategies: either they turn to mergers and acquisitions in order to plug strategic holes and accelerate operational improvements, or they remain independent and put a concerted focus on near-term performance-improvement. Whether merging or not, pharmaceutical companies have to face lots of revolutionary changes on the horizon. The challenge is to weather short-term pressures, while at the same time rethinking fundamental questions of business strategy in light of revolutionary changes ahead.

An essential change is related to the discovery and development of new drugs. Because the specific causes of certain diseases were more or less unknown the natural and chemically derived compounds were screened for potential therapeutic impact. This approach of R&D is also referred to as 'random screening'. Traditionally, the discovery of new chemicals entities (NCEs) has been a rare, very expensive and serendipitous event, and has long been the principal bottleneck in the pharmaceutical value chain. Nowadays, new technologies are supposed to put R&D in a more reliable and stable way. First, Genomics aims at establishing the connection between genes and diseases. Second, through combinatorial chemistry companies are able to produce thousands of chemical variations from one known chemical building block. Third, High throughput screening (HTS) speeds up the processing of biological assays used to screen chemical libraries for potential drug leads. Fourth, bioinformatics is a crucial issue because information technology is critical to successful drug discovery due to the tremendous amount of data involved. Bioinformatics provides the computational tools to identify genes and proteins from DNA sequence data.

Hence, success will require pharma firms to develop new capabilities on many fronts. First, they have to dedicate resources in order to stay informed of technology developments and integrate the most promising technologies in-house. Second, the efficient storage and effective retrieval of the vast quantities of data provided by the new technologies have to be assured. Third, companies will have to hire the right talent for each specific task and pay attention that they effectively work together. Fourth, development and marketing must continuously be informed over the advances in discovery because they have to create targeted products for smaller subpopulations of disease. Fifth, pharmaceutical companies will have to create effective tools for portfolio selection and management. Thus, new discovery technologies are leading the way to a world where pharma pipelines are not constrained by a limited number of promising compounds, and the former random screening approach for new compounds will be replaced by a more focused, science-guided screening approach.

The main points which characterize the development in the pharmaceutical industry are again summed-up in Fig. 2 – along a simplified version of the pharmaceutical value chain.

These trends – taken all together – imply that companies must adopt a new way of looking at integration and coordination, assessing the value created in each function, determining what skills are available through partnerships with service providers or technology players, and building an organization capable of coordinating across boundaries. Besides the need to establish a strong financial base that will fund continuing investment in new markets, technologies and customer needs, the acquisition of knowledge in the biotech sector and its understanding are crucial for their future survival. Basically, there are three strategies: first, organic growth, which means that pharma companies have to build up this knowledge on their own, second, any kind of partnership such as strategic alliances or R&D agreements with biotech firms or universities, through which the company can gain access to the required knowledge, and, third, M&A in order to integrate companies which possess the necessary knowledge and capabilities. Thus, M&A is not only a method to close near-term earnings gap and improve operational performance, it is, first and foremost, a strategic possibility to overcome a lack of knowledge in the biotech sector or, in other words, catching-up as a late entrant. Apart from that, it can also be used to reduce R&D costs, to increase the number of potential products in the pipeline, and to close the earnings

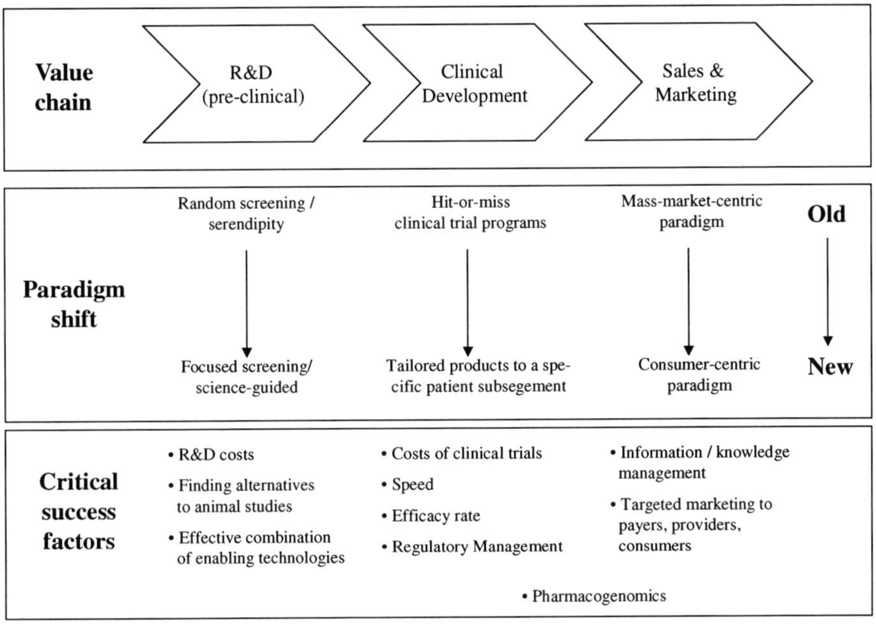

Fig. 2. Trends in the pharmaceutical industry.

gap. Nevertheless, there is still the possibility for mergers between pharmaceutical companies.

Before describing the development of the biotechnology industry from its different perspectives, it is necessary to emphasize the distinction between the pharmaceutical and biotechnology industry – considered from the point of view of this paper. On the one hand, the pharmaceutical industry can – in simplified terms – be subdivided in a non-biotechnology (rather chemical) part, which is loosing more and more of its former importance, and in a biotechnology part, which, obviously, is becoming the most important one. On the other hand, the biotechnology industry can be segmented into (1) red biotechnology dealing with human health care, (2) green biotechnology focusing on agriculture, (3) gray biotechnology dealing with environmentally friendly methods and (4) biotechnological equipment/ devices. The most interesting segment to analyze is the overlap between the biotechnology part of the pharmaceutical industry and red biotechnology.

The development of the biotechnology industry from a scientific point of view

The development of 'new biotechnology' has been characterized by Wirth [35] in four phases, whereas this study is already adding a fifth phase. The first phase, the so-called research phase, lasting from 1970 to 1980, was dominated by two path-breaking discoveries that revolutionized molecular biology. First, in 1973, Herbert Boyer of Stanford University and Stanley Cohen of the University of California at San Francisco reported the discovery of recombinant DNA (rDNA). Second, in 1975, Cesar Milstein and Georges Kohler of the British Medical Research Council discovered monoclonal antibodies (MABs) by fusing cells from a mouse myeloma with cells derived from mouse B-lymphocytes to create a 'hybridoma'. The second phase, from 1980–1985, is considered as being the pioneering phase in which the first product of a biotech company made by recombinant DNA, human insulin, was marketed in 1982 and was soon gaining appreciable market penetration. The third phase, starting with the year 1984, is regarded as being the first prospering phase of biotechnology, because there have been strong indications that the real 'take-off' point for the large corporations came in the years 1984–1985. Big-firm investment in commercial biotechnology in the US increased dramatically. Having remained relatively static through the early 1980s at approximately $200 million a year, it rose to $300 million in 1984 and jumped to $1.2 billion in 1985 [22]. The fourth phase, identified by Wirth [35], has started in 1990 and is perceived as the real prospering phase of biotechnology leading to new opportunities. However, this study puts the end of this phase to the year 1996, due to the fact, that, henceforth, the financing window for biotechnology has been closed.[2] By the end of 1994, more than two dozen biotech drugs and vaccines had been approved by the FDA, more than 200 medicines were in various stags of clinical testing, and approximately two dozen drugs awaited FDA approval [26]. The fifth phase, starting in 1997 and still holding on, is characterized by the discussion about necessary consolidation activities, on the one hand, and, the future 'dream' about the never-ending benefits of biotechnology, on the other hand.

The development of the biotech industry from an organizational perspective

University laboratories have played a critical role in developing the scientific fundamentals of biotechnology. However, it was the dedicated biotechnology firms (DBFs), also referred to as new biotechnology firms (NBFs) or entrepreneurial life sciences company (ELISCO), that commercially exploited the results of the research. The scientific breakthroughs of biotechnology constituted a radical change from previously dominated technologies in the human health care sector. Hence, in the sense of Schumpeter [31], Abernathy and Clark [1], and Tushman and Anderson [33], "biotechnology is a dramatic case of a competence-destroying innovation" [28, p. 368]. Technological change in this case builds on a scientific basis (immunology and molecular biology) that differs significantly from the knowledge base (organic chemistry and its clinical application) of the established pharmaceutical industry [25].

Internally, biotech firms are organized flexible in overlapping interdisciplinary project teams. Thus, the firms have minimal hierarchy and sometimes they have

[2]DeCarolis and Deeds [8] refer to the financing window as "hot markets" which entrepreneurs may use in order to improve their access to capital by going public and taking advantage of investors' optimism.

even created their own postdoctoral fellowship program. Obviously, biotech firms have merged the practices of academy with the requirements of high tech industry in order to create a lean and effective organization for drug discovery and commercial development [26]. Small biotech firms require large financial support and regulatory savvy, while larger pharmaceutical companies desire access to the research prowess of smaller companies. It is evident, that the full range of relevant skills needed to develop therapeutic drugs is not readily found under the single roof of a biotechnology company. The necessary basic and research skills to create a new product are found either in universities, research institutes, or small biotech firms, whereas the cash needed for product development, clinical trials, and world-wide marketing is located in large pharmaceutical companies. Hence, the players in this field have turned to numerous forms of collaboration such as joint ventures, research agreements, or licensing agreements.

The biotechnology industry is more than any other industry characterized by a social network structure[3] which exists in order to ensure the reliability of scientific information due to well defined and socially enforced norms, reciprocity, respect for individuals' intellectual property rights, and honesty in research [5,7,21]. Given that social network structure, a better environment for efficient organizational learning and also an enhanced flexibility for responding to unpredictable changes is provided. Social networks allow the exchanges between legally distinct entities without competitive pricing or legal contracting. A prerequisite for this is that a shift from coordinating the internal activities of the firm through a command and control structure to providing organizational support for internal as well as external exchanges takes place. As a consequence of this, there may be an extend in the scope of organizational learning, a better integration of knowledge in the firms participating in the social network, an increase in the operating, organizational as well as strategic flexibility, and a more efficient self-coordination among the employees involved.

Greis et al. [16] distinguish four different types of partnership agreements: (1) research contracts or minority investments for the purpose of gaining a window on new technologies, (2) licensing and marketing agreements to obtain the use of a particular technology, (3) corporate alliances such as joint ventures with or without the transfer of equity, and, (4) mergers and acquisitions. Interestingly, in the context of their study mergers and acquisitions are regarded as types of 'partnership' agreements. Of course, up to now no real hostile takeover has taken place in the biotech industry. Hence, some may consider M&A as a kind of partnership agreement, however the majority would probably prefer another interpretation. Apart from that, times have changed because the pharmaceutical as well as the biotechnological industry undergoes a radical transition enforcing both sectors to act. Therefore, it cannot be

[3]Liebeskind et al. [20] define a social network as "a collectivity of individuals among whom exchanges take place that are supported only by shared norms of trustworthy behavior. (...) We define a social network that includes members of more than one legally-defined organization as a 'boundary-spanning' social network." (p. 430–431).

excluded that either a big pharma company or even a biotech firm, rich in cash or stock – however feasible and likely this in reality may be – will try to carry out a hostile takeover.[4] Moreover, Greis et al. [16] emphasize the double layer of innovation by pointing out that "the locus of innovative activity is no longer the firm, but a network of inter-organizational relationships which are controlled by different firms" (p. 612). A detailed overview of strategic alliances in the biotechnology industry can be found in Goldman Sachs [15].

The development of the biotech industry from a finance perspective

To date the biotechnology industry has enjoyed more funding by governments, international pharmaceutical companies, the equity capital markets, and the venture capital community than virtually any other high-growth sector in the worldwide economy. Teitelman [32] describes Wall Street's initial attitude to biotechnology as 'biomania'. In 1980/ 1981 biotechnology investments in the US were attracting nearly $100 million of venture capital [18]. Wall Street's overall relationship with biotechnology has, however, been extremely variable, being hot and cold on a number of occasions. In its early enthusiasm for the technology it ensured that many NBFs enjoyed substantial funding. Pierce [23] analyzed the fates of the US industry pioneers – companies that have been public for at least a decade. This study includes 41 biotech companies that had gone public by the end of 1988 and raised nearly $10 billion in venture capital, equity, and debt financing. Of those, 27 are still continuing to exist as stand-alone entities, and barely half are profitable. Large, established pharmaceutical companies were generally slow to become involved in biotechnology, but, nevertheless, have been devoting considerable resources to it, and many also have acquired NBFs.

The restructuring and reorganization within the two primary sources of biotechnology R&D funding – pharmaceutical companies and the institutional investment community – now pose a threat for the continued growth of the industry. On the one hand, the short-term earnings pressure on pharma companies to maintain their valuations will probably result in a reduction of discretionary dollars traditionally used for biotech funding. On the other hand, the bull markets that institutional investors have enjoyed, combined with the inconsistent market performance of biotech investments, have reduced their interests in future investments. From the point of view of the institutional investor, four trends have emerged that force a different set of priorities [30]. One, institutional investors are managing more and more money as a result of continued escalation in equity prices, inflows to mutual funds, and increased merger and acquisition activity. Two, due to the growth in average fund size, fund managers need to take larger and larger positions in order to make investments meaningful to the portfolio's bottom line. Three, volatility in the stock market

[4] Of course, the specific industry structure and the strong dependence on tacit knowledge will make a hostile takeover difficult, but nevertheless not impossible.

has significantly increased the need for fund managers to hold stocks with greater liquidity. Four, Coyler [6] stresses that investors' caution in the biotechnology sector is rooted in its historical return, which means that the additional risk assumed by biotech investors is not being rewarded within a reasonable time. Investors in the average biotech IPO in 1993 have enjoyed on average only an 8% return through 1998, whereas the return to investors in the average US pharmaceutical company over the same period counts for 36%.

The restructuring of these two industries will ultimately provide new opportunities for biotechnology companies if they succeed in adapting to this changing environment. From this it follows, that the dilemma for biotechnology companies is how to manage this new environment, in which the drug companies who still believe in them no longer have excess discretionary dollars to spend and the institutional investors with discretionary dollars to spend are not true believers. The short-term strategic answer is to find ways to give both providers what they need. First, biotech companies have to become as financially innovative in their interactions with pharma partners as they are scientifically innovative by using creative financing structures such as off-balance sheet or product debenture financing. Second, they have to develop a critical mass – either through organic growth, consolidation, or collaborative agreements – in order to meet the needs of the pharmaceutical industry as well as the institutional investment community. Third, they have to become more skillful in addressing the needs of the institutional investors by changing their business model to fit better the risk/ reward profile of potential investors [29,30]. For companies which are not able to survive by following these short-term strategies, they must look at alternative business models to provide them with enough cash to develop their technology and products. One widely discussed solution to this cash-shortfall is industry-wide consolidation – either through a biotech-to-biotech or a pharma-to-biotech merger. Because of pharma companies being rich in cash, the latter one will – from a theoretical point of view – be the most probable solution ahead.

The development of the biotechnology industry has been described from different perspectives: (1) from a technological/ scientific perspective, (2) from an organizational/ management perspective, and (3) from a financial perspective. This analysis of the development of the biotechnology industry leads to the conclusion that a strategic consolidation resulting in fewer but stronger, larger, more market capitalized, and thus more financeable biotechnology companies is only a question of time, because all biotech companies desperately need money in order to ensure their future survival. Basically, biotech companies can choose between two solutions in order to solve this problem: a biotech-to-biotech deal or a pharma-to-biotech solution. Following the line of argumentation of the latest paragraphs it can not be denied that the pharma-to-biotech solution seems to be the most likely one. Let us now consider what empirical evidences can be found for that theoretical argumentation.

M&A-activities in the pharmaceutical industry
(Examples)

1989 Beecham (U.K.)	SmithKline (US)
1989 Dow Merrell (US)	Marion (US)
1989 Bristol Myers (US)	Squibb (US)
1993 Merck & Co (US)	Medco (US)
1994 SmithKline Beecham (GB)	Sterling Drug (US)
1994 American Home (US)	American Cyanamide Products (US)
1994 Sanofi (F)	Kodak Sterling Drug (US)
1995 Hoechst (D)	Marion Merrel (US)
1995 Glaxo (GB)	Wellcome (GB)
1995 Pharmacia (SWE)	Upjohn (US)
1996 Ciba-Geigy (SUI)	Sandoz (SUI)
1997 Hoffmann La Roche (SUI)	Boehringer Mannheim (D)
1998 Hoechst Marion Roussel (F)	Rhone-Poulenc (F)
1999 Pharmacia & Upjohn (US)	Monsanto (US)
1999 American Home Products (US)	Warner Lambert (US)
2000 Pfizer (US)	Warner-Lambert (US)
2000 SmithKline Beecham (UK)	Glaxo Wellcome (UK)

Fig. 3. Examples of M&A activities in the pharmaceutical industry.

3. The inevitable need for M&A – Some empirical evidences and facts

3.1. M&A activities among pharmaceutical companies (Layer 1)

During the last years a lot of M&A activity has taken place in the pharmaceutical industry. Take for example the year 1998, in which Zeneca, the UK drugs group, merged with Astra, the Swedish pharmaceutical company, in a $35 billion deal or Germany's Hoechst and France's Rhone-Poulenc planned in a first step to merge their life sciences businesses in a $22 billion deal to form Aventis which was later on expanded to include all other business areas – not just life sciences. In November 2000, it has been announced that Aventis intends to sell its Agro business and by this realizing the originally planned life-sciences-concept. However, the same year also counts for some planned deals such as American Home Products and SmithKline Beecham or American Home Products and Monsanto that got derailed. Apart from that, also the first merger try between Glaxo Wellcome and SmithKline Beecham failed in 1998, mainly because the two CEOs, at that time, Jan Leschly of SmithKline Beecham and Sir Richard Sykes of Glaxo Wellcome, could not really work together and were unable to agree upon the filling of the top positions of the new company. In the year 2000 they have started a second try, which seems to be much more promising and finally also has been approved by the regulation authorities. The following two figures provides an overview of the major M&A deals in the pharmaceutical industry (Fig. 3) and the development of market capitalization (Fig. 4).

The question is now, what conclusion can be drawn from such a development, which could also be considered as being some kind of a concentration process.

Five of the top-pharmaceutical companies have merged since 1994

Development of market capitalization by 31st of December

1994

™318,1 Billion $

1. Merck & Co. (48,0)
2. Johnson & Johnson (35,2)
3. Roche (34,0)
4. Glaxo Wellcome (31,6)
5. Bristol-Myers Squibb (29,6)
6. Pfizer (24,3)
7. American Home Products (19,2)
8. Eli Lilly (19,2)
9. Bayer (16,5)
10. Schering-Plough (14,1)
11. Hoechst (12,8)
12. Takeda Chemical (10,6)
13. Sankyo (10,1)
14. Smith Kline Beecham (9,8)
15. Shionogi (3,1)

1998

™1.459,2 Billi

1. Merck & Co. (175,7)
2. Pfizer (162,2)
3. Bristol-Myers Squibb (133,0)
4. Novartis (125,9)
5. Glaxo Wellcome (124,6)
6. Johnson & Johnson (112,8)
7. Eli Lilly (97,7)
8. Roche (85,7)
9. Schering-Plough (81,2)
10. Smith Kline Beecham (78,0)
11. Abbott Labs. (74,4)
12. American Home Products (74,3)
13. Warner Lambert (61,8)
14. Astra Zeneca (41,4)
15. Bayer (30,5)

1999

™1.411,0 Billion $

1. Pfizer (incl. Warner Lambert) (196,0)
2. Glaxo Wellcome (incl. Smith Kline Beecham) (174,1)
3. Merck & Co. (157,0)
4. Johnson & Johnson (129,7)
5. Bristol-Myers Squibb (127,3)
6. Novartis (105,3)
7. Roche (83,0)
8. Astra Zeneca (73,5)
9. Eli Lilly (72,5)
10. Schering-Plough (62,3)
11. Abbott Labs. (55,8)
12. American Home Products (51,3)
13. Aventis (45,0)
14. Takeda Chemical (43,9)
15. Bayer (34,4)

Fig. 4. Development of market capitalization of the top pharmaceutical companies.

In a study carried out by Bain [9], one interesting thesis can be found which can partly be supported by the results of a study [10] carried out under the author's supervision at the University of Bamberg. Bain argues that US pharmaceutical companies are on average more successful than European companies and, hence, it is supposed not even to be much more easier for them, but also more likely to acquire their European competitors. Our analysis supports the first part of the Bain study, that US pharmaceutical companies have had a better performance than European companies, however, the conclusion drawn by Bain is somehow misleading. Of course, the logic of this argument seems to be very convincing, but having a look at the M&A activities depicted in Fig. 3, it becomes obvious, that by far most of the mergers are among companies from the same continent and from this it follows, that there is definitely no predominance in US pharmaceutical companies acquiring their European competitors.

The gap in market capitalization between the top-ten pharmaceutical companies and the rest is increasing steadily, making the appearance of M&A in the near future very likely. A very good example for this may be the situation of two German pharmaceutical companies, Schering AG and Bayer AG, which – due to their relatively low market capitalization – have often been handled as takeover candidates during the year 2000. Take for instance Bayer, for months there has already been the rumor that the Swiss pharmaceutical giant Roche might be interested in Bayer, although this was denied regularly. And then, at the beginning of December Bayer announced that

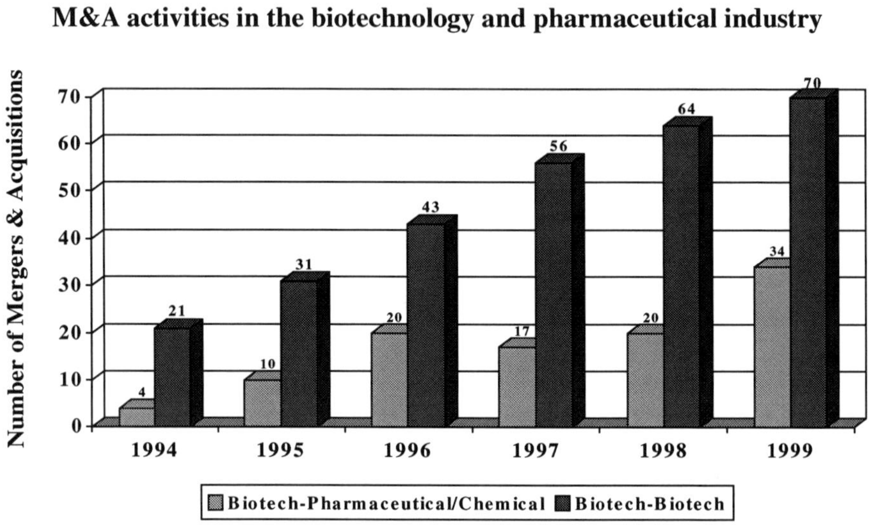

Source: Goldman Sachs (2000)

Fig. 5. M&A activities in the pharmaceutical and biotechnology industry.

it has engaged two investment banks (Credit Swiss First Boston and Deutsche Bank) in order to develop a new corporate strategy for value creation – the rumor that by this a defense strategy for a hostile takeover will be developed has been contradicted [12]. As far as Schering is concerned the rumors for a hostile takeover have been existed for decades. The latest rumor was that US-based Johnson & Johnson was interested in acquiring Schering, but this rumor was also contradicted from the part of Schering. According to their CEO, Giuseppe Vitae, "only good performance protects Schering from a takeover" [11]. And that is what Schering has done – especially also due to their activities in the biotechnology sector – during the last months and what is reflected in a tremendous increase in their stock price, making Schering no longer a bargain. One of the latest news from the M&A-front is that the German chemical giant BASF AG has announced that it has sold its pharmaceutical operations for $6.9 billion to Abott Laboratoires in order to focus more strongly on innovative chemistry [3]. Apart from Abott Laboratoires also some other pharmaceutical companies such as Eli Lilly, Sanofi Synthelabo, Bristol-Myers Squibb and one year before also Novartis, were considered as potential buyers for BASF Pharma [13].

3.2. M&A activities between pharmaceutical and biotechnology companies (Layer 2)

As Fig. 5 shows the number of M&A activities between pharmaceutical and biotechnology companies has increased steadily. Some major deals that have oc-

Table 1
Overview of pharma-to-biotech deals

Target	Bidder	Deal value in million $
1998		
Carnick Laboratoires	Elan	150
Chiron Diagnostics	Bayer AG	1.100
CN Biosciences	Merck KGaA	150
DeKalb Genetics	Monsanto	2.300
International Murex Technologies	Abbott	234
NanoSystems	Elan	150
Mycogen	Dow	325
Neurex	Elan	700
Penederm	Mylan	205
Sequus	Alza	580
Somatogen	Baxter International	188
TheraTech	Watson Pharmaceuticals	300
1999		
Agouron	Warner Lambert	2.100
BioRad Laborities	Sanofi Synthelabo	210
Centocor	Johnson & Johnson	4.900
ClonTech	Becton Dickinson	200
Diatide	Schering AG	130
North American Vaccine	Baxter International	390
PE Corporation	EG&G Wallace	425
SUGEN	Pharmacia & Upjohn	729

curred during the last two years between pharmaceutical and biotechnology companies are depicted in Table 1.

Major pharmaceutical companies have had always big interest in biotechnology companies, primarily to secure access to new technologies and products. However, these companies more commonly operated through licensing agreements rather than outright takeovers. Glaxo Wellcome, for example, has entered into a number of collaborations agreements with biotech companies, but has made no major biotech acquisition since its $538 million purchase of Affymax in 1995.[5] One of the reason for such a behavior has probably been the over-inflated valuations attached to biotech companies in the mid-1990s. In the meantime, these valuations have been adjusted downwards, making acquisitions more attractive and cheaper. Consequently, large biotech acquisitions have multiplied in the last years – as already indicated by the deals in Fig. 5. Pharmaceutical companies are now seeing the possibility to acquire broad-based technologies more inexpensively and cheaper (1) than they could have done before and (2) than they can build internally. In accordance with this argumentation, the total valuations of mergers and acquisitions which involved biotechnology companies have increased steadily from $3.3 billion in 1997, over $8.9 billion in 1998 up to $13.7 billion in 1999.

[5] A more detailed description of this deal can be found in Glaxo Wellcome [14].

Table 2
Overview of biotech-to-biotech deals

Target	Bidder	Deal value in million $
1998		
Molecular Dynamics	Amersham Pharmacia Biotech	256
Penederm	Mylan	205
Molecular Simulations	Pharmacopeia	140
Sequus	Alza	580
Tseng Labs	Cell Pathways	177
1999		
Advanced Inhalation Research	Alkermes	114
Chiroscience	Celltech	535
Collagen Aesthetics	Inamed	142
LeukoSite	Millennium Pharmaceuticals	635
Medeva	Celltech Chiroscience	950
NeXstar Pharmaceuticals	Gilead Sciences	550
Research Genetics	Invitrogen	160
US Bioscience	MedImmune	440

3.3. M&A activities among biotechnology companies (*Layer 3*)

In Fig. 5 – see above – the number of M&A activities between pharmaceutical and biotechnology companies is compared with the number of M&A activities between biotechnology companies – and it is not very surprising that this number has also increased steadily. In Table 2 major M&A activities between biotechnology companies during the last two years are depicted.

But what factors do have an influence on the development of the M&A activity? The financing environment is still not robust for biotechnology offerings. It is estimated that 30% of the public biotechnology companies has less than a year's cash and most of them are in early-stage development of products and will face significant problems in staying solvent as financing options are also relatively restricted [15]. In the year 2000 biotech companies have taken a major role on the M&A front, accounting for nearly 112 deals, and of these 112 deals, almost one-quarter were international, including the first German-British biotech acquisition – EVOTEC BioSystems AG's $474 million purchase of Oxford Asymmetry International plc, completed in October 2000 as well as the first trans-Atlantic genomics M&A between German-based GPC AG and Mitotix Inc., Cambridge, MA.

4. M&A case studies

Bringing the results of the first sections together, this ultimately shows that M&A activities in the pharmaceutical and biotechnology industry are very likely to occur. Thus, there is a triple layer of M&A: the first one focuses on M&A activities between the pharmaceutical companies themselves, the second one treats M&A activities between pharmaceutical and biotechnology companies, and the third one puts its emphasis on the M&A activities between biotechnology companies themselves.

Because of the close interconnections and relationships among these two industries and the companies operating in them, the questions comes up what layer may be the most interesting to analyze. After some research and preliminary discussions with industry experts, it has become evident, that – as already depicted before – neither the development of the industries nor their M&A activities within and between them can be analyzed separately. Hence, in the context of this paper the further analytical focus will be put on two layers: the pharma-to-pharma and the biotech-to-biotech deals, and a case of each layer is described shortly. The remaining layer, pharma-to-biotech, is part of another current, more extensive research project.

4.1. Pharmacia – Upjohn – Monsanto (now: Pharmacia Corp.)

Pharmacia & Upjohn (P&U), under the direction of its 1997 appointed CEO Fred Hassan, has just successfully finished its post-merger-integration process, which was characterized by cultural conflicts between the company's Swedish, Italian, and American components, profit warnings as well as a drop in share price and is now heading towards its next merger with Monsanto. Before having a closer look at the new merger, it seems reasonable and is indeed necessary to make some remarks about the deal between Pharmacia and Upjohn, because this also explains some of the rationale behind the merger with Monsanto. On the one hand, Upjohn was a rather mid-sized company that had some promising tools, but had suffered a prolonged period of poor productivity in its R&D. Furthermore, all processes from R&D over Marketing and Sales were not working well together. On the other hand, Pharmacia was some kind of collection of small Europe-focused boutiques with regional marketers of products focused on specialty customers and little research. This situation forced both companies to act and to become a strong player in the US. Because P&U regards the US market as the key market of the pharmaceutical industry or in the words of Hassan as "the center of gravity in the pharmaceutical business" [17], it moved its headquarter form London to Peapack, New Jersey – while maintaining its strength in Europe. Fred Hassan was the central figure for the successful integration and can really be considered as an integration manager who scheduled many time-consuming one-on-one meetings with P&U managers around the globe, centralized and streamlined the organization. P&U considers itself as being a globally networked company, which is one that has a global attitude, a kind of cross-functional, boundary-less behavior, shares information and works seamlessly across geographical regions. In the terms of Haspeslagh and Jemison [19] we can speak of an absorption approach, in which a high degree of interdependence is required to create the value expected but has low need for organizational autonomy. Integration in this case implies a full consolidation, over time, of the operations, organizations, and culture of both organizations. The central idea behind this reorganization is expressed in the following Fig. 6 at the example of the seamless product flow system of Pharmacia & Upjohn, a concept in which the whole organization is considered as being a product owner and the worldwide responsibility for R&D, Global Business Management and Global

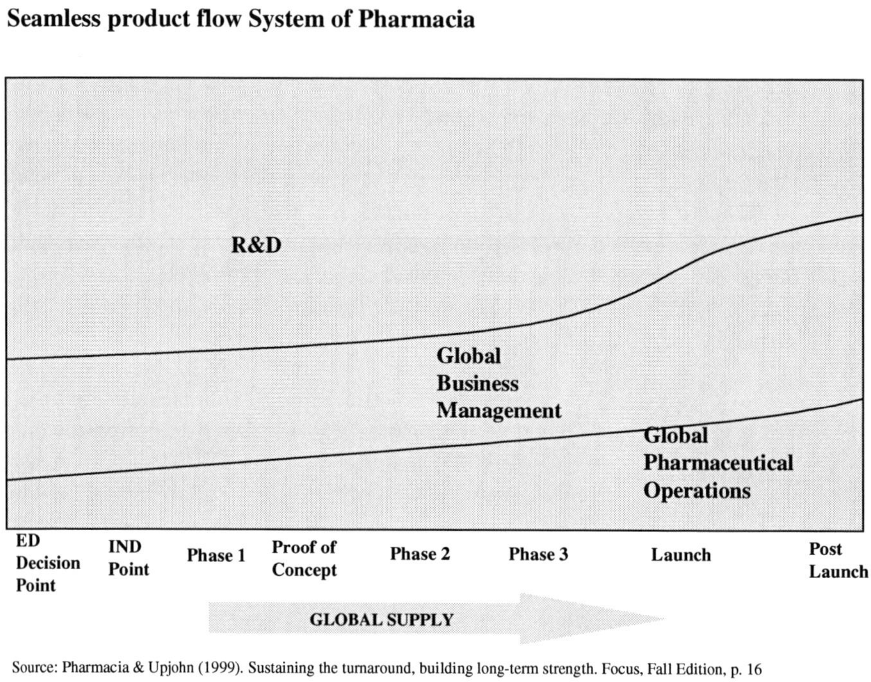

Fig. 6. Seamless product flow system of Pharmacia.

Pharmaceutical Operations lays in the hands of three executives, reporting directly to Hassan.

The merger between Pharmacia & Upjohn and Monsanto that resulted in the formation of Pharmacia Corporation was completed on March 31, 2000. The company estimates total merger and restructuring costs of approximately $2.0 to 2.5 billion for a period of three years.

The short analysis of this merger consists of three different point of views: (1) the benefits for P&U, (2) the benefits for Monsanto and (3) the situation of the combined company, which are discussed briefly. The complimentary drug portfolio of both companies will reduce Monsanto's reliance in Celebrex, by adding several new therapeutic areas, and increase P&U's exposure to new growth products, primarily Celebrex. P&U has a broad international presence while Monsanto derives the majority of its pharmaceutical sales from the US. Moreover, there are potential synergies in the area of marketing and sales as P&U and Monsanto only have one key growth product (Detrol and Celebrex, respectively) for primary care physicians. The combined company has indicated it would have a R&D budget of more than $2 billion, representing approximately 19% of pharmaceutical sales, which is ahead of the average of the industry, estimated at 16%. Furthermore, from the point of view of Monsanto the major benefits are an immediate Earnings per Share accretion for their shareholders, a near-term segregation of their agricultural business, an opportunity for overhead reduction, a stronger balance sheet and, especially, a strengthening of their drug business. Nevertheless, their combined market capitalization of $53 billion is not sufficient to rank among the top-ten pharmaceutical companies.

Referring to an interview with an executive from Pharmacia & Upjohn the major reason for the merger simply was Monsanto's Celebrex, because by this P&U could get a blockbuster. Moreover, Monsanto provides P&U with vast genetic research capabilities and especially with more exposure to the US market, which is perfectly in line with P&U's geographic strategy. During the integration process with Monsanto Hassan also scheduled a lot of one-on-one meetings with Monsanto employees and came up with two 'Hate-to-Lose Lists' for the most valued executives from both companies. Referring to the words of Haspeslagh and Jemison [19], the merger between P&U and Monsanto can rather be considered as a symbiotic acquisition, in which the two organizations first coexist and then become increasingly interdependent. The classification as a symbiotic acquisition seems reasonable, because P&U can be regarded as a fast-growing pharmaceutical group joining forces with a company that had a bigger presence in chemicals and agricultural products than in drugs.

4.2. EVOTEC BioSystems AG – Oxford Asymmetry International plc

EVOTEC BioSystems AG, founded 1993 and headquartered in Hamburg, Germany with a staff of 234 people, is a biotechnology company that focuses on finding new and effective drugs for unmet medical needs for its pharmaceutical and biotechnology partners. It seeks to improve the efficiency and productivity of the pre-clinical drug discovery process. The company is organized in four business units: drug discovery technologies and tools as well as drug discovery services and products. Evotec was listed on the 'Neuen Markt' of the Frankfurt Stock Exchange in November 1999.

Oxford Asymmetry International plc (OAI), founded 1992 and headquartered in Oxford, UK with a staff of 256 people, provides sophisticated chemical services to the worldwide pharmaceutical and biotechnology industries. OAI operates through two divisions: the discovery division, which concentrates on the chemical discovery phase, specializing in an advanced form of combinatorial chemistry, and the development division, which provides services focusing primarily on the development and scale-up of chemical processes. OAI was listed on the London Stock Exchange in March 1998.

The ultimate goal of the merger in a deal worth $474 million is to create a one-stop shop for value-added drug discovery and development services in the pre-clinical phase. By the combination of the two companies – and this represents also the main rationale for the merger – it is assumed that they will realize a sufficient critical mass in order to meet the increasing requirements resulting from the consolidation and outsourcing activities in the pharmaceutical industry. This will be realized by fostering and elaborating the combined position as part of the pharmaceutical value chain. This means, that the new company aims at becoming the first-in-class service provider for pre-clinical development. In contrast to other biotechnology companies, the new company does not intend to cover the whole pharmaceutical value chain, instead it puts its focus on one specific segment, the pre-clinical development phase. Figure 7 provides a schematic overview of the combined activities of the new company and points out how the two companies complement one another. Apart from this main merger rationale, the other reasons can be found in: (1) leveraging customer relationships, (2) repositioning the new entity in order to become the partner of choice for translating raw genetic information into potential drugs, and (3) covering a broader geographical coverage. After the merger the new group will be listed on the German 'Neuen Markt' and the headquarter will be based in Hamburg, however, it is intended that the UK operations will continue to function as they did before the merger. This implies that there will be no real interference from the part of Evotec and the UK operations will operate as a separate entity, so that – in the words of Haspeslagh and Jemison [19] – we can speak of a preservation approach as far as the integration activities are concerned. The boards of the two companies will continue to work together and Edwin Moses, the former Executive Chairman from Oxford Asymmetry, will become President of the new group whereas Karsten Henco, the former Chief Executive Officer from Evotec, will take the roles of Chief Executive Officer and Chief Scientific Officer.

5. Confrontation of theoretical and empirical considerations and findings

Having a closer look at the reasons and key drivers for M&A activities in the biotechnology and pharmaceutical industry one can, at a first glance, consider two fundamental reasons for their appearance: the first one steams from financial necessities, especially from the point of view of the biotechnology companies, which have to ensure their future survival, as well as the pharmaceutical companies, which need to make sure their high profitability margins, and the second one is driven by the need to acquire knowledge in order to remain competitive in the future by having enough promising lead compounds. The financing environment for biotechnology offerings was not robust during the last years and most of the companies are only in early-stage development of products and will face significant challenges to stay solvent. Pharmaceutical companies can mostly acquire broad-based technologies, such as drug delivery, more inexpensively and quickly than they can build the technologies internally. All in all, these are the first two motives which determine M&A activities in both of these industries. Moreover, it becomes evident that the number of M&A deals among biotechnology companies is higher than M&A deals between pharmaceutical and biotechnology companies, although the first ones are much more rich in cash than the second ones. Considering cash and knowledge as the two primary motives of M&A activities, one must also look at where the M&A-Game takes place. Remembering that one-quarter of all biotechnology acquisitions in the year

Contributions of Evotec and OAI in the pre-clinical development phase

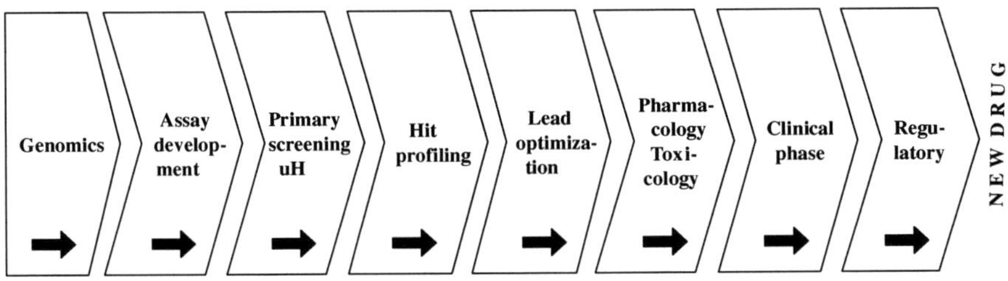

OAI							
(-)	*(-)*	*High Speed chemistry*	*Focused libraries*	*Medicinal chemistry*	*Process R & D*	*Scale-up and manufacturing*	*(-)*
EVOTEC							
Target ID	*Assay development*	*Screening*	*Secondary assays*		*(-)*	*(-)*	*(-)*

Source: Evotec (2000). Background to the proposed merger

Fig. 7. Combined activities of Evotec and Oxford Asymmetry.

2000 were international, it becomes obvious that biotech companies have broadened their reach far beyond their own borders in their search for good science and great scientists, in other words knowledge. The biotechnology industry becomes as global as the capital markets are, because investors are always seeking to put their money where they can expect the best rate of return, wherever in the world that might be and biotech companies – whatever nationality – are quickly looking beyond their own geographic boundaries not only for merger and acquisition possibilities but also for good science, strategic alliances and funding. Taking this into consideration the need for internationalization of the biotech companies matches perfectly with the requirements of capital markets and creates a win-win-situation for both of them.

Apart from that also some other driving forces need to be taken into account for each industry separately. Another effect of this consolidation process is that the market capitalization of the new groups increases and, by this, they are, on the one hand, less vulnerable against unfriendly takeovers as well as, on the other hand, they are at the same time rather able to carry out a takeover attempt on their own. From this it follows, that the struggle for independence or, in other terms, for keeping in control of the company is another important motive.

Moreover, the consolidation of pharmaceutical companies has led to broader product lines and larger sales forces globally. Thus, it becomes increasingly difficult for most biotechnology companies to become fully integrated and, by this, to compete against the pharmaceutical companies directly. Furthermore, with each merger the number of potential partners for biotechnology companies from the pharmaceutical side declines. This bears the consequence that biotechnology companies must build up a critical mass in terms of market capitalization in order not to be taken over as well as in terms of capacities in order to meet the increasing demands resulting from the consolidation process in the pharmaceutical industry, as i.e. Evotec and Oxford Asymmetry did. From a strategic point of view more and more biotechnology companies will focus on a certain step of the pharmaceutical value chain and become a niche player.

What can we learn from an integration point of view? According to the specific situation different post-merger integration strategies (either in an absorption, symbiotic or preservation approach) apply. Furthermore, a lot depends on people and their knowledge, so that the individual/ personal level must be granted a certain degree of importance. In a biotech-to-biotech deal this is not such an extreme crucial issue because there is a combination of two, rather small, entities which after the merger often continue to exist as separate entities as they did before. Additionally, due to the small size of biotechnology companies their organizational structure is clearly laid out, so that a direct and personal communication between the top executives and the rest of the employees is nothing particular but part of all-day work. In big pharmaceutical companies, however, this is surely not the case. But, as one can see at the example of Fred Hassan interpersonal communication is of crucial importance for the success of the integration process. He had to establish the communication situation which is quite normal for biotechnology companies by scheduling a lot of one-on-one meetings all around the world. In the context of such a big integration his role as an integration manger becomes of special significance. Ashkenas/ Francis [2] identified four central roles or activities an integration manager should perform: he has to (1) inject speed, (2) create structure, (3) engineer success, and (4) make social connections. Comparing these four criteria with the activities carried out by Fred Hassan, he perfectly turns out as being an ideal integration manager.

6. Summary and future research

Less than half of all mergers and acquisitions ever reach their promised strategic and financial goals, yet companies spent more on M&A in 1999 than ever before. Companies worldwide spent $3.3 trillion on mergers and acquisitions – 32% more than was spent in 1998 and the pharmaceutical and biotechnological industry are part of this merger wave. From the development of these two industries we have seen that the trend towards an increase in M&A was unstoppable, which has also been proved by empirical data. After that, we considered two M&A case studies in more detail in order to gain a deeper insight into this development by analyzing different motives and integration activities. But, of course, this was just a very first step.

Analyzing one case study among pharmaceutical companies, on the one hand, and biotechnology companies, on the other hand, we have depicted two extremes. Hence, the next step will be to analyze M&A activities between pharmaceutical and biotechnology companies, because there is definitely a greater gap between them as compared to the differences in M&A activities among companies of the same level.

Apart from that a further analysis of the development between M&A activities on the same level is also needed. In this context forthcoming research will deal with the financial success of such deals by analyzing the development of their stock prices before and after the merger. Moreover, it might be interesting to analyze whether M&A activities between biotechnology companies from one country are more successful than international or even trans-Atlantic ones.

References

[1] W. Abernathy and K. Clark, Innovation: Mapping the winds of creative destruction, *Research Policy* **14**(1) (1985), 3–22.

[2] R.N. Ashkenas and S.C. Francis, *Integration Managers: Special leaders for special times,* Harvard Business Review, November-December, 2000, pp. 108–116.

[3] BASF, Pharma business sold for $6.9 billion: "BASF to focus more strongly on innovative chemistry, a highly efficient Verbund and a global presence", Ludwigshafen: Author, Press release December 15, 2000.

[4] BCG, *The pharmaceutical industry into its second century: From Serendipity to strategy,* BCG Report: Author, 1999.

[5] P. Blau, *The organization of academic work,* John Wiley & Sons, New York, 1973.

[6] A. Coyler, Financing as a driver for mergers and acquisitions, *Nature Biotechnology* **17** (1999), BE13.

[7] D. Crane, *Invisible college: Diffusion of knowledge in scientific communities,* University of Chicago Press, Chicago, 1972.

[8] D.M. DeCarolis and D.L. Deeds, The Impact of stocks and flows of organizational knowledge on firm performance: An empirical investigation of the biotechnology industry, *Strategic Management Journal* **20**(10) (1999), 953–968.

[9] J. Duelli, Pharma 2000. Pharmaunternehmen im Fusionsfieber – Die Bedeutung von M&A zur Wertsteigerung [Pharma 2000. Pharmaceutical companies in a fever of merger – The importance of M&A for the increase in value], Bain Report: Author, 2000.

[10] S. Endres, Geschäftsbereiche von Großkonzernen vs. spezialisierte Unternehmen – Ein Performancevergleich am Beispiel der Pharmaindustrie [Business units of big groups vs. specialized companies – A comparison of performance at the example of the pharmaceutical industry]. Unpublished master's thesis, Otto-Friedrich-University of Bamberg, 2000.

[11] Frankfurter Allgemeine Zeitung, *Nur gute Leistungen schützen Schering vor einer Übernahme,* [Only a good performance protects Schering from a takeover], July 25, 2000, pp. 30.

[12] Frankfurter Allgemeine Zeitung, *Bayer feilt an seinem Strategiekonzept,* [Bayer files at its strategy concept], December 9, 2000, pp. 17.

[13] Frankfurter Allgemeine Zeitung, *BASF berät über den Verkauf der Pahrmasparte,* [BASF discusses about the sale of the pharma division], December 13, 2000, pp. 21.

[14] GlaxoWellcome, *Affymax: providing a technology magnet,* GlaxoWellcome World, 1996, pp. 21–23.

[15] Goldman Sachs, *Strategic Alliances in Biotechnology,* Author, New York, 2000.

[16] N. Greis, M. Dibner and A. Bean, External partnering as a response to innovation barriers and global competition in biotechnology, *Research Policy* **24** (1995), 609–630.

[17] V. Griffith, The people factor in post-merger integration, *strategy+business* **20** (Third Quarter 2000), 82–90.

[18] A. Hacking, *Economic aspects of biotechnology,* University Press, Cambridge, 1986.

[19] P.C. Haspeslagh and D.B. Jemison, *Managing acquisitions. Creating value through corporate renewal,* The Free Press, New York, 1991.

[20] J. Liebeskind, A. Oliver, L. Zucker and M. Brewer, Social networks, learning, and flexibility: Sourcing scientific knowledge in new biotechnology firms, *Organization Science* **7**(4) (1996), 428–443.

[21] R. Merton, *The sociology of science,* University of Chicago Press, Chicago, 1973.

[22] OTA see US. Congress.

[23] E. Pierce, The pioneer IPOs: Never say die, *BioCentury* **7**(18) (1999), A1–A4.

[24] G. Pisano, *The development factory: Unlocking the potential of process innovation,* Harvard Business School Press, Boston, 1997.

[25] W. Powell, *The social construction of an organizational field: The case of biotechnology,* Unpublished working paper. Tucson: Department of Sociology, University of Arizona, 1993.

[26] W. Powell, Inter-organizational collaboration in the biotechnology industry, *Journal of Institutional and Theoretical Economics* **152**(1) (1996), 197–215.

[27] W. Powell, Learning from collaboration: Knowledge and networks in the biotechnology and pharmaceutical industry, *California Management Review* **40** (1998), 228–240.

[28] W. Powell and P. Brantley, Competitive cooperation in biotechnology: Learning through networks? in: *Networks and organizations,* N. Nohria and R. Eccles, eds, Harvard Business School Press, Boston, 1992, pp. 366–394.

[29] D.J. Purcell, Navigating biotechnology's new fiscal opportunities, *Nature Biotechnology* **16** (1998), 51.

[30] D.J. Purcell, Financing biotechnology in an efficient market, *Nature Biotechnology* **17** (1999), BE31–BE32.

[31] J. Schumpeter, Theorie der wirtschaftlichen Entwicklung [The theory of economic development] (4th ed.), Duncker und Humblot, Berlin, 1934.

[32] R. Teitelman, *Gene dreams: Wall street, academia, and the rise of biotechnology,* Basic Books, New York, 1989.

[33] M. Tushman and P. Anderson, Technological discontinuities and organizational environments, *Administrative Science Quarterly* **31**(3) (1986), 439–465.

[34] US Congress, Office of Technology Assessment (1988). New developments in biotechnology: US investment in biotechnology – Special Report OTA-BA-360, US Government Printing Office, Washington, DC, 1988.

[35] P. Wirth, Biotechnologie/ Biomedizin – Stand und Perspektiven [Biotechnology/ Biomedicine – State of the art and perspectives], in: *Biotec: Technologieforum [Biotech: Technology forum],* C.P. Hollenberg and V. Hempel, eds, Düsseldorf: Rudolf Stehle, 1994, pp. 53–65.

Pharmaceuticals Policy and Law 5 (2002) 63–78
IOS Press

The convergence of the pharmaceutical and the food industry through functional food: Strategic change and Business opportunity or an illusion?

Malin Brännback, Aart Jan de Heer and Patricia Wiklund
Turku School of Economics and Business Administration/Innomarket, Rehtorinpellonkatu 3, FIN-20500 Turku, Finland
E-mail: {malin.brannback, aartjan.deheer, patricia.wiklund}@tukkk.fi

Currently the pharmaceutical industry is undergoing dramatic strategic changes, affecting the entire life science sector. In this paper the strategic change of the pharmaceutical industry is studied through the convergence of the food and pharmaceutical industry from the point of functional food. Our primary focus is on the European market. Starting from the life-sciences concept, several questions will be discussed: What are functional foods? Does functional food offer real business opportunities for pharmaceuticals? How far apart are the two industries. Are there real synergies to be found or are the two industries antagonistic?

1. Introduction

Advances in biotechnology have not only ignited technological changes within the pharmaceutical industry, but also given rise to entirely new industries, such as biotechnology and in a more broader sense *life sciences* [13]. Massive consolidation is currently taking place where large pharmaceutical companies, small start-up and larger biotechnology companies, food companies, and agri companies are merging or forming strategic alliances in fierce pursuit of maintaining long-term profitability. For example, the current structural change within the pharmaceutical industry is expected to produce a very different industry by the end of 2001. It is estimated that some eight pharmaceutical companies will cover 80 percent of the market [1].

The pharmaceutical industry has since 1994 experienced exceptionally high annual growth rates. In 1999, the global pharmaceutical market grew by 11% with sales estimated to $337.2 billion from a $304.7 billion in 1998. IMS (http://www.imshealth.com/) is expecting this growth to continue despite government pressure and blockbuster drugs going off-patent. As the number of patented blockbuster drugs is decreasing the pharmaceutical industry has recently been attracted to one particular area within the food industry, namely functional food. Functional food appears to be an area where the drug industry can stretch their discovery and development competencies, in particular their knowledge of clinical trials, and therein potentially develop products which have much in common with drugs, but are easier to develop and commercialised. The easiness comes from the fact that food is not subject to the same clinical trial requirements as are drugs. Yet functional food draw on similar disease specific knowledge present in drug discovery processes. Moreover, functional food is an attractive area because food is normally consumed on a daily basis thus representing a huge market potential. The interest for functional foods is also fuelled by an increased health awareness of consumers and their interest in eating healthier food, increased research knowledge of the link between food and well-being, knowledge of how different ingredients of food affect the physiology, increased number of welfare diseases, and an ageing population.

According to Euromonitor 2000 (http://www.euromonitor.com/), the estimated value for the world market for functional foods was worth US$31.661 billion in 1999. The market has grown over the period 1995-1999 by 53.5% in current value terms. More detailed estimations confirm that the largest market in both terms of size and importance is the US, with a lion's share of the world market for functional foods. In 1999 it was estimated 60.5% of the total or US$19.15 billion by value. The corresponding value for the European market accounts for 17.6% of the world market in 1999 (US$5.57 billion). Japan is the third most important market with 16.8% of the world market in 1999, or US$5.31 billion by value. The global forecast of Euromonitor is that the global market for functional foods to reach US$53.9 billion in value by 2004. The overall category growth in the period 1999–2004 is then 70.4%. The market estimations vary drastically and are dependent of the definition of functional food. Despite the differences the message is clear: there is a huge potential and functional food is said to be the connecting link between food, nutrition, and health.

The technological and structural changes are also having significant effects on the strategic management process of both established and emerging organisations. First the concept of an industry is changing, i.e. a new industry recipe emerges. Second, the changes on an industry level will naturally have effects on the strategic management process on a corporate level, i.e. the company paradigm is changing. Finally, the strategic change affects the strategy logic on the individual manager level, i.e. the subjective logic by individual managers on what key issues should be considered is changing. Whether a manager is capable of adjusting to the new situation will in the long run affect the success or failure of the organisation. Therefore, what at first glance may seem as a short cut to success may upon closer analysis fade into an illusion. In this paper, we study the emerging market of functional food and explore in what ways pharmaceuticals and functional foods differ. Are there significant differences that require different considerations and hence can turn a promise of success into shire illusion?

In the next section we describe the emerging life science sector within which both pharmaceuticals and functional foods exist. In the third section we present the strategic changes in terms of industry recipe, company paradigm, and strategy logic. In section four we point at key differences of functional food and pharmaceuticals. In section five we show what the implications of these differences have on the strategy logic of the firm. Finally we conclude and present issues of future research.

2. The emergence of the life-science sector

Similar to what the development of the binary computer code did to previously disparate industries within information and communications technology industry (ICT), the mapping of the human genome is doing for industries focusing on life. All industries dealing with living things and life now have a common language and are converging around this scientific and technological breakthrough and contributing to the formation of what is called the *life science* industry. Since the genetic code is information in itself another convergence is also taking place with the ICT industry.

The phrase *life sciences* is an old concept, which was recoined in 1996 by the US agri-business giant Monsanto and the European pharmaceutical leader Novartis. Disciplines like biotechnology and biosciences no longer seemed broad enough – and life-sciences were thus created to indicate the development of new health care products and markets through open networking of various sciences such as medicine, pharmacy, genetic engineering, food science, agriculture, physics, chemistry, electronics, informatics, and psychology. What orginally started as a human genome mapping project launched by the US government in 1990 [13], has today developed into a cluster of industries which concentrate on developing commercial health care applications for global markets. In Fig. 1 we find an illustration of the synergies between chemistry, biotechnology and genomics in the creation of novel products such as agrochemicals, high-value commodities with enhanced nutritional or industrial uses, and pharmaceuticals. Life sciences companies have developed to capitalize on these complementary technologies. In the cross-section of these technologies, hybrid products with resistant, health promoting and targeted properties are developed. Typical of these products is that they are based on capital intensive, riskful, and long-term R&D and that they developed in a social climate balancing between demands on product safety and product power.

The life science sector is thus emerging out of several previously separate industries and biotechnology is playing a key role. The agriculture business has played an important role, and will continue to do so. However, our focus in this paper is on biotechnology, as the major technological change and pharmaceutical biotechnology and functional food are the two industries within the life science sector subject to closer study due to major structural and strategic change. Pharamceutical biotechnology is accounting for more than 90 percent of global sales and is expected to conitune to do so in the next ten years [33]. Also, functional food is the only sector of the of the food industry projected double digit growth figures. It has been estimated that functional foods will account for ca. 25% of all food products in the next decade, which means a total world market of at least \$300–700 billion [16]. Neverhteless, projections for the agriculture sector are also impressive (see Table 1), which will obviously result from advances in biotechnology [27].

The potential of life-sciences technology in the realm of e.g. pharmacy, agriculture and food industry is enormous: many new medicines with targeted effects will be developed within this decade, food producers will be able to significantly enhance the

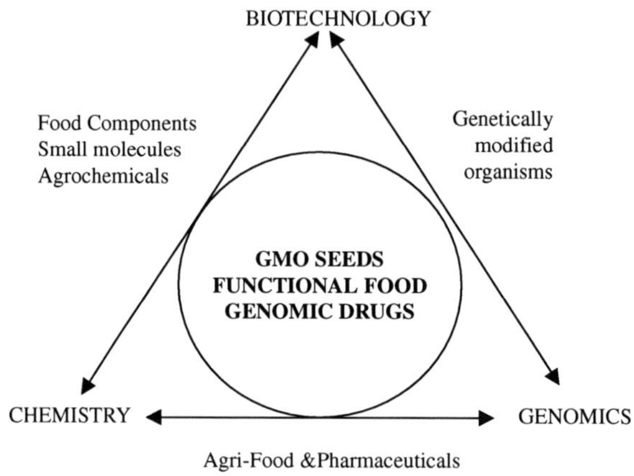

Fig. 1. The interaction between chemistry, biotechnology and genomics (adapted from [5]).

quantity and quality of their crops and livestock, and new organic components will be developed to reinforce the health function of food. Taking into special consideration the future potential of life-sciences in the food industry, it can be expected that the Hippocratic adage *"Let food be thy medicine and medicine thy food"* will come true in a very literary way. Thinking optimistically, future foods may not only prevent, treat or cure single diseases, but may also help regenerating parts or functions of the entire human body. A look at the current state of the life-sciences industry, however, learns that this sector has still a long way to go.

2.1. *Functional food*

Despite promising prospects, the market for functional food is still restricted and unpredictible. Functional food appears to be a very problematic area for a number of reasons. One of the major problems are concerned with the definition of functional food. Functional food is just one term among a number of others indicating the same (pharma foods, medical food, hyper-nutrious foods, smart foods, mood foods, and designer foods, to mention a few). The primary area of confusion surrounds the difficulty in agreeing on what should be included and what not, in this new group of food. Above all the definition varies between countries. In the US the term nutraceuticals is often used and has been defined as "any substance that may be considered a food or a part of a food, and provides medical or health benefits, including the prevention and treatment of disease" [43]. The problem with this definition is that it includes just any food. Vaclavic [40] defines functional food as: "any modified food or food ingredient that may provide a health benefit beyond the traditional nutrients it contains". Functional foods can also be defined depending on from which angle they are approached: scientific, technological or legislative. The first is about food that provides a medical or physiological advantage over and

Table 1
Biotech Global Product Sales and Forecast (2000, 2005, and 2010) in USD billion and US sales (1996 and 2006)[1]

Key Sectors	1996 Actual	2000	2005	2006	2010	'00-'10 Growth ppa
Human terapeutics	7.6	11.7	20.6	24.5	36.3	12
Human diagnostics	1.8	2.5	3.7	4.1	5.4	8
Agriculture	0.3	0.78	1.95	1.7	4.2	18
Specialities	0.3	0.55	1.17	1.6	2.4	16
Non-medical diagn.	0.2	0.32	0.48	0.5	0.7	8
Total	10.2	15.85	27.9	32.4	49.00	12
World total	NA	25.00	35.00	NA	85.00	

above what is expected when consuming normal nutrition. The second is about the natural or processed food product. The last is about when food has a health claim on its package. The difficulties of defining the concept keep companies from wholeheartedly investing in the new market and many decide to 'wait and see'. Currently, a so called consensus definition seems to be emerging, i.e. most important players seem to have adopted this one [10, p. S6]:

> "A food can be regarded as 'functional' if it is satisfactorily demonstrated to affect beneficially one or more target functions in the body, beyond adequate nutritional effects, in a way that is relevant to either an improved state of health and well-being and/or reduction of risk of disease. Functional food must remain foods and they must demonstrate their effects in amount that can normally be expected to be consumed in the diet: they are not pills or capsules, but part of a normal food pattern.
> A functional food can be a natural food, a food to which a component has been added, or a food from which a component has been removed by technological or biotechnological means. It can also be a food where the nature of one or more components has been modified, or a food in which the bioavailability of one or more components has been modified, or any combination of these possibilities.
> A functional food might be functional for all members of a population or for particular groups of the population, which might be defined, for example, by age or by genetic constitution."

Thus, it is unclear what the product actually is and therefore a true definition of the market also becomes unclear. The definitional dilemma gives rise to problems in the area of knowing which regulatory scheme applies with respect to the product as well as the market. There are further problems in defining who the actors are, which directly refers to who the competitors on the market are. Defining the market and the competitors are basic elements underlying the strategic management process of

[1] This table is based on data from two sources. The figures for 1996 and 2006 are taken from Oliver, 2000 and the other figures are based on data from Consulting Resources Corporation. The idea with combining the sources has been to show the magnitude of the US market in comparison with the rest of the world as well as to show that the forecasts are similar in size.

Table 2
The number of patent approvals during the period 1977–1997 [33]

Year	Drugs	Microbiology	Multicellular organisms	Recombinant DNA
1977	660	591	0	14
1982	730	711	1	111
1987	958	1099	19	204
1992	1691	1965	52	356
1997	3372	4178	318	506
Total	7411	8544	390	1191

a company. Finally, there appears to be a very strong cultural aspect of functional food [44,45], which poses considerable problems to many smaller food companies, which traditionally have been and still are operating mainly on domestic markets. The functional food market is global.

2.2. *Biotechnology-based pharmaceuticals*

It is commonly agreed that the biotechnology revolution started in 1973 when Herbert Boyer and Stanley Cohen successfully recombined DNA from one organism with that of another. Only a few years later the results of this scientific discovery began having commercial effects. In 1975, the first biotech company was formed, Genentech, which in 1980 had their initial public offering (IPO). Since then the field has developed rampantly, which is most visibly portrayed in number of patent approvals by the US Patent and Trademark Office (Table 2). Although there is a long way from patent approval to final commercial success of a new product the message is clear.

From 1986 to 1988 the FDA approved only 10 new bio-engineered drugs. Although the number is perhaps low they set the pattern for future. Despite the stock crash in 1987 the industry survived and entered the next decade with a growing number of companies reaching clinical trial stage each month. Companies raised a record $2 billion in the first half of 1991. Actual sales reached nearly $6 billion. In 1993 SmithKline Beecham and Human Genome Sciences made an alliance, which changed the outlook for the entire industry. In 1995 16 bio-engineered drugs were approved and 20 the following year. The number of IPOs increased 537 percent in 1997, market capitalisation increased 60 percent. Globally 1200 antibodies are either on the market or in development. The deal between Genentech and Eli Lilly took place in 1978. In 1998 Bayer made a deal with Millenium worth $456 million. For a 14 percent stake in Millenium, Bayer has the future rights to 256 drug targets. Guilford and Amgen made another deal for $466 million. Market capitalisation for Biogen in 1999 was more than $3.4 billion and Amgen $8 billion.

The biotech revolution did not only change the R&D procedures in pharmaceutical R&D, it also changed the business environment and business operations [7, 23]. Mergers and acquisitions, as well as strategic alliances have become standard procedures in an industry, which used to regard drug R&D (Fig. 2) as proprietary

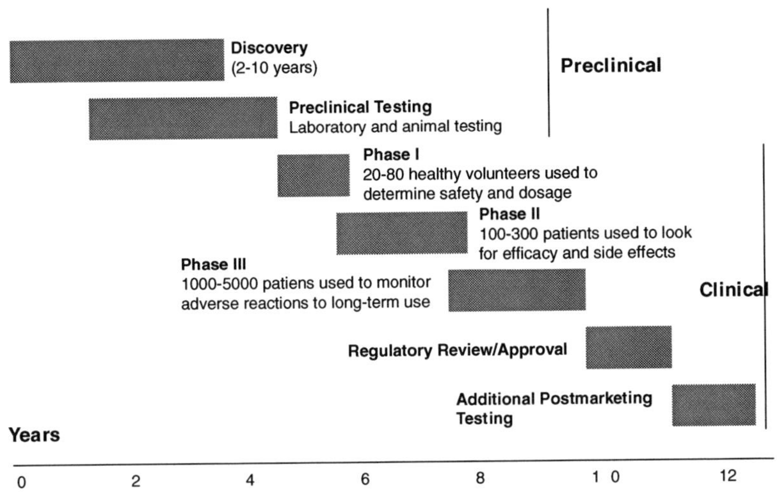

Fig. 2. The drug development process.

knowledge and a core competence. Each phase in the drug R&D process offers separate business opportunities. For several small biotechnology companies the business idea focus on, for example, discovering a drug and taking it through to preclinical trials only, after which the product is licensed to larger pharmaceutical companies. Today networking and collaboration is key to global success.

3. Industry recipe, company paradigm, and strategy logic in the context of change

Traditionally, the concept of an industry has been a way of categorising organisations, which compete in similar environments, i.e. they serve the same market by manufacturing similar products [20,34]. Barney [3] argues that firms within an industry are identical in terms of strategically relevant resources they control and the strategies they pursue. However, the strategies pursued are not necessarily identical and this is due to differences in managerial decision-making processes due to differences in the cognitive orientation of managers, i.e. differences in dominant logic [36].

It is also thought that within an industry there are certain common beliefs and assumptions, which are held as consistent and realistic [17]. These are known as *industry recipe*. Other concepts used by various authors belonging to this same family are e.g. industrial wisdom cognitive maps [11,12,18], dominant logic [36]. A sub-set of an industry recipe is the *company paradigm*, which is a representation of managerial perceptions and views of how to succeed in their business environment. The starting point here is cognition and personal constructs [22] or the idea of a

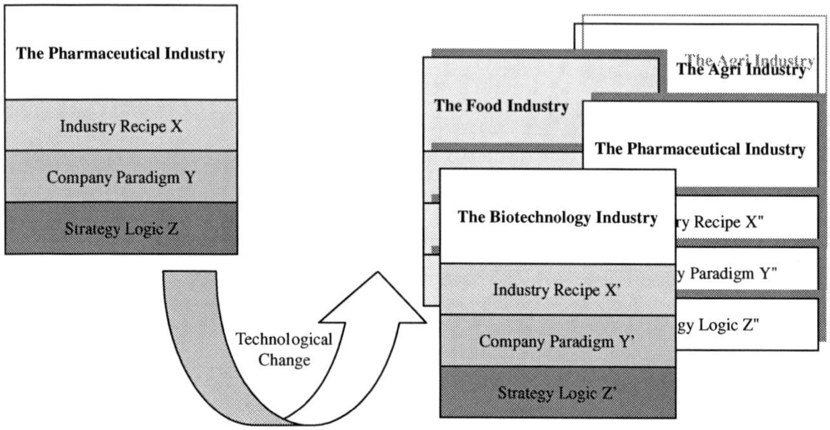

Fig. 3. The impact of technological change on industry recipe, company paradigm, and strategy logic [6].

status quo [2], sometimes also referred to as worldviews [41,42], which develop over time and tend to be persistent (for extensive lists of related concepts see [23]). Company paradigm can significantly impact the success or failure of an organisation. It can provide means for creating a sustainable competitive advantage (SCA) or it can inhibit necessary change [20]. At the core of the company paradigm we find the strategy logic of the firm [23,32] (see Fig. 3). Strategy logic is defined as follows:

> "Startegy logic of a firm comprehends a set of core elements in harmony or coordination, steering the whole of a firm towards survival and successs. Strategy logic is *subjective logic* representing the thinking of key person(s) in the firm ..." ([32, p. 23]; italics added by authors)

According to Näsi et al. [32], the strategy logic of a firm dictates what needs to be done. The nature of the strategy logic changes incrementally hosting dominating ideas and principles, which guide decision-making processes concerned with marketing and product decisions, acquisitions and mergers, investments, etc.

Thus, the strategic way of thinking by executives is generally very stable [4,23, 36,46,47] where the process of retrofitting, i.e. incorporating new insights into established patterns of thought is often nearly overwhelming. This is due to the human nature where people's fundamental beliefs and values change very slowly – if at all. If the firm operates in an industry with a stable industry recipe with a strong company paradigm, there will be considerable difficulties in implementing radical strategic change. Yet, technological change may just require the adoption of a new strategic way of thinking, a new perception of the business per se, provided the company intends to stay in business. And very fast.

In order to understand the relevance of industry recipe to the strategic management process it is necessary to clarify the relationship. As pointed out by several authors ([20,23,25,31,36,46,47] to mention a few) strategy is first and foremost the result of a cognitive process, i.e. it is created by people based on their perceptions of

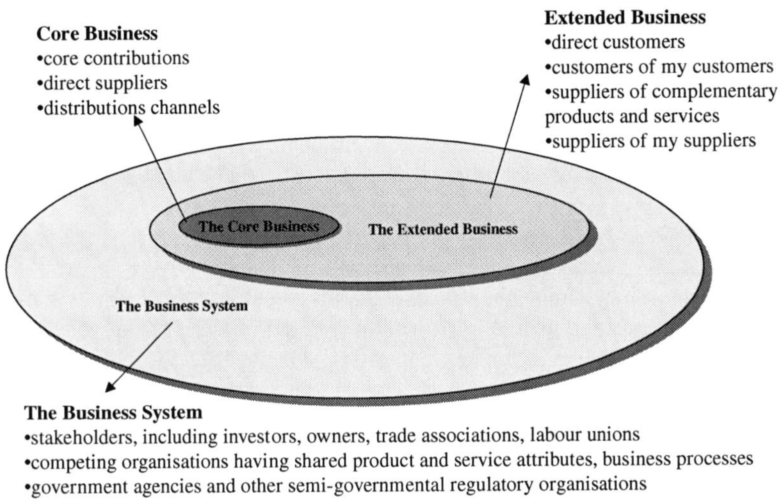

Fig. 4. The business system model (adapted from [29], see [39]).

environmental forces and organisational capabilities where the former generally are regarded as opportunities and threats and the latter as strengths and weaknesses [9]. The recipe becomes the backbone of the strategic management process and a formula for how things 'are done around here'. Johnson and Scholes [20, p. 41] claims that "*... it is likely that purely analytical questioning of the recipe not only will be taken as evidence of the analyst's lack of understanding of the problems of the business but may actually be perceived as an political threat, rather than objective analysis, for it will very likely be perceived as an attack on those most associated with core beliefs ...*".

Moore [29] uses a different set of concepts for the purpose of staking out the boundaries of what we used to call industry. According to Moore, there is the core business at the heart of all activities (see Fig. 4). The core business includes the focal firm, but also direct suppliers and distribution channels. The following level is the extended business, which goes further down in the value system including suppliers of direct suppliers, suppliers of complimentary products and services, direct customers and their customers. The final layer Moore calls a business ecosystem or the business system as used by Suoniemi and Brännback [39] including stakeholders (investors, owners, trade associations, and labour unions), competing organisations having shared product and service attributes and business processes, and government agencies or other semi-governmental regulatory organisations. The model presented by Moore draws on the ideas from stakeholder theory [30], Porter's classical 5-forces model [34], the value chain concept [35], and the concept of strategic groups [6,8, 14,15,24,34] and captures the consequences of changes in an industry or industries, where the relevant issues subject to strategic decision-making also change.

The idea of incremental changes in the strategy process rests firmly outside the high technology, high change industry, such as the information and communications technology industry (ICT) and more recently pharmaceuticals or biotechnology industry. In these industries technological change is the major change driver of the industry with significant implications on the strategic decision-making process and the success of a firm. The technological change can be such that it changes the R&D paradigm giving rise to changes in how firms compete and contributing to new forms of collaborations within the traditional industry. The technological change may even be such that it impacts several other industries through knowledge spill-over, i.e. the new technology may yield profits or other benefits to parties who are not regarded as the original owner of the technology thus blurring the industry boundaries. In such a case the industry recipe, company paradigm, and the strategy logic will change for a number of industries and the definition of the concept of industry will require retrofitting.

Technological change can either lead to process innovation where, e.g. the R&D process is radically changed or it may lead to product innovation or both. The technological change can be incremental at first but have much more dramatic consequences once the technology has won wider acceptance leading to the change of an entire industry. This is called punctuated equilibrium, i.e. strategies develop incrementally with periodic transformational changes [21,38]. As shown in Fig. 3 the technological change in pharmaceuticals has not only impacted the pharmaceutical industry, but also the food industry and the agricultural industry, to mention a few. Oliver [33] adds several other industries, such as the materials industry (both organic and non-organic materials), mining, environmental remediation, forestry, and health services. In fact, Oliver [33] argues that biotechnology will impact every industry within the next few decades leading to the convergence of industries thus forming new business systems (Fig. 4).

Accroding to Moore's rationale the core business can in fact be part of several business systems and the convergence of industries and knowledge spill-over enable an industry to be part of several business systems (Fig. 5). The dotted circles in Fig. 5 depicts this described complexity within which company paradigms, strategy logic are to be formed.

Regardless, of the number of industries, the key point is that the definition of a business becomes cumbersome, in particular if industry membership is regarded as a central variable. In traditional terms the industry has been regarded as a key element because it defines the competitive scope and scale, it provides insights about the product market, and customer segments, i.e. basic elements in strategic decision-making [34]. Now the industry as a unit of analysis may prove unsuitable.

4. Differences and similarities between functional food and biotechnology-based pharmaceuticals

Since functional food is considered to occupy the grey domain between food and medicine, it is necessary to compare some central features of the pharmaceutical

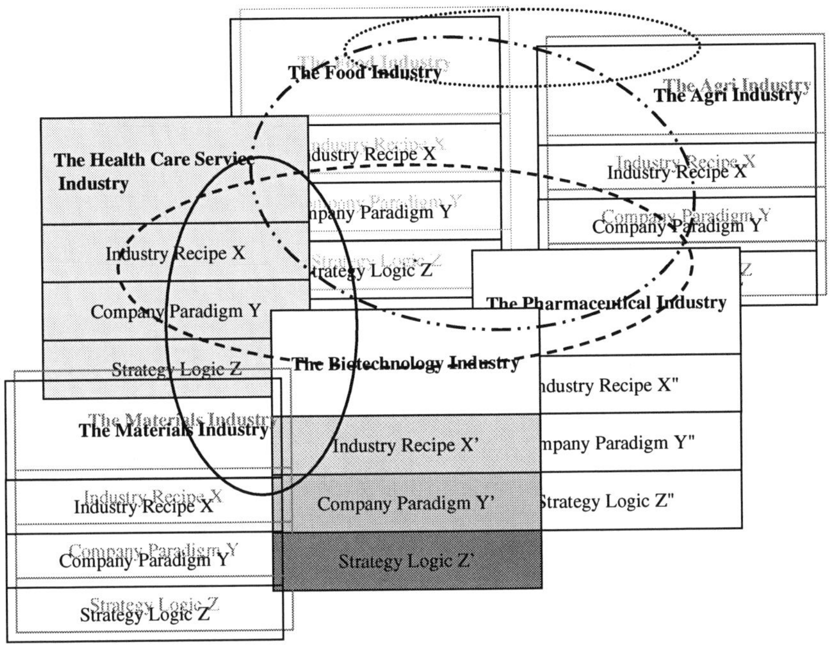

Fig. 5. The formation of multiple business systems from the convergence of industries, where firms in one industry can be part of several business systems. The industries shown are not conclusive, only illustrative [7].

sector and the food industry.

The driving force in both industries is the need to secure growth in long-term profitability, which forces both industries to look for new business opportunities close to their existing core knowledge and core business. The biotechnology revolution has opened up the arena as the technology can be used by both industries, and both industries deal with life and health. Both industries are currently undergoing massive consolidations with large mergers and acquisitions. However, the end-products of the two industries are very different and therefore the served market is very different. The food industry, for example, serves the end-consumer directly whereas, the pharmaceutical industry rarely serves the end-consumer directly (except over-the-counter drugs) but directs its activities to intermediaries, i.e. physicians.

The pharmaceutical industry is one of the most strictly regulated industries. Regulations concern all aspects of drug development, manufacturing and marketing, particularly product safety, intellectual property and pricing control. Although the food industry is also regulated it laggs substantially behind the pharmaceutical industry in terms of rigour and magnitude.

The pharmaceutical industry is truly a high technology industry whereas the food industry is still by and large a low technology industry. There are basically two characterisitics of a high technology industry [33]: (i) the R&D investments as

Table 3
Differences between the food and the pharmaceutical industry in relation to functional food

	Food industry	Pharmaceutical industry	Functional food
Technological intensity	Low	High	Medium/High
Patents	Low	High	High
Regulatory intensity	Less	High	Unclear
Target market	End-consumer	Physicians; Intermediary	End-consumer
Market scope	Local	Global	Local and Global
Pricing	Consumer pays all	Consumer pays a proportion	Consumer pays all
	Low	High	Price premium

percentage of sales, and (ii) number of patents. As shown in Table 2, the number of patents are huge. Also, pharamceuticals and biotechnology are tho most R&D intensive non-defense industries, whereas a typical feature of the food industry is its low R&D profile. On average, the industry has been spending about 1% of its net product sales on R&D, whereas the corresponding figures for the pharmaceutical and biotechnology industries are 10–20% an astonishing 36% respectively [33]. The low level in the food industry has just enabled it to remain abreast of broad developments. Hence the food industry can be characterised as traditionally having been a low technology industry, which through functional food has to go through a radical shift into the high technology sector. The situation is similar to the agricultural business prior to the use of genetic engineering [13]. Moreover, as already pointed out the food industry serves the consumer market directly, whereas the pharmaceutical industry serves the consumer market through an intermediary. The food industry, in general, serves a domestic market although part of it is global. However, in most countries it is still a highly domestic industry. The pharmaceutical market is global although the national health care systems, which govern the served markets, are generally very domestic [26]. From a product development point of view, drug R&D generally starts with a disease for which a cure is sought for, whereas product development within the food industry starts with asking 'who will eat this'. Finally, the pricing issue is different. Pharmaceuticals are generally expensive, but in most western countries some kind of reimbursement system exists, i.e. the end-consumer rarely pays the full price. However, for food the customer pays 100%. In terms of functional food, which has higher R&D costs leading to premium pricing pressures, there is no reimbursement system available. Whether customers are willing to, en mass, pay a premium price appears doubtful. The differences are presented in Table 3.

5. Discussion and issues for future research

Thus, the differences, which we have pointed at, have considerable strategic significance. They show that functional foods, which as a product in terms of R&D may have several traits in common with the pharmaceutical industry, has significant differences with pharmaceuticals, which refer to strategic market management issues.

The strategic market management considerations have an overall aim at creating a sustainable competitive advantage. This means that from a managerial point of view there are different considerations to be made during the strategic decisions-making processes that encompass all key issues decisive for the success of the product, whether a food, functional food, or a pharmaceutical product. It is important to keep in mind that the functional food market is still an emergent market, whereas the pharmaceutical and food market – although under considerable change – are mature markets. Hence the product is in a different stage with respect to the product life-cycle and with respect to consumer acceptance. Following the traditional diffusions of innovations model [37] consumers first become aware, then develop an interest, proceed to potentially try the product and provided it is a positive experience they accept the product. With respect to functional foods the companies launching these products still face the product of making large customer groups even aware of the product, whereas traditional and ordinary food as well as drugs are accepted.

Moore [28] makes a very valid classification of consumers of high technology products, which is well applicable in the context of functional food (Fig. 6). According to this model there are always technology enthusiasts and visionaries who are the first consumers to try the product and even go as far as to accept it. This generates sufficient amounts of sales leading managers in the company to believe that the market – the mass – is really taking on. However, as can be seen from the figure it is a rather small proportion of the market and it is not large enough to ensure long-term profitability but enough to show short-term revenues. The managerial challenge is therefore to cross the chasm and enter into the mass-market segments, which means that the more pragmatic customers have to accept and adopt the new product.

When looking at functional food it is quite obvious that this product concept is at a very early stage and the companies, whether from the food industry or the pharmaceutical industry currently face the challenge of crossing the chasm. Hence the functional food concept is problematic from a product point of view as well as from an industry point of view, i.e. defining the market and the competitors, as pointed out in the previous section. The concept of functional food potentially leverages the R&D knowledge in the pharmaceutical industry towards the food industry and the brand marketing and consumer marketing knowledge enables the food industry to leverage knowledge into the pharmaceutical industry. However, this is much more an idealistic picture in theory and much remains to be done to fully exercise this in practice. It will require a comprehensive understanding of consumer needs and preferences as well as understanding what elements are decisive in the consumer's value proposition with respect to individual health.

It is also obvious that the diffusion of functional food into a wider consumer acceptance will require more sophisticated market communications means. It appears as if functional food will not be marketable in the same way as ordinary food – through massive advertising and promotional activities. On the other hand, it is unclear what impact the use of intermediaries, such as physicians in the role of opinion leaders, will have. That is, will the individual consumer accept a physician as an opinion

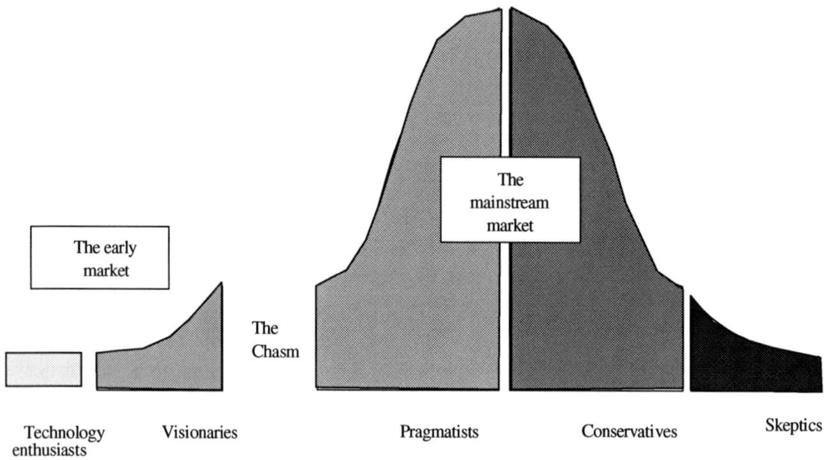

Fig. 6. Classification of consumers in high technology markets (adapted from Moore [28].

leader concerning food despite the fact that functional food clearly shares the health aspect with drugs, which is the traditional domain of doctors.

In this paper, we have described the structural change within the pharmaceutical and food industries due to major technological and scientific advances within biotechnology. We have pointed at the vast impact it has had on strategy, in that markets and competitors are changing. We have also described the similarities that functional have with pharmaceuticals on the one hand and traditional food on the other. Yet, as pointed out there are major differences, which will require a business concept innovation in addition to mere product innovation. The functional food market is however, too nascent and additional research will be required before the huge potential carried in this product concept will materialise.

References

[1] K. Amdjadi, C.D. Herold, S.K. Patel and E.S. Razvi, *The Top 10 Merger & Acquisition Deals in the Biotechnology and Pharmaceutical Industries,* Drug & Market Development Publications, Westborough, the US, 2000.

[2] C. Argyris, R. Putnam and D. Smith McLain, *Action Science,* Jossey-Bass Publishers, San Francisco, 1985.

[3] J.B. Barney, Firm Resources and Sustained Competitive Advantage, *Journal of Management* **17**(1) (1991), 99–120.

[4] R.A. Bettis and C.K. Prahalad, The Dominant Logic: Retrospective and Extension, *Strategic Management Journal* **16** (1995), 5–14.

[5] K.J. Bradford, Seeds: the delivery system for plant biotechnology. Paper presented at the Technical Meeting on Seed Policy Programmers for Latin America and the Carribian, Mérida, Mexico, March 20–24, 2000, http://sbc.ucdavis.edu/Delseeds.htm.

[6] M. Brännback and H. Mäkinen, The structure of the Finnish Pharmaceutical Industry – an evolving cluster, *Innomarket technical reports* **6** (2000).

[7] M. Brännback, J. Näsi and M. Renko, Technological, Structural, and Strategic Change in the Global Pharmaceutical Industry – The Finnish Biotechnology Industry, *Innomarket technical reports* **8** (2001).

[8] K.O. Cool and D.E. Schendel, Strategic Group Formation and Performance: The Case of the US Pharmaceutical Industry, *Management Science* **33** (1987), 1102–1124.

[9] G. Day, *Market Driven Strategy Process for Creating Value,* The Free Press, New York, 1990.

[10] A.T. Diplock, P.J. Aggett, M. Ashwell, F. Bornet, E.B. Fern and M.B. Roberfroid, Scientific Concepts of Functional Foods in Europe: Consensus Document, *British Journal of Nutrition* **81**(1) (1999), S1–S27.

[11] C. Eden, S. Jones and D. Sims, *Messing About in Problems,* Pergamon Press, Oxford, 1983.

[12] C. Eden and J. Radford, *Tackling Strategic Problems,* Sage Publications, London, 1990.

[13] J. Enriquez and R.A. Goldberg, *Transforming Life, Transforming Business: The Life-Science Revolution,* Harvard Business Review, March–April 2000, pp. 96–104.

[14] A. Fiegenbaum and H. Thomas, Strategic Groups and Performance: The US Insurance Industry, 1970–1984, *Strategic Management Journal* **11**(3) (1990), 197–215.

[15] A. Fiegenbaum and H. Thomas, Strategic Groups as reference groups: Theory, Modelling and Empirical Examination of Industry and Competitive Strategy, *Strategic Management Journal* **16**(6) (1995), 461–476.

[16] I. Goldberg, *Functional Foods; Designer Foods, Pharmafoods,* Nutraceuticals Chapman and Hall, London, 1994.

[17] P.H. Grinyer and J.-C. Spender, Recipes, Crises, and Adoption in Mature Industries, *International Studies of Management and Organization* **9**(3) (1979), 113–133.

[18] A.S. Huff, *Mapping Strategic Thought,* Chichester, John Wiley and Sons, 1990.

[19] Internet sources used, www.imshealth.com, www.euromonitor.com, 2000.

[20] G. Johnson and K. Scholes, *Exploring Corporate Strategy,* Prentice Hall, London, 1988.

[21] G. Johnson and K. Scholes, *Exploring Corporate Strategy,* (5th ed.), Prentice Hall, London, 1999.

[22] G.A. Kelly, *The Psychology of Personal Constructs,* W.W. Norton & Company Inc., New York, 1955.

[23] J. Laine, Change in Industry Recipe and Company Paradigm and its Impact on Strategic Change: A qualitative and longitudinal case study on a one-family owned company which moved into the context of a multi-business company, Jyväskylä Studies in Business and Economics, Doctoral dissertation, 2000.

[24] J. McGee and H. Thomas, Strategic Groups: Theory, Research and Taxonomy, *Strategic Management Journal* **7**(2) (1986), 141–160.

[25] H. Mintzberg, B. Ahlstrand and J. Lampel, Strategy Safari. A Guided Tour Through the Wilds of Strategic Management, Prentice Hall, New York, 1998.

[26] E. Mossialos and J. Le Grand, *Health Care and Cost Containment in the European Union,* Ashgate, Aldershot, 1999.

[27] S.W. Morrison and G.T. Giovannetti, *Convergence: Ernst & Young's Biotechnology Industry report,* Millenium Edition, Cleveland OH, 1998.

[28] G.A. Moore, *Inside the Tornado, Marketing Strategies from Silicon Valley's Cutting Edge,* Capstone Publishing Limited, Oxford, 1995.

[29] J.F. Moore, *The Death of Competition,* Leadership & Strategy in the Age of Business Ecosystems, John Wiley & Sons, Chichester, 1996.

[30] J. Näsi, *Understanding Stakeholder Thinking,* Gummerus Kirjapaino, Jyväskylä, 1995.

[31] J. Näsi, The Question of Knowledge Creation and Information Systems in Strategy Design, University of Jyväskylä Department of Economics and Management, Reprint Series No. 44, 1996.

[32] J. Näsi, P. Laine and J. Laine, Strategy Logic in a Megaleader Company, University of Jyväskylä Department of Economics and Management, Reprint Series No. 43, 1996.

[33] R.W. Oliver, *The Coming Biotech Age, the business of bio-materials,* McGraw-Hill, New York, 2000.

[34] M.E. Porter, *Competitive Strategy,* The Free Press, New York, 1980.

[35] M.E. Porter, *Competitive Advantage, Creating and Sustaining Superior Performance,* The Free Press, New York, 1985.
[36] C.K. Prahalad and R.A. Bettis, The Dominant Logic: a New Linkage Between Diversity and Performance, *Strategic Management Journal* **7** (1986), 485–501.
[37] E.M. Rogers, *Diffusions of Innovations,* The Free Press, New York, 1962.
[38] E. Romanelli and M.L. Tushman, Organisational Transformation as Punctuated Equilibrium: an empirical test, *Academy of Management Journal* **37**(5) (1994), 1141–1161.
[39] S. Suoniemi and M. Brännback, Can Elephants and Mice Play? – Organisational and Market Implications of the Restructuring Process in the Drug Industry Innomarket Technical Report No. 2, 2000.
[40] V. Vaclavik, *Essentials of Food Science,* Chapman & Hall, New York, 1998.
[41] K.E. Weick, Cartographic Myths in Organizations, in: *Mapping Strategic Thought,* S.A. Huff, ed., Chichester, John Wiley & Sons, 1990.
[42] K.E. Weick, *The Social Psychology of Organisations,* Addison_Wesley, Reading, 1969.
[43] A.S. Wellner, Eat, Drink and Healed, *American Demographics* **20**(3) (1998), 55–60.
[44] P. Wiklund, H. Korte and M. Brännback, New Challenges for the Finnish Food Industry – a comprehensive report on the iTU-project, Turku, 2000.
[45] M. Brännback and P. Wiklund, A new Dominant Logic and its Implications for Knowledge Management: A Studio of the Finnish Food Industry, *Knowledge and Process Management* **8**(4) (2001), 197–206.
[46] G. von Krogh, J. Roos and K. Slocum, An Essay On Corporate Epistemology, *Strategic Management Journal* **15** (1994), 53–71.
[47] G. von Krogh and J. Roos, A Tale Of The Unfinished, *Strategic Management Journal* **17** (1996), 729–737.

3. Political approaches

Pharmaceuticals Policy and Law 5 (2002) 81–106
IOS Press

Convergence of pharmaceutical policies through heterogeneous social welfare ideologies. A political positive approach

Natalia Martín Cruz[a], Juan Hernangómez Barahona[a] and
Juan Manuel de la Fuente Sabaté[b]
[a] *Universidad de Valladolid, Spain*
[b] *Universidad de Burgos, Spain*

1. Introduction

Pharmaceutical industry represents one of the major public policy worries for safety, efficiency and quality. In any other country these three objectives should push the main actors – pharmaceutical laboratories, national regulators and the interest groups – for a quasi-alignment of interests. Even more, the homogenization process initiated through the ICH (The International Conference on Harmonization of Technical Requirements for Registration of Pharmaceuticals for Human Use) should have, at the same time, an enormous influence on this alignment. However, we observe still some amount of heterogeneous factors influencing each national pharmaceutical drug regulation in different ways.

Those realities related with transactional globalization and transactional homogenization can be explained using transaction cost economics' tools, we hold first, that transaction characteristics provoke costs big enough to influence regulatory results and second, that pharmaceutical drug regulation involve interrelated series of measures ranging from patent protection to consumer protection and affects interest group compatibility. Under New Institutional Economics postulates, national idiosyncrasy is conditioning national regulatory efficiency. Using this perspective we integrate assumptions of the two main regulatory theories: first, the economic theory of regulation allows to explain how different parties being affected by pharmaceutical regulation act in ways to protect their interests and second, public interest theory of regulation considers that any single public decision trying to control pharmaceutical firm activities is related with an increase of the social welfare. All together, these views result in an explanation about the problems and constraints that face regulators working for this pharmaceutical framework construction process.

Our objective is to explain why there is a convergence in the way regulators act on pharmaceutical drug commercialization and consumption creating regulatory

1389-2827/02/$8.00

structures. With this aim we use a model where the multiple influences on the result of pharmaceutical drug regulatory process are represented. Our model specification is generally guided by the institutional approach – transaction cost economics – and the two principal prevailing theories of regulatory behavior – the economic theory of regulation and the public interest theory of regulation –.

2. Towards an integrative explanation for pharmaceutical regulation

Within the last decade there has been a rich flow of regulatory analyses in which we observe an intent for integration. In regard to the limits of any single explanation for intervening an industry, we propose a mix of regulatory theories from an institutional and political economic approach to explain pharmaceutical rules for drug commercialization and consumption. Justifying the role of the government and the efficiency of public rules, the institutional approach has a predominant role in the empirical analyses [15,64,68,78,81–83] and political economics is a powerful approach explaining industry regulation [2,25,51,62,84]. Quoting Serrano Sanz [62, p. 35], our research lean on the claim: 'Public economic questions as rethinking the role of the government into the industry must be answered using an institutional approach. This requires comparative analyses . . . '.

Because the way a drug can be commercialized by laboratories and consumed by patients is not trivial for any of the active actors in the pharmaceutical industry, we must explore the theories helping to understand each factor affecting the behavior of pharmaceutical regulator assuring safety, efficiency and quality. As it is our purpose, we offer an eclectic perspective that helps to understand the large and broad variety of norms used into the industry to control the way transactions are conducted and to value the likelihood to reach an harmonization for drug transaction regulation. Each of those theories introduces some interesting insights to the regulatory process.

2.1. Background for a pharmaceutical industry regulation explanation

From the Public Interest Theory of Regulation, public interest and social welfare are both notions related with practices used by health regulators. While we recognize that regulators are not completely omniscient, neither omnipotent, neither benevolent[1] and they don't try to maximize social welfare, however they have a particular ideology [25] and seek certain public interest [35] in the performance of their activities. In particular, pharmaceutical regulation is partially an answer to market failures to the extent that externalities and asymmetric information; public goods and rent distribution are characteristic for pharmaceutical transactions. Consider each seriatim.

[1]The first normative theories of regulation considered that regulators were individuals with these three characteristics and with an objective of maximizing social welfare [12, p. 8].

First, market failures are certain when externalities are analyzed, even more when asymmetric information is involved. The lack of medical drugs to defy a disease or the lack of information about the drug/disease produces an increase of disease transmission and thus, an increase of long term social costs.[2] At the same time, consumer incapacity of an efficient selection is important enough to consider public policy intervention to yield improved consumer decisions [76, p. 396]. Then, public interest can explain drugs' funding, information control and R&D promotion policies [14, p. 340–341]. The regulator will try to make an easy – fast and flexible – access to the market for these drugs and to facilitate consumption for patients [16].

Second, regulators have incentives to intervene in those transactions in which drugs are considered as public goods, taking into account their two main characteristics: no exhaustively and no exclusivity [14]. Into the pharmaceutical industry, we face a big competition among laboratories to reach the market first and pressures to invest heavily in R&D. The outcomes of this process can be considered public goods when pharmaceutical results are close one to the other and then, imitation and free rider behavior can damage the benefits of this R&D process [12]. While those actions are observed on pharmaceutical firms we can expect two kind of behaviors: first, firms have no longer incentives to do research on those drugs [85], second, firms develop a fast and unnecessary process of new drug's registration. Due to the possibility to observe a lack on production for particular drugs or a enormous amount of new registration claims respectively, regulators have incentives to control these transactions -production and exchange-. Finally, according to public good theory, patients free rider behavior can be observed when drugs are public financed,[3] these opportunistic behaviors -no exhaustively and no exclusivity in consumption- are evaluated as the third reason for regulators to act controlling these kind of drug transactions -production and exchange-. Rent distribution government intervention as a means to reduce market failures in the pharmaceutical industry generates then, this second problem.

At present, there is not doubt that each of these market failures is in the spirit of any pharmaceutical regulator but with different intensities [27]. In a public interest European-US comparison is the European regulator a more public interest-liked while US regulator believe in a more private interest -liked model [21,42]. Holding this last argument some authors started developing a new flow of theories that we are going to develop next.

From the Economic Theory of Regulation, authors claim that interest groups involved in regulatory decisions are an active part of the process and not mere observers [51,66]. Those groups are not banal influences for regulators and their characteristics matter in the final result [26,61]. In pharmaceutical industry examples

[2]Healthy patients are the potential victims of the ill ones, without any previous exposure to the illness [14].

[3]The institutions who develop these policies of drug funding are the 'Seguridad Social' for Spain and most part of the European countries, Medicare and Medicaid for the United States.

are diverse and related with heterogeneous groups conforming the pharmaceutical chain value [61,86]. Other than pharmaceutical laboratories, interests of physicians, pharmacies, insurers and patients among others are not always aligned even though quality, security and efficiency related with drugs is their main objective [14].

Regulators are going to be an active protector of interest groups and constituency interests as substantial voters argue theorists of the demand side of regulation [2, 51,66,87,88]. In particular, actions taken by pharmaceutical regulators referred to strict measures for clinical trials or drug commercialization can be seen from pharmaceutical laboratories as a threat. A backlash could be a decrease in R&D investments, a deviation of investment flows in specific countries or neglecting some therapeutic categories. This feedback usually results in a direct intervention of this group into the regulatory process using activities as lobbying in USA or industry association in Europe.[4] As pharmaceutical companies have developed recently a great industry concentration using a fast process of mergers and acquisitions, variables as cohesion, information and interest of those pharmaceutical groups reveal their increasing power to face pharmaceutical regulators.[5]

Constituency is represented mainly by patients who care about their health and the possibility to have access to the best treatments. As this part of the voters is basically the most significant over intermediates[6] -physicians, nurses, pharmacists- regulators will treat to safeguard their interests. We argue in terms of constituency interests -whom objectives can be measured using potential for health- that they are represented by public interest -disciplining for market failures- when regulators act on pharmaceutical transactions. At present, whereas information technology give access to pharmaceutical drugs for all the patients around the world,[7] regulators act creating a global protection using for all the countries common pharmaceutical registration procedures.[8]

Both, industry globalization and technological development arise as weapons for changes in the utility functions of interest groups and simultaneously pharmaceutical authorities use them to introduce modifications in the rules concerning the paths for drug commercialization and consumption towards a more global pharmaceutical regulatory framework.

---

[4]European firms have copied models of negotiation with regulators of USA firms in Brussels as a consequence of the recent activities of US firms in Europe and the characteristics of European institutions.

[5]The hypothesis that the more cohesion, information and interest of a group reveal the power of the last in the negotiation of the clauses of a regulatory contract is proved by authors as Baron [2, p. 37] or Schuler and Rehbein [84, p. 10].

[6]In each country it is possible to consider the relevance of all those actors. Moreover each country has a different health systems, all participants play a role in national institutions and have a weight in regulator's utility function [104].

[7]The asymmetric information issue in this particular case constitutes a more acute problem for patients: averse reactions of drugs on patients and free rider behaviors of the players in the pharmaceutical chain value can be considered more likely.

[8]See footnote 1.

Once, we have developed the ideas for public interest and economic theories of regulation, it is time to reconsider those attitudes together. Following this purpose, it is interesting to consider the conclusions of P.L. Joskow and N.L. Rose work [24] in which they show the differences of positive and normative analysis of regulation, however those differences are not only the result of the politician intervention but of the constituency negotiation process and the uncertain and complex distributive results from this process. Following this belief, it is not possible to consider pharmaceutical regulators as public interest maximizers nevertheless they are not unaware to their own interests and ideologies and this is related to an unavoidable political behavior of the framer restricted to a specific national endowment [12]. Then, a lack of public interest considerations in all those political economic analysis push to revisit the first maximizing-normative analysis and this time in an integrative manner. This challenging purpose turn the new institutional theory in a very powerful device for driving the research in a coherent explanation of the pharmaceutical regulator's behavior.

From New Institutional Theory, institutional endowment is a basic element in the regulatory process construction. This concept is defined by O.E. Williamson [74, p. 211] as a group of basic rules in political, social and legal aspects that represents the basis for production, exchange and distribution. Analysis focused on these institutional aspects of the regulation usually reflect the regulatory differences among countries based on their specific idiosyncrasy [6,21,32,42,64].

Pharmaceutical regulation is, in particular, a clear example of the institutional endowment influences over time. Regulatory changes in the pharmaceutical industry have to do with factors as the distribution of power among players, political stability -in the legislative, regulatory and judiciary- and changes in the technology [51]. At origin of the pharmaceutical industry in the US, pharmaceutical companies were responsible from R&D to drug consumption, through the registration process, further, regulatory authorities control the whole process [68,89]. [9] In Spain, the beginnings of the industry were very handmade-like and pharmacists were the main players in drug elaboration, however becoming industrial, its evolution was related with international drug developments and a very concerned control of health regulators [104]. As national borders become fuzzy, developed countries reach a political stability and technology evolve, we observe a progressive institutional (EU, Mercosur, NAFTA agreements) and economic (agreements as GATT treaty) homogenization.

In addition to political variables -institutional endowment-, technology -transactional factor- is essential in pharmaceutical regulation development. Connecting with O.E. Williamson [75] argument, transactional characteristics remain

[9] P. Temin [68] studies pharmaceutical industry regulatory evolution in the US, while E. Whitmore [89] refers to the recent regulatory procedures in the US.

the main factors explaining the governance structures.[10] In politics, the same thesis can be applied explaining the issue of regulation/deregulation for some activities. 'Specifically, if the good or service is to be supplied under conditions of uncertainty and if nontrivial investments in specific assets are involved, the efficacy of franchise bidding is highly problematic' [76, p. 41]. In the pharmaceutical industry, there is a long process of R&D investments with sunk costs and uncertainty related, the result of this process is not likely to launch a pharmaceutical drug into the market and the return for the drug marketed is not always warranted. Those particulars provoke the search of laboratories for a protection of their investments from opportunism, moral hazard and free rider behaviors by the means of regulatory procedures as patents or other legal arrangements.[11]

Nevertheless, the specificity and the uncertainty of those investments is largely dependent of the drug and its effects are known by the scientists and the time the drug has been on the market, circumstances that allow regulatory authorities to modify transactional norms and to adapt the new situation [18, p. 2, 17]. From this perspective, efficiency is an objective of health regulators in a remediable fashion, that means the existent regulatory structure in a time and specific moment is efficient; no regulation will change if there is an superior alternative regulatory structure in terms of the expected net benefit for the involved parties [71,72].

From the New Institutional Economics, 'transaction cost economics maintains, ... that all contracting schemes ... need to be examined microanalytically and assessed in a comparative institutional manner' [71,72]. The two aspects already mentioned are clue in the analysis of the governance structures and then, of the regulatory contractual schemas: transaction characteristics and institutional endowment. Finally, '... if we can find a way to measure variations in the choice of governance structure and can match these choices with measures of the associated degree of asset specificity, uncertainty and complexity, we are on our way to being able to test this theory empirically' [24].

However, there is a lack of a real development of positive theory and is related with four ideas, basically: the need of a formalization for the ideas, the superiority of normative models, the disagreement with positive study results and the distinction between norms and Constitutions [12, p. 16—19]. This criticism initiate a change

[10]Those structures are defined as agreements among economic units conceived to manage the way in which those units can cooperate and/or compete [75, p. 457]. 'Transaction cost economics maintains that there are rational economic reasons for organizing some transactions one way and other transaction another'. A predictive theory of economic organization as transaction cost economics identify the principal dimensions with respect to which transaction differ: asset specificity, uncertainty and frequency. 'The first is the most important and most distinguishes transaction cost economics from other treatments of economic organization, but the other two play significant roles'. [76, p. 52].

[11]Other than legal protection, pharmaceutical companies look for an intangible protection using different resources that allow them to create unique, durable, appropiable, nontransferable and nonreplicable capacities and routines [90, p. 111].

in the analysis towards a more integrative trend, the new approach depicts the influences of political history and institutions, as well as economic contributions into the regulatory analysis. From this perspective, -known as transaction cost politics- public intervention will be observed as a process of cycles between regulation and deregulation, intervention and market, or as a last resort public and private [8, p. 58].

2.2. *An integrative approach: Transaction cost politics*

The integrative process of political theories could be assessed in the terminology of transaction cost politics. This approach captures and synthesizes ideas from public interest theory, political capture theory, combining positive and normative analysis in which transaction cost valuation will be essential when designing efficient mechanisms suitable to a dynamic institutional endowment. In general terms, the problem explaining the regulatory process and its results concerns the role of political economy and political process. In particular, the presence of incomplete contracts, player's asymmetric information, long term norms and Constitutions -their effects and evolution- are basic claiming a the normative-positive integration into the regulatory analysis. A.K. Dixit [12, p. 30] describes the situation as follows: '... it is necessary to recognize the process of political economy creation as a dynamic game with uncertainty, change and rules partially created by participants at each moment. Each player will try to manipulate operations of next play in order to gain a result that favors its own results'. From this particular perspective, each group of norms is not an 'absolute' choice made using a maximizing criteria on the social welfare function, instead is a 'relative' part of the game restricted to rules and institutions even thought participants could have free interactions and strategic actions trying to influence or change future rules and institutions.

Experience suggests that intents to get the optimal regulatory system are heading for disaster and it is not possible to seek good results related with the superiority from one organizational formula to another. Authors claim a better knowledge about regulatory mechanisms designed to face problems related with asymmetric information and alignment of incentives. T.M. Moe [40,41], D. North [46], J.Q. Wilson [80] and, more recently, A.K. Dixit [12] are optimistic about the applicability of the new institutional theory and particularly, transaction cost economics to politics.

Transaction cost politics uses a contractual framework analyzing provider-consumer transactions in which both players engage in a bilateral and strong relationship of dependence and justifies public intervention considering players inability to find and execute efficient organizational formulas. Then, this school of thought conduces research about the factors affecting the regulatory process in a positive manner, handling institutional endowment characteristics, transactional attributes and individual behaviors into the analysis.

The pharmaceutical industry provides an intriguing setting within which to examine the hypotheses of transaction cost politics. Pharmaceutical laboratories develop complex, sunk and uncertain processes of R&D, at the same time, those firms shape an industry with strategic features, in the other side, patients face asymmetric information and moral hazard in pharmaceutical choice [14,91]. Both groups are connected by the means of the pharmaceutical exchange, remain the main players in pharmaceutical industry and then, regulators will act based in their behaviors [60].

3. Model and methodology

We develop next the description of the regulatory model and the hypothesis that we derived as well the proposed methodology for the empirical analysis.

3.1. The pharmaceutical regulatory model

Based on the foregoing discussion, research on pharmaceutical regulation has been mainly focused on the effects of norms into R&D investments. [12] Trying to explain the causes for pharmaceutical regulation, authors have considered institutional environment as an important factor affecting the regulatory process [37, p. 234][45, p. 122, 123], or laboratory idiosyncrasy or pharmaceutical drug characteristics [47, 48,56,60,92].

Our model (Fig. 1) tries to explain the regulatory process and regulatory form under the basis of transaction cost politics, using transaction as the unit of analysis. As transaction cost economics proposes 'transaction cost economics maintains that the transaction is the basic unit of analysis ...' [76, p. 393]; '... ascertaining the underlying attributes of transactions, and aligning institutions ... in a discriminating way' [76, p. 385]; 'As compared with other approaches to the study of economic organizations, transaction cost economics (1) is more microanalytic, ...' [76, p. 387]. [13]

Specially in a regulatory analysis 'Transaction cost maintains, however, that all contracting schemes -of which franchise bidding for natural monopoly is one- need to be examined microanalytically and assessed in a comparative institutional manner' [76, p. 41]. The central argument of the explanation for the existence of homogeneous and *ad hoc* regulation on pharmaceutical drugs that I offer here is that into the pharmaceutical industry is possible to observe very active and heterogeneous factors affecting the regulatory process and hence the regulatory result, however pharmaceutical regulation offers homogeneous structures around the world to deal

[12]The results obtain in the analysis of Baily [93], Lasagna [31], Peltzman [51], Wardell [94], Kendall [95], Sarett [96], Grabowski, Vernon y Thomas [16], Grabowski y Vernon [17], Leonard [97], Thomas [98], Wood [99], Peltzman [51], Douglas [100], Magat and Moore [101], Peltzman [51], Viscusi [70], Manning [37], Getzen [14], Ellison y Cockburn show that rules conceived to protect consumer's interests damage or at least delay returns for pharmaceutical companies.

[13]Already Commons (1934, p. 4–8) argued that transaction is properly regarded as the basic unit of analysis and the study of trading at a much more microanalytic level of analysis was thus indicated [76, p. 3, 6].

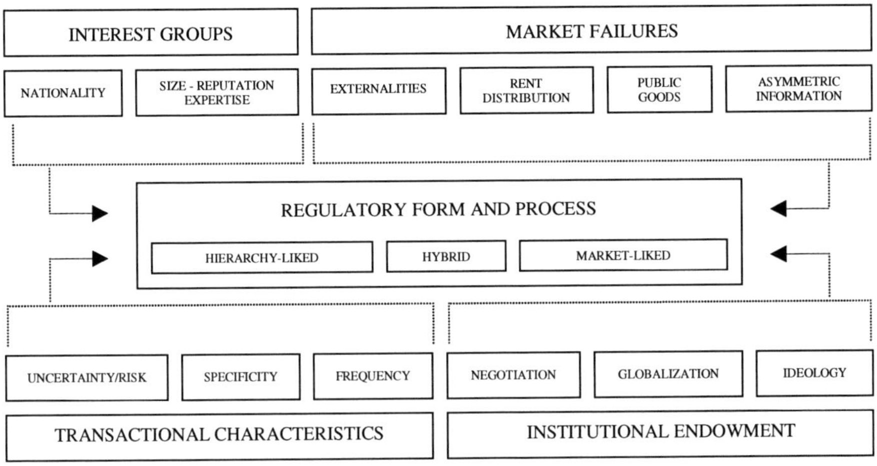

Fig. 1. Regulatory model for pharmaceutical drug commercialization and consumption.

with market failures, interest groups, transactional characteristics and institutional idiosyncrasy.

Each step in pharmaceutical drug transaction introduces the actuation of health authorities. First, R&D process in which after fifteen years a drug can be part of a process of clinical trials for another fifteen years before being launch into the market. Then, the registration process by the means of which the laboratory gain the permission to commercialize the product. Finally, the process of commercialization by the distributor and consumption by the patient. Several variables are suited to control all pharmaceutical transactions, speed in drug approval [48,56,86], speed in generic drug approval [48,60], the need for medical prescription [104], patent protection [102, 103]. Our work is focused on the last, pharmaceutical drug commercialization and consumption taking into account that we use transaction as unit of analysis.

As previously discussed, the analysis of transactions individually could be very instructive. Particularly, we focus in the center of the model and we hold that extreme governance structures are important manifestations of the essence of the contractual problem [78, p. 75]. As it is represented in the model above, we hypothesize:

Into the same industry, regulatory intensity for transactions is dependent with transactional characteristics.

In any institutional endowment, those regulatory structures can be characterized as governance structures in 'transaction cost-fashion' from market to hierarchy structures.

3.2. Sample

Sample selection of drug molecules for the analysis was first, realized from specialized US and Spanish journals using the impact index of different therapeutical categories in the literature; second, for specific pharmaceutical drug sample selection we use the Vademecum (1997) and Medimecum (1997), the Official Classification of Health Department and the Consejo General de Colegios de Farmacéuticos in Spain -US classification is similar[14]-. Finally, we chose those pharmaceutical drugs allowing a characterization of their general, specific or central character into the regulatory figures (Table 1).

The first group is composed by infectious drugs generating externalities, those drugs generate a great interest for regulatory authorities and usually are public financed -more than the rest of the drugs-, other than that, those drugs are R&D intensive, particularly we selected 13 molecules for patients with HIV, using the USP system (1997) and the Merck Index (1997) for their characterization. The second group is composed by drugs for treatment of cancer, we use 7 molecules for cancer, relevant as well as the first group, however those are quite different taking into account the seniority of this disease and the number of patients. Finally, we include therapeutical drugs for neurological disorders (central nervous system, CNS) used for an heterogeneous group of diseases, with a large range of severity for side effects, this last are the main reasons for their inclusion -we include 10 molecules recommended for several treatments related with CNS-. The final sample is composed of 30 molecules, we eliminated 4 from the beginning since they were not sold in Spain. Pharmaceutical drugs included in the sample for those 30 molecules are 1723 for the US and 717 for Spain in the period 1997/98. We didn't use all of them inasmuch as limits for information related with variables. Thus, molecules are represented in the sample with 66 in the US and 171 in Spain.

3.3. Data

In order to construct the regulatory structure (endogenous variable) we are going to use variables related with regulation for drug commercialization and consumption in both countries[15] (Table 2), we leave aside variables as length of treatment, availability and USP requirements, taking into account similarities among national

[14]For disagreements between systems, we use the WHO tables for homogenization.

[15]Web page of Consejo General de Colegios Oficiales de Farmacéuticos (http://www.cof.es). El libro blanco del medicamento; Compendio Legislativo de Productos Sanitarios, serie Monografas de divulgación, segunda edición, Madrid, Ministerio de Sanidad y Consumo, n. 6, 1994; Suñé, José Ma.; Legislación Farmacéutica Española, 7a edición, Barcelona, 1984; Villa, Luis F.; Medimecum, Diaz de Santos, 1997, pp. 683; Ministerio de Sanidad y Consumo; Dirección General de Farmacia y Productos Sanitarios, Diccionario de excipientes de las especialidades farmacéuticas españolas, 1989, pp. 146; Ministerio de Sanidad y Consumo; Secretaría General Técnica. Centro de Publicaciones, Diccionario de principios activos de las especialidades farmacéuticas españolas, third edition, 1995, pp. 236; Generic drug identification guide, compiled by J.R. Swim B.S., RPh., 2 edición, 1988, pp. 245; Handbook of nonprescription drugs, American Pharmaceutical Association, The National Professional society of pharmacists, Washintong, D.C., 1996, pp. 774; Nonprescription products: formulations & features'96–97, A companion to the Handbook of nonprescription drugs, 11 ed., 1996/97, pp. 447; Drugs under patent, A comprehensive guide to FDA-approved pharmaceuticals under patent and marketing exclusivity, 1991 ed., pp. 284; Nursing 98 Drug Handbook, Springhouse Corporation, Pennsylvania, 1998, pp. 1333; The Merck

Table 1
Drug clustering by the American USP

CENTRAL NERVOUS SYSTEM	HEADACHE	MIGRAINE HEADACHES	ABORTIVE THERAPY	ERGOTAMINE TARTRATE SUMAPTRIPTAN DIHYDROERGOTAMINE
		CLUSTER HEADACHES	ABORTIVE THERAPY	ERGOTAMINE SUMATRIPTAN DIHYDROERGOTAMINE
			PROPHYLATIC THERAPY	ERGOTAMINE TARTRATE PREDNISONA
			ALTERNATIVE THERAPY	SUMATRIPTAN DIHYDROERGOTAMINE
		TENSION HEADACHES	ANALGESICS	ASPIRIN ACETAMINOPHEN
			ANXIOLITICS	BUSPIRONE CHLORDIAZEPOXIDE
			ANTIHISTAMINES	CYPROHEPTADINE DIPHENHYDRAMINE
			OTHERS	AMITRIPTYLINE NADOLOL
	PARKINSON'S DISEASE			AMANTADINE
	CEREBROVASCULAR DISORDERS			SULFINPYRAZONE WARFARIN
TREATMENT OF CANCER	CHEMOTHERAPY	BREAST	CMF	CYCLOPHOSPLAMIDE METHOTREXATE FLOUROURACIL
			CAF	CYCLOPHOSPLAMIDE + DOXORUBICIN + FLOUROURACIL[1]
			CMFVP	CYCLOPHOSPHAMIDE + METHOTREXATE + FLOUROURACIL + VINCRISTINE + PREDNISONE[2]
		PROSTATE		DOXORUBICIN CISPLATIN CYCLOPHOSPHAMIDE
	HORMONAL THERAPY	BREAST		TAMOXIFEN
TREATMENT OF VIH (AIDS)	REVERSE TRANSCRIPTASE INHIBITORS			ZIDOVUDINE DIDEOXYNOSINE DIDEOXYCYTIDINE STAVUDINE LAMIVUDINE
	NONNUCLEOSIDE REVERSE TRANSCRIPTASE INHIBITORS			NEVIRAPINE ATERVIDINE DELAVIRDINE
	PROTEASE INHIBITORS			SAQUINAVIR RITONAVIR INDINAVIR

[1,2]It is a combined therapy of pharmaceutical drugs above indicated. Source: Based in USP Dictionary of USAN and International Drug Names (1997), European Drug Index (1995), The Merck Index, 11 edition (1989) and Nursing 98 Drug Handbook, Springhouse Corporation (1998).

Table 2
Regulatory comparison between pharmaceutical drug in Spain and US

PHAREMACEUTICAL DRUG REGULATION	SPAIN	US
PATENT	20 years (change in 1992 from process to product patent)	20 years (from 17 to 20 years)
PRICES	Laboratories return rate control	Not price control
DISTRIBUTION	Pharmacy monopoly	Rx/OTC
FINANCIATION	Social security. Negative lists	Medicare/Medicaid. Positive lists
REGISTRATION	Three procedures: Centralized procedure/ Mutual recognition procedure/ National procedure	FDA centralized process through Center for Drug Evaluation and Reserach (CDER)
ACCELERATED REGISTRATION	Compassionate use	Accelerated registration. Orphan drugs.
INDUSTRY NEGOCIATION	Farmaindustria	Lobbies
ADVERTISING	OTC (for patients)	Not limits ("ex-post" control)
GENERICS	1992 (from patent product approval)	1984 (fast access for generics from approval of Drug Price Competition and Patent Term Restauration Act
TERAPEUTICAL EQUIVALENT	Same composition	A and B equivalent categories
PHYSICIAN PRESCRIPTION	Total freedom for prescription	Cost control and drug substitution

pharmaceutical systems.

Only there is complete coincidence for patent protection in both countries considering the eleven pharmaceutical regulatory tools. For the rest of mechanisms there are several degrees of dissimilarities. This descriptive analysis shows a global freedom for drug commercialization and consumption in the US above the Spanish one for the same exchanges. Coexistence for both national systems provoke an unavoidable question related with the regulatory mechanisms remediableness in order to reach health purposes. An historical interest for social welfare in Spain drives drug regulation into a traditional institutional endowment, while market rules have controled public health system and thus, pharmaceutical regulatory process in the US.

Applying transaction cost economics to the search of the efficient regulatory limit and efficient regulatory form, we argue that there is a bunch of regulatory structures ranging from market-liked to hierarchy-liked structures adapted to transactional characteristics of each pharmaceutical transaction. Other than differences among regulatory structures for pharmaceutical transactions, we argue that national regulatory dissimilarities due to idiosyncratic institutional endowments are not enough to find

index, 11 ed., centennial ed., Merck&Co., USA, 1989, pp. 1606; USP System, Taunton, US Pharmacopoeia Convention, USA, 17 ed., 1997, vol. I. Drug information for the health care professional, vol. II. Advice for the patient, vol. III. Approved drug products and legal requirements; USP Dictionary of USAN and international drug names, US Pharmacopeia, Rockeville, USA, 1998, pp. 1006; Mutschler, E.Y. Derendorf, H.; Drug Actions, basic principles and therapeutic aspects, Medpharm, Scientific Publishers, Stuttgard, 1995, pp. 799; European Drug Index, 4 ed., European society of clinical pharmacy, Muller/Dessing ed., 1997, pp. 1456; Physician's desk reference, Medical Economics Company, 52 ed., 1998; Drug Evaluations, Annual 1995, American Medical Association, USA; 1995, pp. 2536.

Table 3
Pharmaceutical drug regulation in Spain [2 axes (33.23% of the information)]

internalized. AXE 1. (21.61%) [eighteen value 0.2881]. Inertia corrected percentaje: 47.76% (negative extreme of the axe).				aligned. AXE 2. (11.62%) [eighteen value 0.1549]. Inertia corrected percentaje: 13.50% (negative extreme of the axe).			
Variable contribution	SPAD-N category	Variable	Signification	Variable contribution	SPAD-N category	Variable	Signification
17.4	AE	REG13	Farmacy	18.2	AK	REG10	Controlled substance
11.6	AH	REG7	Multiple	12.9	AJ	REG9	Rx
11.3	AF	REG3	No USP	18.2	AD	REG12	Low price
9.6	AB	REG2	No risk	17.4	AA	REG1	Fast approval
10.6	AC	REG5	Oral	8.0	AL	REG11	Discontinuity
7.3	AJ	REG9	OTC	6.0	AH	REG7	Multiple

but small regulatory distinctions for similar transactions.

4. Empirical results

4.1. Factor analysis

Two axes result relevant in Spain (Table 3) and we baptized as *internalized structures* (axe 1) and *aligned structures* (axe 2).

For the *internalized regulatory structure*, we observe the relationship between nature of the transaction and regulatory form. This axe represents regulatory structures used by government to limit or facilitate drug commercialization and consumption. From the negative extreme, where we see market structures, to the positive extreme, where we observe drugs controlled much more rigid or hierarchy. Then, it is possible to interpret a maximum and a minimum regulation for drug commercialization and consumption within which there are hybrid structures. The *aligned regulatory structure* reflects an alignment between regulatory process and regulatory structure. The ex-ante and ex-post regulatory process has a parallelism with a regulatory structure in which it is mandatory a physician prescription and warrants low prices. The clue for a good interpretation of this axe holds in regulatory decisions interdependence that push regulatory authorities to solve ex-post, problems generated ex-ante. For those drugs with high demand and high risk – negative extreme of the axe – regulators will balance between regulatory flexibility and regulatory rigidity, in opposition, drugs without a special interest for the regulator – oral availability, one molecula in composition and with low levels of risk – are related with a large registration timing, less ex-post control (OTC) and without market discontinuities. The global results have a signification related with the aim of the regulator, to control risk, quality and efficiency and at the same time to promote firm's competition.

Flexible regulatory structure, can be interpreted as follows: taking into account safety, the regulator will try to warranty flexibility in drug commercialization and

Table 4
Pharmaceutical drug regulation in US [2 axes (32.89% of the information)]

flexible. AXE 1. (16.89%) [eighteen value 0.2252]. Inertia corrected percentaje: 35.24% (positive extreme of the axe)				competitive. AXE 2. (16%) [eighteen value 0.2134]. Inertia corrected percentaje: 29.62% (negative extreme of the axe)			
Variable contribution	SPAD-N category	Variable	Signification	Variable contribution	SPAD-N category	Variable	Signification
12.7	AB	REG2	Pregnancy Risk	30.4	AA	REG1	Fast registration
24.1	AF	REG6	Not equivalents	13.1	AH	REG10	Not controlled substance
16.9	AD	REG12	Not generics	13.1	AD	REG12	Generics
15.1	AH	REG10	Controlled substance	11.9	AG	REG7	Not multiple

Table 5
Significance of factors as regulatory structures

PHARMACEUTICAL DRUGS	SPAIN		US	
	Internalized structure		Flexible structure	
	−	+[16]	−	+
	MARKET	HIERARCHY	MARKET	HIERARCHY
	Aligned structure		Competitive structure	
	−	+	−	+
	HIERARCHY	MARKET	MORE VALUE/ HIERARCHY	LESS VALUE/ MARKET

consumption. This way, patients and companies interests are aligned with regulatory structures well-suited for both group of actors. *Competitive regulatory structure* represents the added value of the drug for the regulator. It seems that monopoly-liked regulatory structures and fast registration procedures allowing a rapid investment recovering fit with high value drugs and competitive regulatory structures when there is low value drugs.

Thus, -Regulatory formulas- are the factors:[97] internalized and aligned regulatory structure for Spain and flexible and competitive regulatory structure for the US (Table 5).

Factorial analysis for the US, as well in Spain, shows specific regulatory structures related with specific drugs, as we postulated from transaction cost politics in our fisrt hypothesis. Comparing those results with the ones in Spain, we observe different motivation for each regulator, the Spanish one emphasize ex-ante and ex-post regulatory alignment and harmonizes, at the same time, regulatory structure and drug nature adaptation, while, the Northamerican concentrate in flexible and competitive structures for drugs. Even the most important objective for a regulator is patient's

[16]The sign for the represents the value for factorial axes in the ACM analysis and it is not the sense for regulation under which pharmaceutical transaction are subjected to.

[97]The process and results for the factorial analysis exhibit in Appendix 1A.

Table 6
Cluster analysis of pharmaceutical drugs in Spain. Decomposition of the inertia in two axes

	INERTIAS		NUMBER OF INDIVIDUAL	
	BEFORE	AFTER	BEFORE	AFTER
INERTIA BETWEEN GROUPS	0.3043	0.3058		
INERTIA INSIDE THE GROUP				
GROUP 1 / 3	0.0529	0.0513	74.00	73.00
GROUP 2 / 3	0.0387	0.0407	51.00	53.00
GROUP 3 / 3	0.0472	0.0453	46.00	45.00
GLOBAL INERTIA	0.4431	0.4431		
INERTIA BETWEEN GROUPS / GLOBAL INERTIA	0.6868	0.6902		

safety, public costs concerns are one of the important engines for pharmaceutical regulation in Spain, while in the US regulators try to favor pharmaceutical firm's incomes.

Both countries have a large range of regulatory structures suited to each drug, from total flexibility to total control, even these regulatory structures are not completely similar. Differences are due to regulatory tools and exogenous variables that motivate their behavior. This last circumstance is the heart of the following title and we will conduct a cluster analysis using as variables the regulatory structures coming from factor analysis. We anticipate that the result of the grouping is ranging from market to hierarchy structures, with hybrid structures within those extremes.

4.2. *Cluster analysis*

Sample of 171 pharmaceutical drugs in Spain is separated into three groups of 73, 53 and 45 medications with an inertia coefficient of 69% (Table 6). Since there is a quasi-identical equivalence with sample' therapeutical categories, we choose three categories.

The basic characteristics for a separation is the provided by the two axes - internalized and aligned structure-, allowing to identify those medication used for cancer and aids (group 3) and those related with central nervous system (groups 1 and 2). The last groups -pharmaceutical drugs in an oral availability, no risk and no prescription drugs- are facing the rest of pharmaceutical drugs -fast registration procedure- (axe 2) grouped in cluster 3 and composed by 45 pharmaceutical drugs: 24 for aids and 16 for cancer, 4 pharmaceutical drugs for cardiovascular problems and one for neurological disorders joint the group. This first disunion for drugs, taking into account transactional characteristics -nature of medication for cancer and aids and its patients-, is largely anticipated.

The rest of the sample, 126 medications, from which almost 60% are drugs for neurological disorders, was divided in two cluster. Cluster 2 with 53 medications for neurological disorders -15 from Acetaminophen, 18 from Aspirin, 9 from Ergotamine, 1 from Buspirone, 5 from Chlordiazepoxide and one from Dihydroergotamine-, plus two for respiratory system -Diphenhydramine-, and two for cancer -Prednisone and

Table 7
Cluster analysis of pharmaceutical drugs in the US Decomposition of the inertia in two axes

	INERTIAS		NUMBER OF INDIVIDUAL	
	BEFORE	AFTER	BEFORE	AFTER
INERTIA BETWEEN GROUPS	0.3599	0.3616		
INERTIA INSIDE THE GROUP				
GROUP 1 / 4	0.0111	0.0111	10.00	10.00
GROUP 2 / 4	0.0168	0.0168	17.00	17.00
GROUP 3 / 4	0.0327	0.0327	17.00	17.00
GROUP 4 / 4			22.00	22.00
GLOBAL INERTIA	0.4386	0.4386		
INERTIA BETWEEN GROUPS / GLOBAL INERTIA	0.7283	0.7395		

Ciclophosphamide-. Finally, cluster 1 represented by 73 pharmaceutical drugs for neurological disorders -18 from Aspirin, 45 from Acetaminophen and one from Sumatriptan-, 2 for digestive system -Cyproheptadine- and 7 hormonal -Prednisone-. The most representative variables for this second separation are: place for sale -axe 1- and prices and time for registration -axe 2-. Clearly, pharmaceutical drugs in the second group are commercialized in pharmacies and the ones in the first group are caracterized by high prices and slow registration.

The aligned structure -axe 2- seems to separate cluster 3 -formed by pharmaceutical drugs relevant for the regulator- to the rest of the drugs. The first is more flexible ‘ex-ante’ and subordinated to higher control ‘ex-post’ that means facing to regulatory hierarchy, the last medications are polarized by internalized structure -axe 2-, since those pharmaceutical drugs can be considered as hybrid in the second cluster and market-liked drugs for the first cluster.

Grouping the 66 medications in the US, as we did in Spain, from the two axes -flexible structures and competitive structures-, we got a 74% of the inertia (Table 7). The same reason we argue for Spain apply in here to group pharmaceutical drugs in four clusters, with 10, 17, 17 and 22 pharmaceutical drugs. From the initial group (cluster 1), formed by 10 drugs for neurological disorders to the last created (cluster 4), formed by 22 pharmaceutical drugs, mostly for aids, we got two more groups with an heterogeneous background, taking into account the rest of the seven pharmaceutical categories inside the groups. However is necessary to point out that in the third group is basically cancer drugs (cluster 3). Interpretation for the separation of pharmaceutical drugs is related with less rigidity and more competitiveness of regulation for the first (cluster 1) and the more rigidity and less competitiveness for the last (cluster 4).

The first aggregate (10 drugs) is related with medication for neurological system but the main characteristic is the controlled substance condition. This category, inside the axe 1, is the heaviest in the composition for the first group. The second group (17 drugs) has a more heterogeneous composition and, other than 7 molecules for neurological system, appear 5 for cancer, 3 hormonal and one for cardiovascular system. The heaviest therapeutical category in this group is the neurological system one, however there is not controlled substances inside and the main characteristic is the profusion of generics and therapeutical equivalents approved in 10 years on average, axe 1. The third group, with a rigid regulatory structure, has ten medication for cancer, five for neurological disorders, one for blood and another one for digestive system. The reason to separate those medications from the group number 4 is low interest of regulatory authorities to give them a fast registration, and high interest for controlling their commercialization and consumption. The last group (22 drugs), we found 8 molecules for aids, four for cancer and one for neurological disorders with a different regulatory structure than the rest due to both axes: flexible and competitive structures. Basically, it seems that medication for infectious diseases has a more rigid regulation than the rest of pharmaceutical drugs, both in the way those are registered (access to commercialization) and the way those can be purchased.

Groups of medication in the US has been obtained after the four grouping while in Spain this grouping was stopped in the third one. That means a more clear and homogeneous group definition in Spain. It seems that axes in the US define regulation in a more sequential or gradual fashion than in Spain. Those results validate the second of our hypothesis. Results show a clear separation of medications by the way those are regulated. The way grouping is developed show manifest similarities in both countries as well, even regulators do not use identical variables. Groups relate with regulatory structures ranging from market structures to hierarchy structures in several forms of hybrid regulations. Thus, even though both countries have different regulatory tools, groups of medications have similar regulatory structure.

Differences in national regulations are due basically to those differences in regulatory national mechanisms and objectives on health policies. However, similarities are stronger than dissimilarities in national regulations, that means that the institutional endowment is not so important than transactional characteristics for pharmaceutical drug regulation for commercialization and consumption. Health regulator is clearly concerned by intrinsic drug's characteristics and treats homogeneous medication in a homogeneous manner. Thus, we can conclude that those national regulatory differences are more outward than inward ones.

5. Conclusions

The microeconomic analysis of regulation using transaction as unit of analysis allows to identify alternative regulatory structures and confirms the existence of different degrees of public intervention for each transaction in any particular country. Specific transactional regulatory structures has some differences in any country due to the institutional endowment. In Spain, each regulatory structure is adapted to the intrinsic characteristics of pharmaceutical drugs and then, those are more rigid and there is higher alignment between registration procedures and consumption control 'ex-post' as risk associated with the drug increases. While, in the US, the regulatory structure to control pharmaceutical drug commercialization and consumption shows clear preferences for flexibility and competition. Regulator tries to get flexibility in order to satisfy patient and laboratories interests simultaneously when pharmaceutical drugs have high therapeutical interest; tries to promote competition when pharmaceutical drug market is not new any more and value of drugs is only incremental. We can argue that even each specific national transactional regulation is different, however in any country this regulation can be characterized in a more flexible or rigid manner, that means using the same constructions than institutionalists in the analysis of governance structures: market, hybrid and hierarchy structures.

This comparative analysis of regulatory structures is complemented with a comparative institutional analysis of regulation. In the last, it holds that regulatory structures are dependent on the institutional endowment for transactions. Our analysis shows that grouping by pharmaceutical drug regulatory structures we get a similar structure in Spain and in the US. Medication related with aids and cancer groups homogeneously in both countries, medication related with neurological disorders are inside a more heterogeneous group in Spain and in the US there is a possibility to separate clearly into two more homogeneous groups. As a consequence, we observe that the regulatory structures by transaction does not show big differences in both countries. Then, we can argue that there is a more and more homogeneity in the way regulators act on transactions -with similar tools for regulators- within the international pharmaceutical industry. Transaction characteristics have increasing weight in the search of remediable regulatory structures than institutional characteristics, even those have important differences.

Finally, we can consider regulations as governance structures with different features from market to hierarchy, adapted to transaction cost generated in the development of transactions in each country.

Appendix

Variables For Regulatory Analysis

Variable	Description	Values
REG1j	Number of years on average from first registration of the molécula to the next one.	[0-number of years in the market for registration j]
REG2j	Pregnancy category risk.	[1:A. 2:B. 3:C. 4:D. 5:X. 6:NR]
REG3j	Dummy USP requirements.	[1:Light. 2:Cold. 3:Light and cold]
REG4j	Dummy Generic condition.	[0:Generic. 1:Brand] [not for Spain]
REG5j	Drug availability.	[1.Effervescent tablets/ 2.Chew tablets/ 3.Dispersion tablets/ 4. Covered capsules/ 5.Capsules/ 6.Sirop/ 7.Elixir/ 8.Drops/ 9.Solution/ 10.Granules/ 11.Capsules/ 12. Injection/ 13.Lyophilized injection/ 14.Effervescent injection/ 15.Suspension/ 16.Inhalation/ 17.Powder/ 18.Suppository/ 19.Cream]
REG6j	Dummy Therapeutically equivalents available.	[0-number of therapeutically equivalents for drug j]
REG7j	Dummy Multiple substance.	[0-number of component for drug j]
REG8j	Dummy Drug for long term treatments.	[0:drug is not 'long term'. 1:drug j is 'long treatment'] [not for US]
REG9j	Dummy Prescription condition for the drug.	[0:drug j OTC. 1:drug j Rx]
REG10j	Control condition for the drug.	[Spain: 0:drug j is not controlled substance. 1: drug j is controlled substance] [US: 0:drug j is not 'controlled substance'.1: drug CI. 2:drug CII. 3:drug CIII. 4:drug CIV. 5:drug CV]
REG11j	Dummy discontinuity status.	[0:drug j on the market. 1: drug j discontinued]
REG12j	Price of the drug.	[0. NA. Rest: price of the drug for consummer]
REG13j	Establishment for selling the drug.	[1:Pharmacy. 2:Hospital I. 3:Hospital II] [not for US]

Basic Statistics

	Original Variables. Spain (sample: 171 pharmaceuticals).					
	Media	Standard deviation	Minimum	Maximum	Skenness	Kurtosis
Reg 1	15.000	15.156	0.000	48.000	0.467 (0.186)	−1.078 (0.369)
Reg 2	3.000	0.833	1.000	6.000	0.524	−0.102
Reg 3	0.000	0.706	0.000	3.000	3.797	12.561
Reg 4	–	–	–	–	–	–
Reg 5	11.000	4.688	1.000	19.000	−0.115	12.561
Reg 6	1.000	7.022	0.000	37.000	3.359	12.752
Reg 7	0.000	2.048	0.000	10.000	1.370	1.626
Reg 8	0.000	0.266	0.000	1.000	3.228	8.518
Reg 9	1.000	0.445	0.000	1.000	−1.051	−0.906
Reg 10	0.000	0.212	0.000	1.000	4.330	16.951
Reg 11	0.000	0.386	0.000	1.000	1.669	0.796
Reg 12	400.000	19689.562	0.000	120448.000	3.500	12.877
Reg 13	2.000	0.568	0.000	4.000	0.773	3.121

	Original Variables. US (sample: 86 pharmaceuticals).					
	Media	Standard deviation	Minimum	Maximum	Skenness	Kurtosis
Reg 1	0.000	213.491	−1978.000	12.000	−9.271 (0.260)	85.966 (0.514)
Reg 2	4.000	1.219	2.000	6.000	0.293	−0.627
Reg 3	2.000	0.542	1.000	3.000	−0.123	−1.076
Reg 4	1.000	0.471	0.000	1.000	−0.758	−1.460
Reg 5	4.000	2.860	4.000	13.000	1.905	2.073
Reg 6	1.000	0.860	0.000	2.000	0.285	−1.621
Reg 7	1.000	0.855	0.000	4.000	0.815	0.437
Reg 8	–	–	–	–	–	–
Reg 9	1.000	0.185	0.000	1.000	−5.160	25.214
Reg 10	0.000	1.211	0.000	4.000	1.786	1.707
Reg 11	0.000	0.185	0.000	1.000	5.160	25.214
Reg 12*	49.680	179.046	3.500	979.670	3.720	14.871
Reg 13	4.000	1.219	2.000	6.000	0.293	−0.627

	Transformed Variables. Spain (sample: 171 pharmaceuticals).					
	Media	Standard deviation	Minimum	Maximum	Skenness	Kurtosis
Reg 1	2.000	0.822	1.000	3.000	0.033 (0.186)	−1.521 (0.369)
Reg 2	2.000	0.507	1.000	3.000	−0.185	−1.639
Reg 3	1.000	0.235	1.000	2.000	3.797	12.561
Reg 4	–	–	–	–	–	–
Reg 5	1.000	0.577	1.000	3.000	2.755	5.870
Reg 6	2.000	0.371	1.000	2.000	−1.834	1.378
Reg 7	1.000	0.500	1.000	2.000	0.130	−2.007
Reg 8	1.000	0.266	1.000	2.000	3.228	8.518
Reg 9	2.000	0.468	1.000	2.000	−0.770	−1.423
Reg 10	1.000	0.212	1.000	2.000	4.330	16.951
Reg 11	1.000	0.386	1.000	2.000	1.669	0.796
Reg 12	2.000	0.893	0.000	3.000	−0.127	0.186
Reg 13	2.000	0.488	1.000	3.000	−0.230	1.045

	Transformed variables. US (sample: 66 pharmaceuticals).					
	Media	Standard deviation	Minimum	Maximum	Skenness	Kurtosis
Reg 1	1.333	0.591	1.000	3.000	1.609 (0.295)	1.605
Reg 2	2.076	0.590	1.000	3.000	−0.013	−0.041
Reg 3	–	–	–	–	–	–
Reg 4	1.742	0.441	1.000	2.000	−1.135	−0.736
Reg 5	1.333	0.751	1.000	3.000	1.831	1.393
Reg 6	1.682	0.469	1.000	2.000	−0.799	−1.405
Reg 7	1.833	0.376	1.000	2.000	−1.831	1.393
Reg 8	–	–	–	–	–	–
Reg 9	–	–	–	–	–	–
Reg 10	1.182	0.389	1.000	2.000	1.689	0.877
Reg 11	1.076	0.267	1.000	2.000	3.282	9.042
Reg 12	2.197	0.827	1.000	3.000	−0.386	−1.433
Reg 13	–	–	–	–	–	–

VARIABLES TRANSFORMATION (I).

REG1

SPAIN

$L_{i-1} - L_i$	n_i	N_i
≤6.00	33.3	58
>6.00 y ≤23.00	33.3	58
≥23.00	33.3	55
	100	**171**

U.S.

$L_{i-1} - L_i$	n_i	N_i
0.00 <10.00	62.8	54
≥10.00	32.6	28
	4.6	4
	100	**86**

REG12

SPAIN

$L_{i-1} - L_i$	n_i	N_i
≤295.0	33.3	60
>295.0 ≤545.0	33.3	55
≥545.0	33.3	56
	100	**171**

U.S.

$L_{i-1} - L_i$	n_i	N_i
≤24.3	62.8	54
>24.3 y ≤88.8	32.6	28
≥88.8	4.6	4
	100	**86**

Transformation from REG1 and REG12 implies the use of the formula:

$$Q_{r/k} = L_{i-1} + \frac{\frac{r}{k} \cdot N - N_{i-1}}{n_i} \cdot c_i$$

where $k = 3$ and $r = 1,2,3,\ldots$ we have three groups.

REG2

- A, B } 1:no pregnancy risk
- C, D } 2:benefits outweight risks
- X, NR } 3: risks outweight benefits

REG3, REG4, REG6, REG7, REG8, REG9: *dummies*

REG11: transformed in *dummy*

REG13

- 1: Pharmacy.
- 4: Pharmacy and H.D.
- 3:Hospital diagnosis.
- } 1: Pharmacy; pharmacy and H.D.
- 6: Pharmacy and hospital.
- 7: Pharmacy, hospital and D.H.
- 2:Hospital.
- } 2: H.D.; pharmacy and hospital; farmacia, hospital and H.D.
- 5: Hospital and H.D.
- } 3: Hospital; hospital and H.D.

VARIABLES TRANSFORMATION (II).

REG5

AVAILABILITY CATEGORIES		TRANSFORMED AVAILABILITY CATEGORIES
1:Tabletas efervescentes. 2:Masticable. 3:Tabletas dispersables. 4:Cápsulas recubiertas. 5:Cápsulas. 6:Jarabe. 7:Elixir. 9:Solución. 10:Gránulos. 11:Cápsulas. 15:Suspensión.	1:Oral.	1
18:Supositorios.	5:Supositorio.	1
19:Crema. 17:Polvos.	7:Tópica.	1
8:Gotas.	2:Oftálmica; 3:Otica.	2
16:Inhalación.	6:Aerosol.	2
12:Inyección. 13:Inyección liofilizada. 14:Inyección efervescente.	4:Inyectable.	3

REG10

CI CII CIII	3
CIV CV	2
No control:	1

References

[1] E. Anderson and D. Schmittlein, Integration of the sales force: an empirical examination, *Rand Journal of Economics* (1984), 385–395.

[2] D.P. Baron, Design of Regulatory Mechanisms and Institutions, *Handbook of Industrial Organization* **2** (1989), 1347–1439.

[3] A.P. Bartel and L.G. Thomas, Direct and Indirect Effects of Regulation: A New Look at OSHA'S Impact, *Journal of Law and Economics* **28** (1985), 1–25.

[4] Y. Barzel, *Economic Analysis of Property Rights,* Cambridge University Press, NY, 1989.

[5] F. Bator, The Simple Analytics of welfare maximization, *American Economic Review* **47** (1957), 22–59.

[6] M. Bergara, Network access pricing and 'light handed' regulation: a comparative institutional analysis, presentado en el BPP seminar, Universidad de California, Berkeley, 1997.

[7] R.H. Coase, The problem of social cost, *Journal of Law and Economics* **3** (1960), 1–44.

[8] R. Coates, Electoral Support and the Capture of Legislators – Evidence from North Carolina vote on Radioactive Waste Disposal, *Rand Jornal of Economics* **26**(3) (1995), 502–518.

[9] K.J. Crocker and S.E. y Masten, Regulation and administered contracts revisited: lessons from transaction-cost economics for public utility regulation, *Kluwer Academic Publishers*, 1996, pp. 5–39.

[10] L.E. Davis and D.C. North, *Institutional change and American economic growth,* Cambridge University Press, Cambridge, 1971.
[11] H. Demset, Why regulate utilities, *Journal of Law and Economics* **11** (1968), 55–56.
[12] A.K. Dixit, *The making of economic policy, a transaction-cost politics perspective,* The MIT Press, 1996, pp. 192.
[13] J.H. Dunning, *Governments, globalization, and international business,* Oxford University Press, 1997, pp. 507.
[14] T.E. Getzen, *Health economics, fundamentals and flow of funds,* John Wiley & Sons, NY, 1997, pp. 467.
[15] V.P. Goldberg, Regulation and administered contracts, *The Bell Journal of Economics* **7**(2) (1976), 426–448.
[16] H.G. Grabowski and J.M. Vernon, Consumer protection regulation in ethical drug, *American Economic Association* **67**(1) (1977).
[17] H.G. Grabowski and J.M. Vernon, The regulation of pharmaceuticals: balancing the benefits and risks, *American Entreprise for Public Policy Research,* Washington y Londres, 1983, pp. 74.
[18] W.B. Gray and R.J. Shadbegian, Environmental regulation, investment timing, and technology choice, *NBER Working Paper*, 6.036, 1997, pp. 1–37.
[19] H.K. Gruenspecht and L.B. Lave, The economics of health, safety, and environmental regulation, *Handbook of Industrial Organization* **2** (1989), 1507–1551.
[20] J.T. Hamilton, Politics and Social Costs-Estimating the Impact of Collective Action on Hazardous Wastes Facilities, *Rand Journal of Economics* **24**(1) (1993), 101–125.
[21] A. Hillman and G. Keim, International Variation in The Business-Government Interface: Institutional and Organizational Considerations, *Academy of Management Journal* **20**(1) (1995), 193–313.
[22] G. Holburn, Regulatory Rules and Procedures: The Determinants of Electricity Rate Structures, presentado en el seminario del BPP Group, Haas School of Business, Universidad de California, Berkeley, 1998.
[23] G. John and B.A. Weitz, Forward integration into distribution: an empirical test of transaction cost analysis, *Journal of law Economics, and Organization* **4**(2) (1988), 337–354.
[24] P.L. Joskow, Vertical integration and long-term contracts: the case of coal-burning electric generation plants, *Journal of Law, Economics and Organization* **1** (1985), 33–79.
[25] J.P. Kalt and M.A. Zupan, Capture and Ideology in the Economic Theory of Politics, *American Economic Review* **74**(3) (1984), 279–300.
[26] Kaserman, L. David, Mayo, John W. Pacey and L. Patricia, The Political Economy of Deregulation: The Case of Intrastate Long Distance, *Journal of Regulatory Economics* **5** (1991), 49–63.
[27] T.E. Keeler, *Theories of regulation and the deregulation movement,* (Vol. 44), Martinus Nijhoff Publishers, Dordrecht, 1984, pp. 103–145.
[28] B. Klein, R. Crawford and A.A. Alchian, Vertical integration, appropriable rents, and the competitive contracting process, *Journal of Law and Economics* **21** (1978), 297–326.
[29] K. Krehbiel, Information and legislative organization, *Ann Arbor: University of Michigan Press* **1**(5) (1991), 1–22, 151–192.
[30] J.J. Laffont and J. y Tirole, *A Theory of Incentives in Procurement and Regulation,* MIT Press, Cambridge, MA, 1993.
[31] L. Lasagna and W. Wardell, The rate of new drugs discovery, in: *Drug development and marketing,* R.B. Helms, ed., Washinton, 1975, pp. 155–164.
[32] D.T. Levy and P.T. Spiller, The Institutional Foundations of Regulatory Commitment: A comparative Analysis of Telecommunications Regulation, *Journal of Law, Economics & Organization* (1994), 201–246.
[33] B. Levy and P.T. Spiller, *The institutional foundations of regulatory commitment,* Cambridge University press, 1995.
[34] D.T. Levy and P.T. Spiller, The institutional foundations of regulatory commitment: a comparative analysis of telecommunications regulation, *Journal of Law, Economics & Organization* (1994), 201–246.

[35] F. Lotter, Coûts de transaction et fondements de l'intervention publique, *Révue d'économie industrielle* **71** (1995), 163–180.

[36] S. Maijoor and A. Witteloostuijn, An empirical test of the resource-based theory: strategic regulation in the dutch audit industry, *Strategic Management Journal* **17**(7) (1996), 549–569.

[37] R.L. Manning, Products viability and prescription drug prices in Canada and the United States, *The Journal of law and Economics* **XL** (1997).

[38] S.E. Masten and K.J. Crocker, Efficient adaptation in long-term contracts: take-or-pay provisions for natural gas, *The American Economics Review* **75**(5) (1985), 1083–1093.

[39] S.E. Masten, J.W. Meehan and E.A. Snyder, The costs of organization, *Journal of Law and Economics* **25** (1982), 321–328.

[40] T. Moe, The politics of structural choice: toward a theory of public bureaucracy, en Organizational Theory, O.E. Williamson, ed., Oxford University Press, NY, 1990, pp. 116–153.

[41] T. Moe, The New Economics of Organization, *American Journal of Political Science* (1984), 739–777.

[42] T. Moe and M. Caldwell, The Institutional Foundations of Democratic Government-A Comparison of Presidential and Parliamentary Systems, *Journal of Institutional and Theoretical Economics* **150**(1) (1994), 171–195.

[43] K. Monteverde and D.J. Teece, Supplier switching costs and vertical integration in the automobile industry, *Bell Journal of Economics* (1982), 206–216.

[44] R.G. Noll, Economic perspectives on the politics of regulation, *Handbook of Industrial Organization* **2** (1989), 1253–1282.

[45] R. Nonell and J.R. Borrel, Mercado de medicamentos en España. Diseño institucional de la regulación y de la provisión pública, *Papeles de Economía Española. La prestación farmaceútica en España: Evolución y control* **2** (1998), 113–132.

[46] D.C. North, *Institutions, Institutional Change, and Economic Performance,* Cambridge University Press, New York, 1990.

[47] M. Olson, Regulatory agency discretion among competing industries: inside the FDA, *Journal of Law, Economics, and Organization* **11**(2) (1995), 379–405.

[48] M. Olson, Firm characteristics and the speed of FDA approval, *Journal of Economics and Management Strategy* **6**(2) (1997), 377–401.

[49] M.S.R. Palmer, Toward an Economics of Comparative Political Organization, *Journal of Law Economics & Organization* **1**(1) (1995), 164–188.

[50] B.P. Pashigian, The Effect of Environmental Regulation on Optimal Plant Size and Factor Shares, *Journal of Law and Economics* **27** (1984), 1–28.

[51] S. Peltzman, Toward a more general theory of regulation, *Journal of Law and Economics* **19** (1976), 211–240.

[52] A.C. Pigou, *Introducción a la economía,* Editorial Ariel, 1974, pp. 262.??

[53] K.T. Poole and H. y Rosenthal, Patterns of Congressional Voting, *American Journal of Political Science* **35**(1) (1991), 228–278.

[54] R.A. Prager, Franchise bidding for natural monopoly: the case of cable television, *Journal of Regulatory Economics* **1** (junio 1989), 115–132.

[55] R.A. Prager, Firm behavior in franchise monopoly markets, *Rand Journal of Economics* **21** (verano 1990), 211–225.

[56] P.J. Quirk, Food and Drug Administration, in: *The Politics of Regulation,* J.Q. Wilson, ed., Basic Books Inc., NY, 1980.

[57] K. Ramaswamy, A. Thomas and R.J. Litschert, Organizational performance in a regulated environment: the role of strategic orientation, *Strategic Management Journal* **15**(1) (1994), 63–74.

[58] M.V. Russo, Power plays: regulation, diversification, and backard integration in the ekectric utility industry, *Srategic Management* **13** (1992), 13–27.

[59] Samuelson, 1963.

[60] F.M. Scott Morton, The strategic response by pharmaceutical firms to the Medicaid most-favored-customer rules, *Journal of Economics* **28**(2) (1997), 269–290.

[61] F.M. Scott Morton, The objetives of the FDA's Office of generic drugs, NBER Working Paper Series, National Bureau of Economic Research, 1997, pp. 32.
[62] J.M. Serrano Sanz, La regulación del Estado como instrumento de política económica, in: *Regulac'on y competencia en la economía española,* Civitas, ed., Biblioteca Civitas de Economía y Empresa, 1995, pp. 21–31.
[63] K.A. Shepsle and B.R. Weingast, *Positive theories of congressional institutions,* cap. 2, University of Michigan Press, 19, n. 2, 1996, pp. 5–35.
[64] P.T. Spiller, Politicians Intesest Groups and Regulators: A Multiple Principals Theory of Regulation, *Journal of Law and Economics* **33** (1990), 65–101.
[65] P.T. Spiller, A positive political theory of regulatory instruments-constracts, administrative law or regulatory specificity, *Southern California Law Review* **69**(2) (1996), 477–515.
[66] G.J. Stigler, The theory of economic regulation, *The Bell Jorunal of Economics and Management Science* **2** (primavera 1971), 3–21.
[67] J.A. Stuckey, *Vertical integration and joint ventures in the aluminium industry,* Harvard University Press, 1983, pp. 347.
[68] P. Temin, Technology, regulation, and markets structure in the modern pharmaceutical industry, *The Bell Journal of Economics* **10**(2) (1979), 429–446.
[69] Tirole, 1991.
[70] W.K. Viscusi, Frameworks for analyzing the effects of risk and environmental regulation on productivity, *American Economic Review* (1983), 793–801.
[71] O.E. Williamson, Public and private bureaus, presentado en el IDS-270 seminar, Haas School of Business, Universidad de California, Berkeley, septiembre, 1997, pp. 52.
[72] O.E. Williamson, Economics and organization: a primer, *California Management Review* **38**(2) (invierno 1996), 131–146.
[73] O.E. Williamson, Economic organization: the case for candor, *Academy of Management Review* **21**(1) (1996), 48–57.
[74] O.E. Williamson, *Organization theory,* Oxford University Press, 1995, pp. 268.
[75] O.E. Williamson, Calculativeness, trust, and economic organization, *Journal of Law and Economics* **XXXVI** (1993), 453–485.
[76] O.E. Williamson, *The economic institutions of capitalism,* Free Press, 1985, pp. 450.
[77] O.E. Williamson, Transaction-cost economics: the governance of contractual relations, *Journal of Law and Economics* **2** (1979), 233–261.
[78] O.E. Wiliamson, Franchise bidding for natural monopolies-in general and with respect to CATV, *Bell Journal of Economics* **7**(11) (1976), 73–104.
[79] R.D. Willig and E.E. Baley, Income Distribution Concers in Regulatory Policymaking, in: *Studies in Public Regulation,* G. Fromm, ed., MIT Press, Cambridge, 1981.
[80] J.Q. Wilson, *Bureaucracy: what Government Agencies do and why they do it,* Basic Books, NY.
[81] M.A. Zupan, The efficacy of franchise bidding schemes in the case of cable television: some systematic evidence, *Journal of Law and Economics* **XXXII** (1989), 401–459.
[82] W.J. Henisz and B.Z. Zelner, The institutional determinants of infrastructure growth in telecommunications, a cross-national study, *BPP Group Seminar*, Haas School of Business, Universidad de California, Berkeley, 1997.
[83] G.R. Barker and R.B. Chapman, Evaluating labor markat contracting and regulation: a transaction costs perspective with particular reference to New Zealand, *Journal of Institutional and Theoretical Economics* **145** (1989), 317–342.
[84] D.A. Schuler and K. Rehbein, Uncovering the dimensionality of corporate political involvement, *Conference on the positive political theory of business strategy,* California, October, 1998, pp. 36.
[85] I. Herberts Scheinberg and J.M. Walshe, *Orphan diseases and orphan drugs,* Manchester University Press, 1986.
[86] D. Dranove and D. Meltzer, Do important drugs reach the market sooner? *Rand Journal of Economics* **25**(1) (1994), 402–423.
[87] J.M. Snyder, On buying legislatures, *Economics and Politics* **3**(2) (1991), 93–109.

[88] K.T. Poole and H. Rosenthal, Patterns of congressional voting, *American Journal of Political Science* **35**(1) (1991), 228–278.
[89] E. Whitmore, *Product development planning for the health care products regulated by the FDA,* A.S.Q.C. Quality Press, Wisconsin, 1997, pp. 159.
[90] R.M. Grant, *Contemporary Strategy Analysis,* Blackwell Business, Cambridge, Mass, 1991.
[91] B. Spielker, *Multinational drug companies. Issues in drug discovery and development,* Raven Press, New York, 1995.
[92] D. Dranove, Medicaid drug formulary restrictions, *Journal of Law and Economics* **XXXII** (April 1989), 143–162.
[93] M.N. Baily, Research and development cost and returns: the pharmaceutical industry, *Journal of Political Economics* **80** (1972), 70–85.
[94] W.M. Wardell, Introduction of new therapeutic drugs in the United States and Great Britain: An international comparison, *Clinical Pharmacology and Therapeutics* (1973), 773–790.
[95] M.C. Kendall, *FDA regulations, patent lives and the pharmaceutical industry,* paper submitted to PhMa, Washington, DC, 2 de abril, 1974.
[96] L.H. Sarett, FDA regulations and their influence on future R & D, *Research Management* **27** (1974), 18–20.
[97] H.J. Leonard, *Are environmental regulations driving US industry overseas?* The Conservation Foundation, Washington, DC, 1984.
[98] L.G. Thomas, Regulation and firm size: FDA impacts on innovation, *RAND Journal of Economics* **21** (1990), 497–516.
[99] D.J. Wood, Business and public policy in the progressive era: the Food and Drug Act of 1962, in: *Research in corporate social performance and policy,* L.E. Preston, ed., JAI Press, Greenwich, CT, 1984, pp. 213–252.
[100] G.F. Douglas, *Industrial organization and public policy,* McMillan Publishing Company, NY, 1992, pp. 736.
[101] W.A. Magat and M.J. Moore, Consumer product safety regulation in the United States and the United Kingdom: the case of bicycles, *Rand Journal of Economics* **27**(1) (1996), 148–164.
[102] N.J. Clark, *Rx-to-OTC switching-new indications, new opportunities,* Pharmaceutical & Healthcare Publishing, 1996, pp. 130.
[103] M. Alvargonzález Figaredo, Mercado interior y productos farmacéuticos: patentes y autorización de comercialización, *Noticias de la Unión Europea* **148** (May 1997), 41–48.
[104] F. Lobo, La evolución de las patentes sobre medicamentos en los países desarrollados, *Revista del Derecho Industrial* **11**(32) (May–August 1989), 311–341.

Pharmaceuticals Policy and Law 5 (2002) 107–123
IOS Press

Medicines in Europe: Scientific convergence and political divergences

Virginie Godet[a] and Sabine Ferrand-Nagel[b]
[a]*CREGAS-U 537 / Université Paris I Panthéon-Sorbonne, 80 rue du Général Leclerc, 94276 Le Kremlin-Bicêtre Cedex, France*
[b]*ADIS / Faculté Jean Monnet / Université Paris Sud, 54, boulevard Desgranges, 92331 Sceaux, France*

1. Introduction

The pharmaceutical sector is one of the key sectors of the European manufacturing industry (ranked 5th), representing 3.5% of added value in Europe in 1995, and making a strong contribution to its balance of trade ($US 16,201 million). Europe used to be the primary source of new molecules to have been granted marketing authorisations since 1975, and it continues to hold its own against its leading competitors on the world market, ranking behind the USA but ahead of Japan.

Whilst this market was at first strictly regulated within each member state, in accordance with the three principles of effectiveness, safety and quality of the products, it is now in the process of becoming an integrated European market. Over recent years, the authorities have allowed the market to converge in certain areas such as the authorisation to market, transparency, patents, research programmes, etc. – centralised procedures for authorising biotechnological and/or radically innovative medicines are one example of this desire for unification. Conflicting objectives nevertheless remain; countries are trying to achieve a single market and generalise the free circulation of goods, whilst simultaneously maintaining their political autonomy. Unification is continuously hindered by each member state's desire to preserve its sovereignty with regard to health policies. This situation is the result of the strong national identity of health and social protection systems. Several decades after the failed attempts to standardise social security systems (1962), the community's ambitions are now restricted to co-ordinating the systems, and have essentially returned to competitive pressure make the system evolve.

Our objective is to look at the extent to which medicine policy has converged in Europe, and to demonstrate that whilst we can certainly talk about European convergence with regard to objectives and to technical and scientific standards, we have to accept that there is divergence regarding healthcare policies and medicines. We can also try to see whether or not the current trends in the reforms adopted by member states comply with guiding principles and/or common legislation.

To begin with, we analyse national specifics for the social welfare systems in four European countries. We then attempt to highlight the main aspects of scientific convergence and regulatory divergences within the European medicine market. Finally, we make sure that we qualify our opinion by showing that current reforms in medicine policies are following common guiding principles.

2. European health systems with strong national specificities

In order to characterise the different medicine markets among the member states and to highlight their heterogeneousness, we have chosen four countries (France, Germany, Italy, and the United Kingdom) using an analysis grid to identify the mechanisms and principles behind the different systems.

2.1. The physical heterogeneousness of these member states

If we are to analyse how the European pharmaceutical market works we must make it clear that it is developing within a "physically" diverse space. The macro-economic characteristics of the member states are very different, illnesses have diverse effects and prevalences, medical practices and treatments often have a national character and the different segments of the market are also very specific to each country, especially in terms of size. Here are a few figures to illustrate the extent of these variations:

Firstly, the size of each market in 1999 (total sales of pharmaceutical products):

- The first of the four is Germany (ranked 3rd in the world behind the USA and Japan) with $18,500 million, followed by France (4th in the world) with $17,751 million, then Italy (5th) with $11,332 million, and finally the UK (6th) with $11,029 million.

The expenditure on medicines[1] in the four countries can be resumed as follows:

	France	Germany	Italy	United Kingdom
Share of expenditure on medicines compared to total healthcare expenditure in 1997	20.9%	12.2%	17.5%	16.3%
Rate of growth of expenditure on medicines[2]				
1996	2%	8%	11%	12%
1997	3%	2%	7%	7%
1998	8%	n.c.	n.c.	n.c.

If we now look at the different market segments:

[1] OECD Health Data 2000.

[2] Last year in which OECD Health Data gave figures for the four countries.

- In all member states, prescribed medicines represent the main share of medicine consumption: in 1997 for example, they represent 67% of overall expenditure on pharmaceutical products in France, and 69% in the UK. The essential differences between the countries in fact relate to whether or not the other market segments are expanding.
- The share of generic medicines out of all prescribed medicines is thus extremely variable: in 1997 it stood at 2% in France, at 3% in Italy, 22% in the United Kingdom but 39% in Germany. If we look at the volume shares (number of prescribed medicines), given the major differences in price, the latter two countries exchange rankings, with 38% in Germany and 40% in the UK. [3]
- In 1997, Over The Counter (OTC) medicines – which are difficult to measure with any real accuracy due to the lack of any standard definition in Europe – represented 14.2% of the total medicine market in Italy, as against 24.6% in France and 33.7% in Germany [9].

These figures support the "physical" heterogeneousness of the European countries that we are considering. This is essentially the result of the different historical and economic changes to the social welfare systems in these countries.

2.2. *Different systems despite common referents*

The diversity of the social welfare systems in Europe, and more particularly in the four countries we are examining, can be demonstrated by looking at the way in which they are organised and work. The standard grid thus distinguishes systems in the Bismarck tradition from those in the Beveridge tradition.

As Lambert [18] reminds us, Bismarckian, social security and social welfare systems were the initial common denominator in Europe. As in Germany, the first six countries in the common market thus had social security systems which were financed by contributions based on salaries. Indeed, at the end of the 19th century, Bismarck's Germany was the first country to generalise, by statute, a social insurance system which, in varied and partial forms was gradually implemented more often than not within a context of professions and of mutual aid associations. The Bismarckian systems thus have the particularity of having closely linked the protection of individuals to the world of work (exercising a profession and joint participation from employers and employees).

The generalisation of social security systems in the rest of Europe was longer to come, after the Second World War, and it was universal systems which saw the light of day, first of all in England (created in 1948 in application of the Beveridge plan of 1942), and in Scandinavian countries. The reforms made in England from the 1980's onwards to diversify revenue, make the system more flexible and control expenditure. But the common principles have not really changed since the beginning.

[3] From "Policy Relating to Generic Medicines in the OECD", European Commission Report, 2000.

Table 1
Germany / France: two Bismarckian systems

	Germany	France
Social contributions	– 1/2 employers and 1/2 employees – Increases lower for the employers	– 2/3 employers and 1/3 employees – Increases higher for the employers
Benefit of social insurance	– Employees with lower incomes, the other choose their insurer	– Every employees, because egalitarian notion prevails
Decision making	– Decentralised	– Centralised
Patient's contribution	– High	– Low, but variable (with private insurance or mutual funds)

These systems, based upon redistribution rather than insurance, offer a total, free and uniform cover to the entire population; funding comes from taxes; and the health system is a public monopoly with salaried employees. They correspond to a period marked by intervention by the state, whose economic role was considerably developed, particularly with regard to healthcare. So we find at this time national welfare systems. During the two phases following the growth of the EEC, it was these countries which joined – England and Scandinavia followed by countries from southern Europe (Spain, Portugal and Greece), which, like Italy, chose to move from one system to the other by nationalising their welfare systems. The result was that the split between the two types of organisation changed: two thirds of the countries in the Fifteen have Beveridgian systems with salaried doctors; but as the most populated countries have a Bismarckian organisation, two third of the European population are concerned by this type of organisation.

The question of organisational choice will continue in the years to come, in as much as Europe will continue to grow, with the arrival of countries such as Poland, Hungary, the Czech Republic, etc., whose public welfare organisations have been diminished and whose public authorities are faced with the choice of a new welfare system. Nevertheless, as Lambert point out, a generalisation of public health monopolies seems unlikely as it is not compatible with the re-evaluation of the welfare state.

Without going into the details, the following tables highlight the main themes to illustrate the organisational diversity in European systems.

This brief look at the health systems in these four countries demonstrates the national positions which still prevail. Depending on the political context, the power of the players and individual cultures, the models developed by Bismarck and Beveridge vary considerably. The resulting diversity hinders the construction of a single medicine market.

Analysis of how medicines are regulated – and this is only one part of the healthcare system – leads us to reflect upon the interdependency of the measures which directly concern medicines and upon the role of this policy within a country's health policy.

Table 2
UK / Italy: two Beveridgian systems

	UK	Italy
Financial regulatory	Centralised power: – Low patient's contributions – Supply severely restricted by budgetary constraints	Decentralised power: – Powers transferred to the municipalit ies (two-speed system)
Co-ordination	– Complementarity of local practice and hospital medicine (filtering, and waiting lists)	– Contractual system between the local health authorities and healthcare providers (public or private)

3. Convergence versus divergence on the european market of medicines

3.1. Successful standardisation of the scientific and technical aspects

The pharmaceutical market is now a European market, and has had to restructure itself around the criteria of the global European market. The main economic objective of the European Community is to guarantee four fundamental freedoms: the free movement of goods, labour, services and capital. The convergence of objectives required a panoply of legal acts: mutual standardisation and recognition, and the creation of new institutions [3]. This economic community, which was being built around the notion of a market, had a highly liberal connotation, and state interventions – aside from the Common Agriculture Policy – were extremely limited. The two pillars of this new Europe were freedom of movement and free competition [11]. In addition to these basic principles, supporting policies were developed. [4]

So over a period of approximately forty years, we have moved from a multitude of markets juxtaposed within Europe to the European Union, which is to date the most accomplished form of the integration of different countries. The question we are asking is what place does the medicine market have within this new integrated space?

3.1.1. The realities of successful convergence in the European medicine market

We wish to demonstrate that, with regard to the technical and scientific aspects, standardisation has been successful, and has led to improvements in the free movement of goods.

a. Marketing authorisations and the European Agency

In order to remove the obstacles (created by the national nature of marketing authorisations) to the free movement of pharmaceutical products, the legislators came up with a regulation in July 1993. [5] This regulation enables the conditions

[4] Tools of intervention within the community's economy, which amongst other things protect it from certain excesses of capitalism (CAP, competition policy, industrial policy, tax policy, etc.).

[5] EEC regulation n°2309/93; Directives 93/39/CEE, 93/40/CEE and 93/41/CEE of the Council, 14th June 1993.

under which marketing authorisations are granted to be standardised, and lays the ground for one or more countries to recognise an authorisation granted by another country. This convergence of standards was decided and organised with a view to protecting public health and international credibility.

There are in fact two distinct procedures, depending upon the composition of the medicine: a centralised procedure for biotechnological medicines or medicines designated by the European Medicine Evaluation Agency as being radically innovative, and a decentralised procedure, referred to as mutual recognition, for all other medicines. This Agency is a new European institution, and was also created to co-ordinate centralised and decentralised authorisations. In essence it is an advisory body, even though its scientific influence is by no means negligible.

b. Monitoring and pharmacovigilance

The principle of monitoring – which is a control mechanism – naturally complements that of marketing authorisations and requires that the company responsible for placing the medicine on the market must ensure that the medicine is manufactured and controlled in accordance with approved scientific methods.

It is linked to pharmacovigilance,[6] an alarm mechanism, which deals with the analysis, exchange and compilation of information relating to the side effects of medicines and to any steps which might be taken as a result of this information. Companies and member states are thus required to set up a rapid alarm system, all information of which is centralised in Sweden.

This construction of a standardised Europe has led to a pan-European organisation which is the guarantor of the safety of the products for which authorisations are granted.

3.1.2. Partial convergence

Other scientific and technical aspects are in a convergence phase, but this phase is not completely finished. These rules, which relate to the information and rational use of the medicine, as well as to patents, are once again justified by the notion of protecting public health and removing obstacles to the free movement of goods.

On the one hand, the information aimed at the medical profession and the public – in particular in the instructions for use and on labels - comes from the evaluation report that accompanies every request for a marketing authorisation, and is in the process of being standardised. Differences in scientific standpoints and medical semantics between countries nevertheless remain, and standardisation has not been fully achieved. Rational use means the standardisation relating to the wholesale distribution, to the issue and to the advertising of medicines.[7] Such standardisation was required because differing national regulations were likely to hinder the free

[6]Regulation 2309/93 and directive 93/39.

[7]Directive 92/25/CEE of the 31st March 1992.

movement of products. It was also necessary to ensure that medicines are stored, transported and handled under proper safety conditions.

On the other hand, patents are an integral part of industrial policy, and the standardisation of European patent rights has ensured the free movement of products. Patent protection is not proper to medicines,[8] but it is vital because it gives the holder a monopoly to market the product over a certain period. There are currently two systems in Europe, but neither of them is based upon community legislation: the national patent systems and the European system,[9] completed by the Supplementary Protection Certificate[10] for pharmaceutical products.

The community patent on which the experts are still working[11] will produce the same effects throughout the Community and any issue, transfer, cancellation or termination will be valid in all countries of the Community. The creation of such a patent would appear to be vital, in order to remove the distortions in competition that can arise from national patents; it is also one of the most appropriate ways in which to ensure free movement of goods that are protected by a patent. It will allow companies to adapt their production and distribution activities to suit the European scale. This system will coexist with the national and European patent systems, and inventors will be free to choose how they wish to be protected. However, it has not yet been implemented, as experts believe that it is too costly.

It is nevertheless important to mention that this technical and scientific convergence has its limits. The name and brand, for example, are aspects currently being standardised, but there are now major disputes between manufacturers and the community's authorities, particularly with regard to unresolved language problems. Nor must we forget corporate differentiation strategies, for which the brand name is a crucial element.

The standardisation which has already taken place and which is now in operation is mainly of a scientific and technical nature; in other words, it meets the criterion of freedom of movement. Although these aspects were undoubtedly the easiest to converge, they are already having repercussions in the sector's industries: new entrance barriers, but shorter durations and lower marketing costs, scientific recognition of the reliability of marketing authorisation dossiers, etc.

3.2. Divergent regulatory policies

European healthcare systems are currently undergoing a financial crisis, and governments have introduced "medicalised" policies to control the cost of healthcare and medicines. Such regulation is legally the responsibility of each individual member state, thus hindering free competition. The questions of price and reimbursement are

[8] With the exception of the Supplementary Protection Certificate.
[9] Introduced by the Munich Convention on the 5th October 1973.
[10] EEC regulation n°1768/92 of the Council, 18/06/92.
[11] New proposal for regulation by the council for community patents. COM(2000) 412 final.

intimately linked to the way in which each health system works, and for the moment (though there is no reason to believe it will not continue) each country refuses to see any reason to change. This is the main obstacle to any process for creating a single market for pharmaceutical products.

3.2.1. The question of price

Prices and levels of reimbursement are the stumbling block of the single medicine market: they crystallise the divergent economic stakes. On the one hand, it is vital for a pharmaceutical company that the initial price of a medicine be properly set, as it determines the company's return on investment, and thus its profits and its future capacity to self-finance its R&D. On the other hand, it is in the government's interests to encourage scientific progress, in order to develop innovative therapies which will, in the long term, reduce expenditure whilst continuing to satisfy the population's healthcare requirements. Whatever the member state, the prices of pharmaceutical products are directly or indirectly set, which involves economic distortions – like parallel trade- and tension in the relationships with manufacturers.

The European texts concerning the price issues are relatively timid, even though the Community wants to supervise prices and reimbursement rates on the pretext of allowing pharmaceutical companies to innovate, whilst simultaneously organising the policies which control healthcare expenditure. These attempts fall within the context of the liberal Europe that has been created, and are more often than not based upon studies which show that the lack of innovation in the European pharmaceutical market is mainly due to the pricing policies in force in some countries. The Community has nevertheless had to give in to pressure from the member states and to recognise their sovereignty with regard to social welfare. [12]

However, as early as 1988 the Community set its economic text: the Transparency Directive.[13] Its purpose is not to standardise the conditions for controlling prices and the criteria for reimbursing medicines; it simply establishes a certain level of transparency. Above all, it is a way of gathering information on the different regulatory systems, and thus of protecting free competition within the European Community. We are therefore a long way from measures which aim to unify pricing systems in Europe; this is no more than a form of acceptance of the current situation, which we are nevertheless trying to control.

3.2.2. Fundamentally heterogeneous characteristics

We wish to demonstrate that whilst the need to control healthcare expenditure is common to all the countries we are studying, the ways in which the offer and demand

[12] Art.1 §2 of EEC regulation n°2309/93 of the 22/07/93 and Art.1 of the 93/39/CEE directive of the Council, amending the 65/65/CEE directive of the Council. The respective clauses from the Council and the Commission do not affect the competency of the authorities within the member states, either with regard to setting the prices of medicines, or with regard to their inclusion within the scope of application of the national healthcare systems.

[13] 89/105/CEE directive of the Council of the 21st December 1988.

for pharmaceutical products are regulated are essentially heterogeneous, especially with regard to price and reimbursement policies, and co-payment.

3.2.2.1. Pricing policies

There are three major types of pricing policy in Europe: direct policy, such as the administered price system in France; indirect control policy using the reference price method as in Germany and to a lesser extent in Italy, and another indirect control policy via profit control, as in United Kingdom. Truly free prices existed in Germany until 1989, but have now disappeared as far as ethical medicines are concerned; on the other hand, they still exist for OTC medicines and often for hospital medicines too (with the exception of the United Kingdom).

In France, the state – which supervises the healthcare system – has a long history of interventionism where medicines are concerned. The prices for reimbursable specialised medicines (hospitals excepted) are established by the Comité Economique des Produits de Santé and are among the lowest in Europe. The Committee signed a sector-wide accord with the SNIP[14] on 19 July 1999 to introduce a global financial regulation system designed to be compatible with ONDAM.[15] The system controls prices pre-market and volumes post-market. The margins of wholesalers and pharmacists are also determined by regulation: the former are in proportion to manufacturer's prices while the latter are established according to a system of tapering rates. In hospitals the prices are unregulated: since 1987, the sale of medicines is governed by public contract procedure.

In Germany, manufacturers are free to set and revise their prices. The retail price is then determined by applying the wholesalers' mark-up, which has a regulation ceiling. The price of medicines is nonetheless indirectly controlled by a system of reference prices, defined in successive waves from 1989 onwards. One crucial restriction is that they do not apply to patented medicines, nor to those that contain a new active ingredient and which offer improved treatment or attenuate side effects. The products concerned are grouped into three classes on the basis of similarity. Each medicine from a therapeutic group is attached to one of the three classes, and 66% of the total drug market is listed. A fixed health insurance (Festbetrag) cover charge is then established for each group. When one of these medicines is sold for more than the reference price, the patient has to make up the balance. While the prices of the listed products have tended to come down, the manufacturers have stepped up their promotion efforts and accordingly increased the average price of products outside the scope of the Festbetrag [4].

In The United Kingdom, the prices of medicines covered by the NHS[16] have, since 1977, been laid down by the Pharmaceutical Price Regulation Scheme (PPRS).

[14] Syndicat National de l'Industrie Pharmaceutique = national syndicate for the pharmaceutical industry.

[15] Objectif National des Depenses d'Assurance Maladie = national objective for healthcare expenditure, set by parliament and allocated by the government to the various different types of healthcare expenditure. (Government orders of 24 April 1996).

[16] National Health Service.

Price control is indirect, acting on profits and sales volumes. The government and the representatives of the pharmaceutical industry (ABPI) regularly negotiate an authorised profit margin, calculated for each company on the basis of the turnover of branded products it sells to the NHS. If it exceeds its profit margin, the company must either pay back the excess to the NHS or reduce its prices. Only generic medicines, for which the price is set by the Department of Health and Social Security, fall outside the scope of this system. Wholesalers are free to set their own mark-ups and dispensing chemists are paid on the basis of services rendered, regardless of the price of the products delivered.

In Italy, the system initially consisted of assigning each product a European price, calculated on the basis of the price obtained on several selected markets, of which at least two had to have a direct pricing system. In 1995, the government tried to bring in a reference price system on the German model, but with a difference: if the price of the product was superior to the reference price, the patient had to pay not only the balance but the full price of the product. This system is due to be reviewed in the coming months. For radically innovative medicines and, since 1998, for products resulting from the European decentralisation procedure, a new pricing system has been developed by contractual negotiation between the industry and the government.

3.2.2.2. Reimbursement and co-payment

Each of these pricing models corresponds to a particular reimbursement mode and co-payment policy, both of which are closely bound in with the overall workings of the welfare system.

All the Member States now use a list system to register medicines for reimbursement. The technical criteria for inclusion are very similar. At the end of the day there are two types of list: positive, for reimbursable medicines (France) and negative, for those which are not covered by the system (Britain). Some systems, including the German and Italian versions, combine the two.

In France, reimbursement is calculated on the basis of categories of medicines or types of illness and corresponds to a percentage of the product price: 35, 65 or 100% depending on the gravity of the condition and the therapeutic effect of the medicine. Additionally, to benefit from healthcare services, patients must usually pay for treatment up front before being reimbursed at a later date. They must nonetheless pay a contribution from their own pockets. For medicines, this contribution corresponds to the balance left after subtracting the percentage reimbursed per type of medicine and type of beneficiary. The great majority (85%) of French people, however, subscribe to private insurance which covers this remaining charge. For obvious reasons, then, co-payment is relatively ineffective at fostering responsibility among patients and staunching the flow of healthcare spending.

In Germany, the reference price implies that the sum reimbursed for each group of medicines is fixed. However, patients pay not only the difference between the price of the prescribed medicine and the reference price for the class, but also a fixed charge that varies according to the size of the packaging (DM 8, 9 or 10 since 1999).

Patients cannot take out supplementary insurance, but there are a range of exemptions based on age, income, etc.

In The United Kingdom, all the products prescribed on the NHS and in receipt of an authorisation to market are fully covered, and the patient has nothing to pay. Since 1952, however, a prescription charge system has been in operation. This involves a fixed contribution for all types of medicine, per prescription item (currently £6). When the cost of the prescribed item is lower than the franchise, and the item belongs to the category of medicines available from chemists without prescription, then the consumer has the option of paying the price of the product. The franchise is very high, but there are numerous exemptions based on age, income and other economic criteria, covering slightly over one half the population, who consume 88% of prescription items [20]. Successive increases in the franchise would seem to have been effective in dissuading non-exempt users.

In Italy, as in France, reimbursement is based on categories of medicines or types of illness and corresponds to a percentage of the product price,[17] the balance being down to the patient, who usually pays the charge up front anyway. Co-payment is dual in nature: there is a ceiling rate which determines the co-payment in accordance with the number of prescribed items and a variable reimbursement rate (0, 50 or 100% depending on the class to which the medicine belongs) linked to the product price. Exemptions – based on precise criteria of income, household size, specific illnesses and age – cover 36% of the population.

Regulatory policies, especially as regards pricing, are therefore heterogeneous in the countries we have been examining. In as far as this heterogeneity is the legacy of history and the corollary of specific national healthcare and welfare systems, it may seem reasonable to assume that it is irreducible. We would like to qualify that opinion, however, by demonstrating that the reforms currently under way in these Member States share a common inspiration and are therefore being implemented in accordance with common guiding principles.

4. The common guiding principles behind the current reforms

4.1. European public policies

The construction of Europe has contributed in a number of ways to redefining the nature of state intervention in the economy. From the outset, in the Treaty of Rome, the role of the European institutions was designed to restrict the scope of state intervention in the economy. Integration thus went hand in hand with the ascendancy of liberal economic policies (competition policy, tight monetary policy, etc.) – one reason why Europe social policy is still in its infancy. Whether the construction of

[17] 0, 50 or 100%, depending on the gravity of the condition and the therapeutic effect of the medicine.

Europe has helped harmonise public policies in Europe, or whether it has preserved and even accentuated national specificities – especially in the health sector – is indeed a moot point.

The community's jurisdiction on health is very limited and non-exclusive. As we noted earlier, issues involving the financing and organisation of the healthcare system remain very much under state control, and the Member States can be regarded as a form of expression of national identity. Community policy is mainly there to promote the public health policies and programmes already implemented in the Member States and to adopt measures to encourage best practise and make recommendations, notably with regard to preventive care. The Community's role here is essentially one of co-ordination.

As for policy on medicines, it is worth pointing out that certain aspects of healthcare spending controls are part of an overall trend in Europe towards restricted state intervention. There is a general tendency throughout the Member States to restrict reimbursement of so-called "comfort" treatments, which attack the symptoms rather than the underlying illness and which, when covered by the various social security systems, have proved a rich source of profit for the laboratories. Recently, in France, the state introduced a policy of re-evaluating "medical services rendered" which, it hopes, will save 10 billion francs over 3 years. The diminishing percentage of people's medical expenses covered by France's social security system can also be interpreted as a move to restrict reimbursement. The figure fell to a low of 54.9% in 1995, although its has since risen slightly to 57%.

4.2. Cost awareness: Targeting the prescribers

A strong common tendency in the policies adopted by the various states is the introduction of regulatory mechanisms into systems that had previously had few or none. With free or heavily subsidised healthcare coming to be considered an inflationary factor, many governments sought to develop regulation by introducing a pricing system for the services and products dispensed. In an initial reaction against the principle of free healthcare at the point of delivery, the policies of the 70s and 80s were aimed mainly at healthcare consumers, increasing – sometimes significantly – the proportion of the overall cost borne by the patient. None of the countries that followed this path achieved any convincing results. In the 90s the strategy therefore took a different tack, targeting the doctors as the prescribers, and thus the initiators of healthcare spending.

This policy, now becoming widespread in Europe, is based directly on the findings of Arrow (from 1963 onwards) which highlighted the specificity of healthcare, linked not only to the size of the risk and the uncertainty inherent to the medical domain, but also to the asymmetry of information in the doctor/patient relationship. It was demonstrated that the patient is rarely sensitive to considerations of cost and the price cannot therefore play the role of moderator or clearly reflect healthcare preferences (attempts at estimating price elasticity have proved less than conclusive: the results are highly variable and on the whole yield near-zero values). In consequence, the doctor, with a near-monopoly on information, is deemed to be the key decision-maker in lieu and in place of the patient, who merely applies the doctor's decisions. It is upon the doctor, then, as the real initiator of spending, that the recent cost awareness campaigns have focussed.

4.2.1. Overall budgets

These policies are at their most developed, and restrictive, in Britain and Germany, where prices are said to be free. The main purpose of this type of constraint is thus to make prescribers aware of costs and limit the drug consumption.

Britain's prescription regulation system was introduced in 1989: it aims in fact to target growth in spending rather than to set fixed budgets. Since 1993, the structure of the patient population has been factored in. This prescription regulation system is based on the transmission of information to doctors (on the safety, effectiveness and price of medicines) and the provision of information by doctors, who have to declare their medical acts. The system then returns a set of statistics[18] enabling doctors to compare their prescriptions with those of a theoretical practice of similar age structure and geographic location.

In Germany, the Seehofer reform of 1992–1993 [19] introduced a binding global budget setting a fixed sum for the reimbursement of pharmaceutical products applicable to all doctors. This is in fact a ceiling which only comes into effect if the spending levels exceed the threshold. The resulting financial sanctions are covered by the accredited professional associations up to a limit of DM 280 million; for anything beyond that, the pharmaceutical industry itself is forced to contribute. But the lack of visibility for the doctors, who were often unable to situate their own activity relative to the overall budget allocation, led to the adoption of an individual-budget solution in 1997. German doctors now evidence greater price flexibility in terms of demand: faced with this constraint, they have been prescribing a larger number of generics and fewer drugs of uncertain effectiveness [20].

In France and Italy, the systems are less restrictive, so the volume of sales is high. Administrative controls on prescriptions have been in place in France since 1993, and tied in to ONDAM since 1996, but compliance is hard to enforce. A set of guidelines known as Références Médicales Opposables[20] was drawn up for certain categories of drugs and has been in force since March 1994. These offer guidance on best practice and on diagnostic or therapeutic strategies designed to help the practitioner and patient decide on the most appropriate course of treatment. The guidelines are binding: non-compliance can lead to financial penalties for the prescribers, but in

---

[18]This information system (1988) is known as PACT (Prescribing Analysis and CosT information system).

[19]Gesundheitsreformgesetz 1992–1993.

[20]These recommendations were drawn up by the National Heath Accreditation and Evaluation Agency or, in the case of pharmaceutical products, by the Agence du Médicament.

fact checks are rarely made [19]. In Italy, this type of control is currently the object of discussion, and the health system is seeking to introduce incentives to encourage GPs to pay attention to the cost of their prescriptions. A proposed system that involved redirecting some of the resulting savings into doctors' personal incomes came in for severe criticism; other solutions are now under consideration.

4.2.2. Generics and OTCs

The focus here is on product portfolios, both from the industry standpoint and from that of health insurance. In the context of a fixed annual budget, the general idea is that savings have to made on current products in order to "make way" for newer, innovative products, usually very expensive, but always in great popular demand due to media coverage of medical research. The policy of developing generic medicines is aimed at a particular niche in the market: that of drugs for which the patents are about to run out. The production of generics therefore relies on older, familiar technologies not subject to licensing, and leads to selling prices significantly lower than those of products still under patent (by some 30 to 40%). The United Kingdom and Germany were quick to take this route, while France and Italy have only just embarked on it. The delay in France is largely due to the low regulatory prices and the absence of incentives for prescribers.

OTC (Over The Counter) drugs are freely available for purchase, but under conditions that vary widely from one country to another. In Britain they are available from the dispensing chemist or drugstore, whereas in France the pharmacist still enjoys a monopoly. In France the category is somewhat fuzzy around the edges: are they non-prescription drugs, or prescription drugs that are not reimbursed? In any case, they are not listed among the reimbursable products. This leaves the manufacturers free to set their own prices and advertise their products, and it is in this particular segment that we find a competitive market situation where the pharmaceutical firms can develop independent strategies, without governmental supervision except for the quality controls. Given the heavy constraints that weigh on the pharmaceutical sector, this small free-market segment is now clearly an instrument of negotiation between the manufacturers and the public authorities.

4.3. Innovation: A crucial factor for Europe's pharmaceutical industry

Innovative products make up the third market segment that focuses the attention of manufacturers and public authorities. At stake is the current and future capacity of the European pharmaceutical industry to bring to market the medicines of tomorrow, especially now that – as the above developments imply – the companies can no longer count on getting a high price for older drugs. Fostering and protecting innovation is therefore an issue of prime importance for the pharmaceutical industry, especially given the substantial research and development costs referred to earlier. The joint policy on Research and Innovation, absent from the Treaty of Rome, was made a priority in the Maastricht Treaty. Its main objective is to maintain and reinforce the international competitive edge of European industry over its global rivals in high-technology sectors. Although the pharmaceutical industry can benefit from these programmes, the subsidies are often insufficient, and the policy offers less incentive than the companies had hoped. For the most part it simply offers a framework and guidelines for national initiatives that are of likely benefit to the whole European Community. To this should be added the section of industrial policy dedicated to protecting innovation, as discussed earlier, which is currently at the harmonisation stage. The purpose of patents is of course to facilitate innovation (in this case clinical innovation) by guaranteeing a better return on R&D costs, but these advances don't seem to have gone far enough to provide real encouragement for innovation.

It is therefore up to the Member States to give a policy lead in this field with the right incentives, and notably by means of pricing policies: this inevitably raises the question of fair remuneration for pharmaceutical innovation. As we have seen, the different pricing systems make the European market heterogeneous, with regard to policies as well as prices. It should be remembered, though, that this is especially true for older and "me-too" products. Indeed, the question of innovative medicines is usually considered outside the pricing system, being based instead on a contractual relationship, notably on case-by-case agreements between manufacturers and governments. This has been the situation in France since the framework agreement between the government and the SNIP in 1994, and the more recent accord in July 1999, but also in Italy and Germany. It amounts to implicit recognition by the various Member States of the need to provide a proper reward for innovation, i.e. to enable the manufacturers to obtain prices that ensure an adequate return on investment for innovative products. This is effectively one way to encourage upcoming research.

These issues are the subject of a growing number of debates involving representatives from industry, the Member States and the European institutions, all of whom are seeking to define a framework for a fairer and more consistent approach to the remuneration of medicinal innovation in Europe. Such an approach would draw widely on medico-economic or pharmaco-economic studies. The economic evaluation of medicines and healthcare services, based on comparative cost analyses and strategy modelling, is a useful decision aid for the manufacturers and for the bodies that set drugs prices. The studies currently produced are often of unequal quality, lacking in uniformity and transparency, which prevents decision-makers from using them, especially when it comes to evaluating innovative products. We could rectify this problem and ensure the use of high-quality studies by standardising methods, not only at national level but also Europe-wide. This would require all those involved, at the European level, to work out a skeleton methodology acceptable to all, in order to make transnational comparisons as objective as possible and to institute a fair and homogeneous price for innovation across Europe. The 'natural' convergence of prices for innovative drugs that we see today would be further encouraged, although the issue of the price levels would remain.

While the ongoing reforms within Europe concerning healthcare policy, especially as regards medicines, are still very much the business of the individual Member States, it should be clear from the above that they share a number of guiding principles.

5. Conclusion

This article presents our factual and conceptual analyses of the convergence of medicine policies in Europe, based on an overview of four countries: France, Germany, Italy and the United Kingdom.

We have sought to demonstrate that European convergence of scientific and technical standards, justified by the principles of public health protection and free movement, is now practically complete.

Its operation remains hampered, however, by marked national differences between European healthcare systems: the newly reaffirmed autonomy of the Member States in the domain of healthcare regulation policy, and particularly with regard to medicines, entails significant heterogeneity in Europe's regulatory systems and therefore in the markets. The main focus of these divergences lies in the prices and levels of reimbursement of pharmaceutical products. There are those who see this as one of the main causes behind the European pharmaceutical industry's competitive shortfall vis-à-vis the United States and Japan in the 1990s.

This argument calls for some reassessment, however: the analysis of recent healthcare system reforms – concerned with fostering responsibility on the demand side and above all on the supply side, and with questions of innovation and the remuneration of innovation – shows that these reforms have been conducted in accordance with a common set of guiding principles.

References

[1] K. Arrow, Incertainty and the Welfare Economics of Medical Care, *American Economic Review* **53** (1963), 941–973.

[2] V. Atella, Drug cost containment policies in Italy: are the really effective in the long-run? The case of minimum reference price, *Health Policy* **50** (2000), 197–218.

[3] M.A. Barthe, *Economie de l'Union Européenne. Manuel,* Economica, Paris, 2000, pp. 362.

[4] S. Blersch-Raillard, La régulation du système de santé allemand, Thèse pour le Doctorat en Sciences de l'Organisation, Université Paris IX-Dauphine, 1996.

[5] A. Bocognano and A. Couffinhal et al., Mise en concurrence des assurances dans le domaine de la santé, *CREDES* **1243** (1998).

[6] J.P. Buisson and D. Giorgi, *La politique du médicament,* Montchrétien, clés économie, Paris, 1997.

[7] M.L. Burstall, The management of the cost and utilisation of pharmaceuticals in the United Kingdom, *Health Policy* **41** (1997), S27–S43.

[8] S. Caporal, La maîtrise des dépenses de santé en Italie, in: *La maîtrise des dépenses de santé en Europe et en Amérique du Nord,* ENSP, juin 1996.

[9] A. Casiraghi, F. Cilurzo, P. Minghetti and L. Montanari, The situation of OTC drugs in Italy compared to the other EU states, *Pharmacological Research* **42**(1) (2000), 25–31.

[10] G. Fattore and C. Jommi, The new pharmaceutical policy in Italy, *Health Policy* **46** (1998), 21–41.

[11] J.P. Faugère, *Economie Européenne,* Paris, Presses de Sciences Po et Dalloz, 1999, pp. 311.

[12] J.P. Faugère et al., *Convergence et Diversité à l'heure de la mondialisation,* ADIS-Université Paris-Sud, Economica, Paris, 1997, pp. 290.

[13] J.-M. Graf Von Der Schulenburg, Management of cost and utilization of pharmaceuticals in Germany, *Health Policy* **41** (1997), S45–S53.

[14] C. Hénin, *Le médicament en droit communautaire,* Editions de santé, Paris, 1997, pp. 603.

[15] C. Huttin, Prix et Remboursement des médicaments dans l'Union Européenne, *Journal d'Economie Médicale* **14**(7–8) (novembre–décembre 1996), 439–453.

[16] C. Huttin, Drug price divergence in Europe: regulatory aspects, *Health Affairs* **18** (1999), 245–249.

[17] P. Kavanos and E. Mossialos, Les aspects principaux de la régulation sur le marché pharmaceutique européen, *Pharmacoeconomics* **15**(6) (juin 1999), 519–533.

[18] D.-C. Lambert, *Les systèmes de santé. Analyse et évaluation comparée dans les grands pays industriels,* Seuil, Paris, 2000.

[19] A. Le Pape and C. Sermet, Les références médicales opposables sur le médicament: bilan de trois années d'application, *Credes, Série analyses* **1237** (1998), 192.

[20] T. Lecomte and V. Paris, Le contrôle des dépenses en médicament en Allemagne, en France et au Royaume-Uni, *Economie et Statistique* **312–313**(2/3) (1998), 109–124.

[21] G. Majone, *La Communauté Européenne: un Etat régulateur,* Montchrétien, clefs politique, Paris, 1996, pp. 158.

[22] OCDE, *La réforme des systèmes de santé dans 17 pays de l'OCDE?* OCDE, Paris, 1994.

4. Distribution and demand

Pharmaceuticals Policy and Law 5 (2002) 127–133
IOS Press

Pharmacists and governmental medicine policy

B.A. Chansarkar
Middlesex University Business School, London, UK

No one can deny that pharmacists and pharmacies play an important part in the health of the nation. The pharmacists need to face up to the changes in entrepreneurial needs more than others because of their professional nature and the marketing strategy they need to adopt to keep up with the competition. This group of entrepreneurs due to increase in prescription charges in the last few years had to undertake a close examination of the service being offered, and how it can be improved or changed. This paper investigates the implications of Government's medicine policies and entrepreneurial skills, the business attitude of the pharmacists and the new skills they will need in the future. The present government policy of increasing the real cost of prescription charges and of imposing budgets on GPs is resulting in help being sought by a significant number of patients from sources other than GPs. To take advantage of this opportunity it is important for pharmacists to undertake a close examination of the service being offered, to see how it can be improved and changed. Certainly the government seems intent on the eventual setting of a very high prescription charge which will encourage self-medication in non-exempt patients, and budget restrictions on GPs will help to reduce prescriptions usage in the exempt population. It could also lead to a major role change to 'pharmacists as doctor' in which responsibility is transferred from GPs for a range of illnesses and offer an extended range of services.

1. Introduction

Entrepreneurial needs of businesses are undergoing changes due to changing economic conditions, keen competition and availability of internet/web facilities. One group of businesses – the pharmacists – need to face up to these changes more than others because of their professional nature and the marketing strategy they need to adopt to keep up with the competition. In addition, this group of entrepreneurs due to increase in prescription charges in the last few years had to undertake a close examination of the service being offered, and how it can be improved or changed. It is known [3] that the general expansion of the managerial capability of the entrepreneurs begins with a conscientious effort to acquire knowledge and skill in management.

This paper investigates the implications of Government's medicine policies and entrepreneurial skills, the business attitude of the pharmacists and the new skills they will need in the future. Additional demand for new skills for the pharmacist is created due to the impact [1] of the rate of increase in prescription charges and the proposed abolition of the recommended retail price (RRP). Prescription charges have fluctuated since their introduction in 1952, but the significant increase coincided with the Conservative Party taking office in 1979. Prescription charge is the money a patient pays to get a single medicine (prescription) from a pharmacist. Certain groups of patients – as below – are exempt from paying prescription charges.

Categories of patients exempted from the prescription charges are:

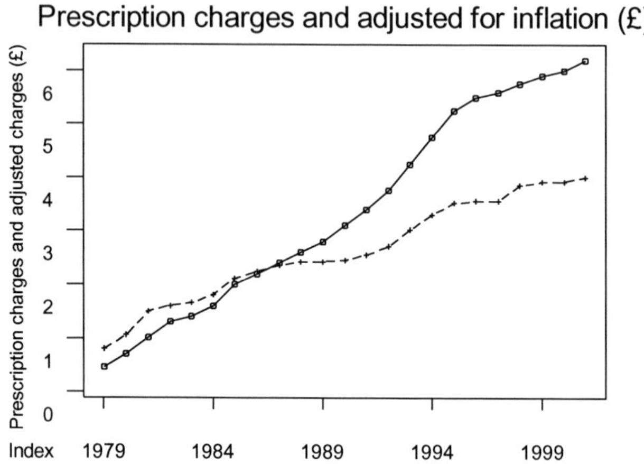

Key: 0 Prescription charges
+ Prescription charges adjusted for inflation

Fig. 1.

- Children under 16 years of age.
- Full time students aged 16, 17 0or 18 years.
- Men and women aged 60 years and over.
- People with a current exemption certificate (Form FP92).
- People with a current pre-payment certificate (Form FP95).
- People (or their partners) receiving Income Support.
- People (or their partners) receiving Family Credit.
- People (or their partners) receiving Disability Working Allowance.
- People (or their partners) with a current NHS Charge Certificate for Full Help (Certificate AG2).
- War/Service pensioners with an Exemption Certificate.

A large section of the population, 85% in 1999, is exempt from prescription charges [4]. Variations in prescription charges do not affect their behaviour, and so the majority of frivolous use will not be discouraged. Nor, of course, will any extra revenue be generated from this group. There have been regular increases well above the rate of inflation and the recently announced revised charge of £6.10 is a rise over the rate of inflation in the last year. The prescription charges adjusted for inflation have been steadily increasing throughout (see Fig. 1), though the rate of increase has slowed down in the past few years.

In the United Kingdom, the prices of medicines covered by the NHS have, since 1977, been lid down by the Pharmaceutical Price Regulation Scheme. Price control is indirect, acting on profits and sales volumes. The government and the representatives of the pharmaceutical industry (Association of British Pharmaceutical Industry) regularly negotiate an authorised profit margin, calculated for each company on the basis of the turnover of branded products it sells to the NHS [6]. If it exceeds its profit margin the company must either pay back to the NHS or reduce its prices. Only generic medicines, for which the price is set by the Department of Health and Social Security, fall outside of this system. Wholesalers are free to set their own mark-ups and dispensing chemists are paid on the basis of services rendered, regardless of the price of the products delivered.

No one can deny that pharmacists and pharmacies play an important part in the health of the nation. A large majority of the independent outlets are either owned or managed by the Asians. It is interesting to note that chemists shops are visited on a daily basis by around six million people, and it is estimated by the Pharmaceutical Society that 10% of these are likely to seek medical advice from the pharmacist. Pharmacy businesses are of different kind compared to the other businesses such as tobacconists, newsagents and general grocery outlets. To be a pharmacist, individuals should have a professional qualification and have to be registered with the British Pharmaceutical Society. In many cases they need to have a good understanding of the local conditions to provide necessary support and service essential in their geographical areas of work.

The role of pharmacists and the skills required is of course defined by their position in the distribution of pharmaceutical products. A distinction is made between prescription only medicines (POM) which are usually dispensed by pharmacists on production of a prescription signed by a GP, and over the counter medicines (OTC) which can only be bought from pharmacists. Thus GPs are the major influence in the POM market whereas pharmacists are more dominant in the OTC market. Links between these two sets of professionals are not as strong as they might be, and Turnball and Leung [11] advocate more co-operation and communication so that a pharmacist will know exactly what to stock (POM), and can also help to keep a busy GP up-to-date on new pharmaceutical products. OTC medicines then are largely the domain of pharmacists who seem most likely to be asked for advice on their use. Further, currently there is an on-going debate on the proposed abolition of the RRP, which will adversely affect the independent pharmacists.

2. Method of investigation

Face to face interviews lasting for about half an hour each were conducted with independent pharmacists using structured questionnaires. The areas investigated dealt with the background of the pharmacy, the pharmacists, method of purchasing and dispensing medicines, participation in rota system, use and availability of computing facilities, training activities and effect of the increase in prescription charges on the behaviour of the patients in terms of purchasing the prescribed medicines, asking the pharmacists' advice, and relationship with the local GPs.

3. Empirical analysis

The nature of the pharmacy management and the pharmacy practice will have direct bearing on the skills needed by the pharmacists due to the changes in acquiring supply of products and the impact of the increase in prescription charges. In this context it is interesting to observe that 60% of the turnover of the pharmacists comes from dispensing.

In the UK, pharmacists spend most of their time in dispensary. Every prescription dispensed is individually labelled and all data may be stored on computer for later reference. Generally tablets are not available in ready-made packs, but the required amount has to be counted into a container, and liquids have to be measured and bottled. These procedures are extremely time-consuming and have the disadvantage that patients very rarely receive a package leaflet informing them about the prescribed drug. The pharmacist's time is mainly taken up by counting and labelling, leaving little scope for other services. There is, however a proposal to move away from this tradition and towards the practice of easy to serve methods as other European partners.

Keeping patient medication records is not a legal requirement but according to Pioch et al. [10] nearly half of the pharmacists do so using IT equipment and the number is increasing. A quarter of the pharmacists is also using the computers to track and study interaction of medicines dispensed. The Internet and electronic commerce is likely to benefit small and medium marketing to a wider geographic audience. Technological developments may also make it easier for businesses to collaborate with other companies, although there are risks for those falling behind [8]. These developments will have special relevance in buying products for independent pharmacists, though they have to be watchful with the pitfalls (limited merchandise ranges, erratic delivery, lack of security etc.) of such retailing.

The survey shows that all pharmacists have some link with other pharmacists in the area and nearly a third also have links with pharmacists in other areas. The nature of business and the lack of time permitted only a quarter of them to attend training courses, though more would like to do so. This is acting as a barrier in acquiring professional skills essential for meeting the changing needs of the consumers. An improved networking of the pharmacists may alleviate the problem by acting as relief pharmacists when on training.

4. Effect of prescription charges

It is anticipated that the increased prescription charges result in patients' choosing which of the prescribed medicines they should buy to reduce the total cost of the prescription. It is known [9] that the average number of prescriptions per person rose from 9.2 to 9.4 in 1994 compared to 1993. Majority of the pharmacists (75%)

Table 1
Effect of increased prescription charges

	Greatly increased or increased	Stayed the same	Greatly decreased or decreased
Number of patients using prescription only medicines	–	55%	45%
Number of patients seeking advice	75%	25%	–
Sales over the counter products	70%	28%	2%
Workload	42%	54%	4%
Links with the local GPs	20%	80%	–

reported patients seeking help in choosing alternatives to the prescribed medicines due to the total cost getting the prescribed medicines.

Table 1 shows the effect of increased prescription charges.

The increased prescription charges have resulted in decreased usage of POM by patients and this is true for nearly 40% of the independent small pharmacists. This decrease in POM usage is accompanied by increase in patients' seeking advice from the pharmacists and sales over the counter. The overall effect of increased prescription charges has change the role of the pharmacist, increasing the workload by about 10 hours per week and requiring professional knowledge previously handled by the GPs. This is further accentuated by the need to provide alternate complimentary medicines, which have become popular and advocated strongly by the practitioners.

5. Implications

The present government policy of increasing the real cost of prescription charges and of imposing budgets on GPs is resulting in help being sought by a significant number of patients from sources other than GPs. Further, a recent survey (Doctor, 2001) by the British Medical Association has shown that as some patients cannot afford to pay for the prescriptions, the GPs are advising patients to buy medicines which are cheaper on the market. Some GPs are even paying themselves for the medicines for those patients who are unable to pay for the essential medicines they need. To take advantage of the opportunity of patients seeking help form those other than the GPs, it is important for pharmacists to undertake a close examination of the service being offered, to see how it can be improved and changed.

Investigation of consumer needs will give guidance on how to achieve greater effectiveness at fairly simple levels, for example the need for a private area for consultation, a patient record database, or an insight into the symptoms which result in a visit to the pharmacy instead of the GP. This will need additional professional training and knowledge for small pharmacists. A reorganisation of work schedule, availability of relief pharmacist would go long way in meeting these needs.

Sadly, if the results of recent surveys are to be believed, it seems that many pharmacists are finding it difficult to attain even the simple level of meeting the customer needs. An extension of the advisory role would depend on the improvement in overall standard of advice.

More market research, both qualitative and quantitative, needs to be carried out, and here there would seem to be some threat to small independents, as multiples, with resources to invest in research and development, begin to modify and adapt to offer a more comfortable, desirable, user friendly, and efficient customer-pharmacist interaction. Pharmacists may like to construe the future in terms of offering some services currently available only from GPs, but this is unlikely to occur in a 'cosy' protected system such as the NHS, and competition is likely to become increasingly important. Clearly those who can adapt to the new environment will thrive.

Lessons may be learnt from the results of research into the changing role of the pharmacist in Sweden, in which there is an increased emphasis on giving advice on medicines and health issues in general. The concept of consumer medication behaviour [7] has been used to refer to the processes involved in the obtaining, possession, and use of medicines, and clearly a deeper knowledge of these processes will lead to a better service and increased profitability. A judicial use of Internet for marketing activities will give these small ethnic businesses wider possibilities for expansion.

Certainly the government seems intent on the eventual setting of a very high prescription charge which will encourage self-medication in non-exempt patients, and budget restrictions on GPs will help to reduce prescriptions usage in the exempt population. This will lead to what Turnball and Leung [11] refer to, as "major opportunities for retail pharmacists" as OTC medicine usage becomes the norm for a range of ailments.

It could also lead to a major role change to 'pharmacists as doctor' in which responsibility is transferred from GPs for a range of illnesses, and this has been the basis of government thinking for some time. Certainly more pharmacists would like to offer an extended range of services, for example:

- Tests, for instance on blood pressure and pregnancy, normally carried out by GPs
- Home visits to disabled people
- 24 hour access to prescription drugs
- Extended services on the premises, such as chiropody, and homeopathy (EIU, Retail Business, 1991)

However individual differences will occur and it is argued that being aware of and sensitive to the needs of different consumer groups is the route to an improved service, that is, customer segmentation.

References

[1] B.A. Chansarkar and J. Colwell, Prescription charges and Independent Pharmacists, *Middlesex University Business School* **20** (1995), 1–19.

[2] Chemists and drugstores, *EIU Retail Business* **401** (1991), 48–54.
[3] T. Cohn and R.A. Lindberg, *Survival and Growth: Management Strategies for the Small Firm*, New York, AMA, 1974.
[4] Department of Health, Health and Personal Social Services Statistics, 2000.
[5] Survey of GPs by the BMA, Doctor, April 2001.
[6] V. Godet and S. Ferrand-Nagel, Medicines in Europe: Scientific convergence and political divergences, 5th Workshop on Challenges for Pharmaceutical Policies in the 21st Century, Brussels, January 2001.
[7] M. Hedvall, Consumers and self-medication. A model for the self-medication process. Swedish School of Economics and Business Administration, Research Report No 16, Helsinki, 1988.
[8] V. Holder, *Financial Times*, Management, 22nd October 1996.
[9] *The Pharmaceutical Journal* **255** (August 1995).
[10] E.A. Pioch, B.J. Davies and D. Bennison, Pharmacies: The SEM and Retail Harmonisation, *International Journal of Retail & Distribution Management* **20** (1992), 29–35.
[11] P.W. Turnball and S. Leung, New product adoption by pharmacists, *Journal of Marketing Management* **2** (1986), 73–94.

Pharmaceuticals Policy and Law 5 (2002) 135–149
IOS Press

Innovative marketing

Changes in the pharmaceutical marketing and selling; Direct to consumer (DTC) or the new P's of marketing

F. Harms[a], S. Rohmann[b], M. Heinrich[a], M. Druener[c] and V. Trommsdorff[c]
[a]*CEO OncoScore Basel, TU-Berlin*
[b]*International Marketing Oncology Merck*
[c]*TU-Berlin, Lehrstuhl Marketing I, Germany*

1. The problem: High-grade pharmaceutical innovations don't sell. (Example: Mifegyne)

The launch of the abortion pill Mifegyne, also known as RU 486, on the German market in 1999, was accompanied by controversial social and political discussions. The procedure, which is internationally approved and considered to be especially mild, was encountering common consent in many places. However, on the part of the church vehement protest was raised and numerous compromises were to be made before approval was possible at all. As a result of these compromises the launch of Mifegyne has turned out to create no value in Germany to date. The drug is applied in just 3% of all cases, whereas in France and Sweden almost every third abortion is carried out by this procedure. Most likely, in consequence of the poor sales figures Femagen, which is the company responsible for the German marketing of Mifegyne, has announced to return their license by the end of 2000. [1]

This example illustrates that the success of a pharmaceutical product may not only depend on its effectiveness, but is also affected by a great number of external factors, too. Correspondingly, only 3 out of 10 new preparations generate the expected gains. Because innovative drugs have a great influence on the profitline – 50 percent of the sales pharmaceutical enterprise are achieved by drugs that were not yet authorised a decade ago – the timely alignment with the needs of all participants of the health care market gains increasing importance for the new product development [1–3].

[1] Product Information Contragest GmbH, Mörfelden-Walldorf.

2. The innovation pressure is unprecedentedly high

Innovations form the basis of successful enterprises. Durable growth and occupation can only arise, if enterprises constantly manage offering new products and services, which meet the requirements of the market at the best possible rate [4–6].

In order to keep pace with the rising individual and social needs, pharmaceutical companies have continuously increased their total expenses for research and development from 11 billion US-$ to approximately 40 billion US-$ from the mid eighties to the year 2000 [1–3,7–9].

Simultaneously, the time from start of development to approval of a new drug extended from an average of two to twelve years. Within this process statistically only one in 5000 substances initially screened for development is finally approved. As a result the development costs for pharmaceutical innovations average 350 million US-$, with an annual increase of 7.5% [1–3].

At the same time, the development competition around therapeutics is continuously increasing, in particular in common diseases. As for the field of oncology, neurology, and heart and circulation, in 1999 more than 3.400 research projects were initiated. In Germany currently more than 160 drugs are in the clinical phase III or in the approval process. In order to achieve priority and guarantee a one-year privilege for a patent application, pharmaceutical companies must submit the application for the corresponding substance at a very early stage. Consequently, the pre-clinical and clinical investigation of the substance as well as the evaluation of the study results for approval takes place within life of the patent. In addition, the approval process itself, which according to law is not supposed to take more than seven months, usually requires more than two years. The time span for exclusive marketing of a drug is therefore considerably shorter than the actual patent life of 20 years. In the case of Propranol in 1968 this meant 12 years, while in the case of Saquinavir the residual period of exclusive marketing amounted to no more than three months [3,6,9,10] (Fig 1 and 2).

Additional innovation pressure arises from a duplication of the medical knowledge every 5 years, generally resulting in more costly diagnostic and therapeutic procedures. These will put the national health care systems, which are already fighting with increasing bottlenecks, under a heavy financial strain. Therefore, it is to be supposed, that the previously observed development of budgeting and fixed amounts combined with service exclusion and additional payments will be reinforced in future [11,14].

In the case of Mifegyne the limited budget resulted in an amount of 130 to 170 US$ being available for the procedure, only 80 US$ of which being paid for the drug. This is reason why from the physicians' point of view the Mifegyne induced abortion turned out to be a losing bargain, particularly, because it also requires an intensive psychological support. Consequently, physicians apply the conventional operative procedure in most cases.

Beyond this the pharmaceutical market is characterised by a lack of customer sovereignty: The ones, who make the decisions are not identical with those, who

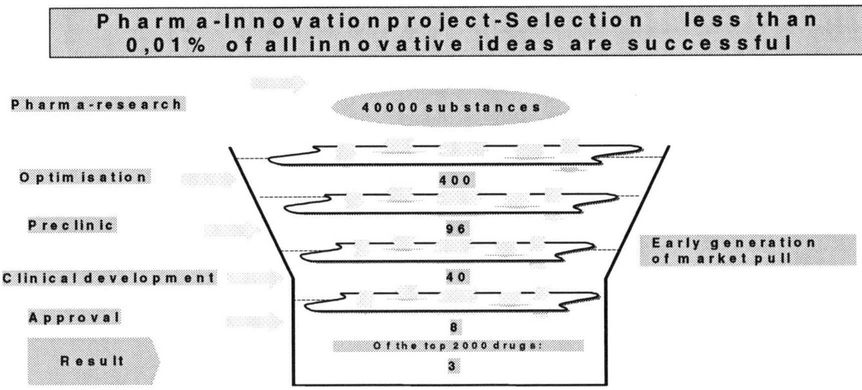

Fig. 1.

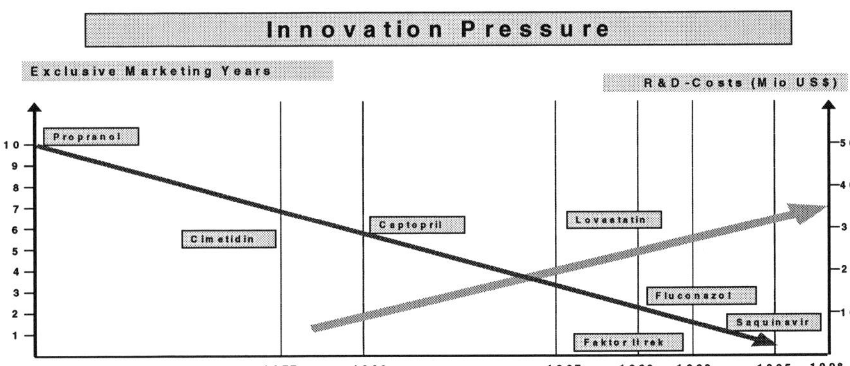

Fig. 2.

receive the service and/or pay for it. A comprehension of the health care system and its different values is a prerequisite for development of suitable tools to cope with these aspects. The system is currently in a stage of a radical revolution [12,13].

3. Physicians, patients, multipliers ...

At present more than 60% of the marketing costs of pharmaceutical enterprises account for the communication with physicians. In many cases intensification of marketing only means augmenting the field sales force with the objective of improving the relationship with physicians. Very often this relationship actually is the major determinant of the drug chosen by the physician [15,16].

While up to now the physician was the deciding opinion leader with respect to certain medications, the pressure of the patients onto the prescription habits continuously increases. Especially when suffering from chronic diseases they no longer appear as individual patients but rather as a part of well-informed and -/organised associations. These national and international associations increasingly intervene with the forming of opinion. The patient leaves his passive position and is no longer only consumer of prescribed drugs but rather wants to discuss the necessity of the therapy with the physician [17–19].

In response to this risk-benefit-ratio, physicians are forming communication networks to improve the information exchange. Up to now approximately 200 of such networks are under construction in Germany. Sixty percent of these projects have not yet exceeded the informal stage; however, 10% already operate in the intended way. The Evidence Based Medicine (EBM), providing databases containing up-to-date research results and state-of-the-art therapies, contributes an important part of the construction of such networks. The decisive factors for prescription habits will increasingly be based on these information as well as i) on the extended communication between physicians, ii) on the existence of network internal lists of recommended drugs (positive lists), iii) on economic demands of the network manager, and iv) on the realisation of high-quality circles of certain drugs [20,23].

4. Society, politics, multipliers ...

The rising costs of innovations cause increasing social discussions that exceed the relation between physician and patient. Market acceptance and success do no longer solely dependent on the participants that are directly involved, but rather on the impact of different lobbies. The example of Mifegyne illustrates the number of the different parties deciding about success or failure of a new drug. Next to physicians, patients and health insurance's particularly politics, the jurisdiction as well as temporal and spiritual communities of interest proved to be factors of wide influence. The far reaching impact of the genetic research, consumer protection movements and health services through electronic media will further increase the number of parties involved [21,22].

5. The underestimated service component

Consequently, innovative drugs are no longer fast-selling items – their value must be proved as a debt to be unambiguously discharged at creditor's domicile. Considerations about the social demands and therapeutic relevancy of the expected result of the treatment must precede the actual study.

6. Processes

The shift from component management to disease management is one long-term objective of the initiated co-operations in the health sector. Components in this connection mean individual links of the supply chain as administration, prevention, diagnostics, ambulant treatment, stationary treatment and rehabilitation. Previous measures against curbing cost expansion were specifically targeted at those components of the health care system that should yield the cost reduction. However, up to now this concept was ineffective, because the individual components attempted to optimise their profit by shifting off their cost loads to other components. In addition the component management completely ignores the individual characteristics of a disease; an economic medical optimisation in the component management is left to chance [25].

Disease management, however, represents an integrated approach for prevention of diseases, the sole criterion for success being the result of the therapy. Through this the health care is undergoing a change from the input perspective to the outcome perspective. A prerequisite is the existence of an adequate base of medical and economical expertise. The existing pilot projects are predominantly found in the fields of those indications that can be unambiguously diagnosed and treated with a defined therapy. Particularly diabetes, heart and circulation diseases, asthma, depression and cancer are counted among those [26–28].

Disease management attempts to elaborate individual applications and standardised therapy guidelines for every stage during the course of a disease. First steps towards an improvement may already be observed. In experimental groups the annual costs for the processing of asthma patients were reduced by a third using an integrated disease management approach [29,30].

7. The communication was established ineffectively and poorly placed

Even though debates about positive and negative lists, price and profit controls, fixed prices and additional payments by the patients run counter to the general values, one should strive for the communication with institutions, that are important for the forming of political opinion. Due to the increasing pressure and the influence of politics onto the development of the pharmaceutical market, the close contact to all politically active communities of interest is of eminent importance. The typical challenges of a modern innovation management are perfectly mirrored in the pharmaceutical field [12,31,36].

8. Strategy: Innovation marketing management

Innovation marketing must consider relevant future developments in due time: direct customer contact, building up of confidence, set-up of pharmaceutical brands, competition oriented positioning. The customer becomes the pivotal element within the own product design, and/or the satisfaction of the market demands becomes the hallmark of the overall strategic planning. The principal marketing tools are communication and co-operation [12,13,32–34].

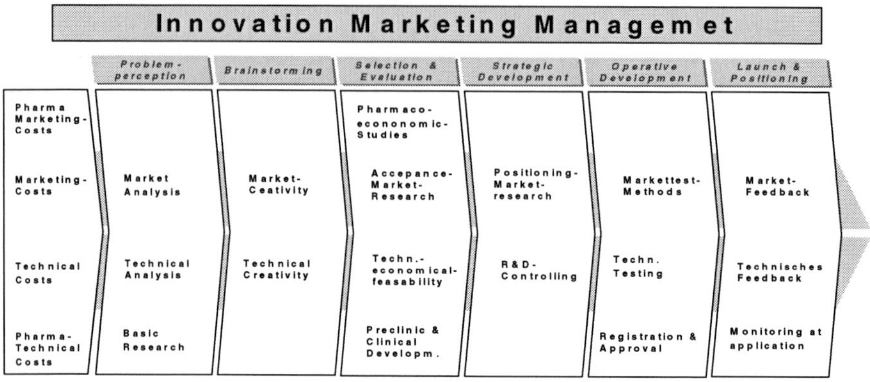

Fig. 3.

9. Innovation marketing

Unlike inventions, which are time-related, innovations are rather development processes. Due to the different managerial functions during this process, it is useful to divide innovative processes into typical phases. Within these phases different communication and co-operation strategies need to be developed. The phases of pharmaceutical innovations already existing in development have to be transferred to the marketing now. This includes the definition of a communication- and marketing concept for early phases of the innovations, the clinical phases and the launch, respectively, in order to build up the targeted market positioning in parallel to development [12,13,28] (Fig. 3).

A new consciousness was created through the rise of budgeting in conjunction with a broad discussion about the sense of specific medications and therapies (evidenced based medicine). "Value for money" advances to the decisive model of the survivability of whole sections. In a time of decreasing product differentiation the key for the success is an improved understanding of the customers' demands. Currently more than 90% of all activities of the pharmaceutical industry are addressed to physicians, pharmacists, hospitals, and wholesale. In future this spectrum will extend to the different patient groups, national and international authorities, insurance companies, social associations, political parties and any form of medical interest associations. The comprehension of the health care system and its values from the viewpoint of the market is of decisive importance. Unlike the seventies and eighties this system is no longer prepared to support the medical progress with all consequence. In the past the crucial question was: What will a new medication cost? Thus, in the commencing 21st century the question reads: How much is the social system willing to pay for a new therapy [27–29] (Fig. 4).

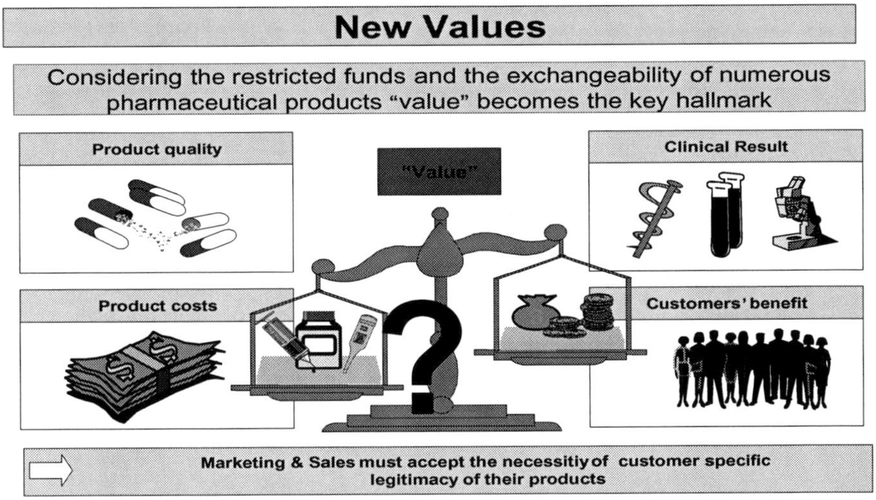

Fig. 4.

10. Concepts for innovative marketing: The new Ps of marketing

10.1. Positioning

Due to the changing health care market the importance of positioning is continuously increasing. In the future the marketing must be ready to tackle with critical questions of the market. Only those companies that contribute constructive solutions may successfully extend their market shares. Companies that are in the position of establishing a close-partnered relationship with their clients attain the necessary renown to be equal to the challenges and the increasing complexity of the pharmaceutical market [12,28].

Due to the increasing self-confidence of the market participants, the customer selects between different enterprises when deciding about a purchase. Namely between those, that only sell medications and those that give special emphasis to the service idea. With the aid of this idea and the resulting satisfaction of the customers' demands a positive image is built up continuously. This continuity creates a form of social prestige by which the necessity of the application of innovative therapies may be imparted [12,29,30].

10.2. Politics

The medical supply is increasingly subjected to a cost benefit analysis and the sense of established therapies, medications, diagnostic procedures and surgical interventions is crucially scrutinised. For this reason health care economics become the second central dimension of positioning aside from the contribution of the product itself. Consequently the cost-benefit-optimisation becomes the essential success factor for the survivability of innovative product design. Due to the increasing pressure which politics put onto the development of the pharmaceutical market the close contact to all politically active associations of interests will be of far-reaching significance [12,37,38].

Since the nineties the budget restricted distribution competition is a typical feature of the structurally reformed health care system. With respect to the marketing of innovative products the changing political circumstances lead to a new product understanding. It is no longer a matter of producing a good product in a sensible quality for a high price but of providing an acceptable cost/benefit ratio. The marketing is challenged to include social trends into its development plans. Because politics propagate the exchangeability of drugs resulting in cost minimisation, the concept of value creation is a pivotal factor for political decisions [12,39].

10.3. Patients

At the outset of the 21st century the pharmaceutical marketing is going through a time of upheaval. The above mentioned increasing influence of the patient on decisions about medication and therapies requires a flow of information, which is no longer restricted to pharmaceutical companies and physicians alone. If this information is made available to the patients in posted form in agreement with the specialised medical organisations, the marketing of innovative substances can be established as a constructive service provider in the market. Through construction and care of these electronic service exchanges it demonstrates its obligation and responsibility for the reasonable use of the limited resources within our health care system. With the patients the corresponding confidence is acquired in order to propagate the benefit of new therapeutic options. Furthermore the marketing should be eager to make close contact with its potential customers. Thus conversation platforms could be established for all institutions of our health care system with the focus of interest being the patients. One should proceed with informational activities and advertising measures in co-operation with the different opinion leaders. A patient adapted means of communication would satisfy concrete demands and obtain the understanding of innovative therapies and/or present a platform for the need for their application. For this reason an advertising campaign set directly to the customer could help to satisfy these information demands [22,24] (Fig. 5).

10.4. Communication and co-operation

Communication and co-operation in all innovation and market phases is decisive about flop or top. Many impulses for innovations arise from informal communication among employees, e.g. between R&D and marketing specialists or between customers and service persons. Particularly, within initial phases of an innovation the

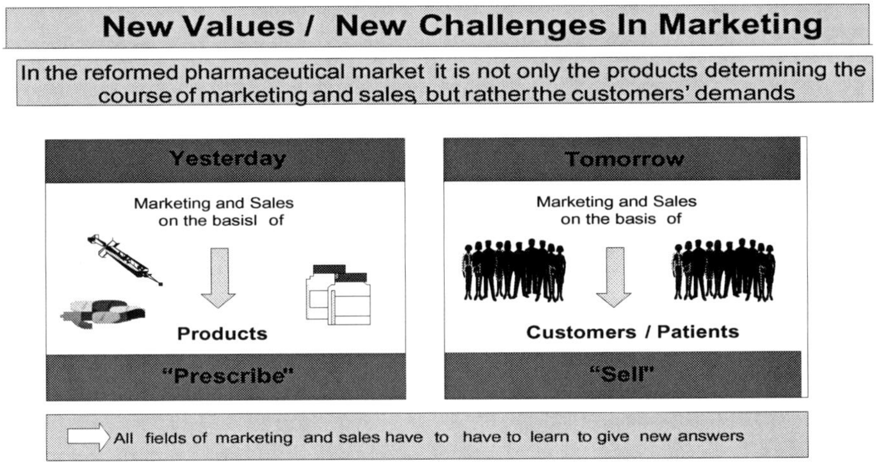

Fig. 5.

communication must not be regularised. As for the pharmaceutical field this is especially valid for service-oriented extra options. In the course of further development a transition to structured information supply should proceed in order to minimise the costs of superfluous communication. During the entire process information should not only flow top down, but rather within a network [15,16,36–39].

The investigation of success factors of new products indicates that the strategic competitive advantage remains the key prerequisite for innovative achievements. And also in the pharmaceutical industry success is no longer generated solely through the effectiveness of a product. For the pharmaceutical field this includes not only the co-operation with patients in the clinical stages, but also the well-timed co-operation with all players subsequently implicated in these innovations, including health insurance's, physicians, departments of health, etc. The integration of target customers in the sense of "Lead Users" or "Lead Co-operation" may simultaneously be considered as measure of and impact on the engendered acceptance [27,28,30] (Fig. 6).

Pharmaceutical companies provide their most important market partners with problem solving and services. The services to be produced include education, support during construction of physician networks, information services and communication/advertising-partnerships. Particularly pharmacies already need this communicative support, because with respect to prices 50% of their product range is already competing with self-service department stores, discounts, and drugstores [4, 5].

10.5. The basis for information: Innovation market research

The above-mentioned approach of the 4+3P-marketing allows consideration of all health care market participants and their interactions. However, with the increasing

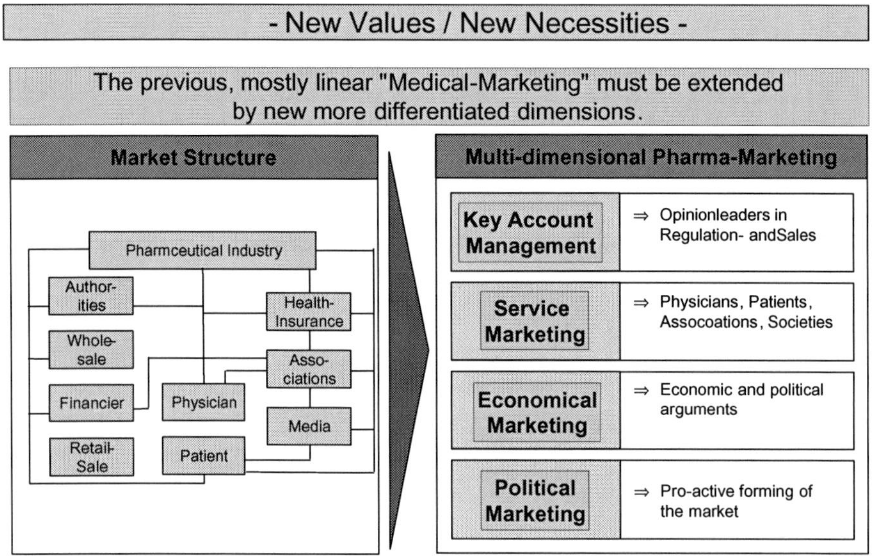

Fig. 6.

number of players the complexity of such systems increases too. The understanding of this complexity requires dealing with players in such a way as to obtain new communicative approaches through innovation market research.

It is assumed, that flop rates of new products range between 40 and 90%. Is the innovation market research failing? Is the conventional market research with its rather quantitative-functional and linear-retrospective tools ill conditioned for strategic decisions? Does it supply decision-makers with information from yesterday for the problem solving of tomorrow [12,13]?

Standard market research with basic technologies is often efficient, yet it is not necessarily effective. Efficiency specifies, whether a task is carried out correctly, whereas effectivity specifies, whether the correct task is carried out. Present-day market research is efficient, yet not effective, because it is not adequately integrated into the strategic decision process. Traditional market research primarily deals with simple rather than complex questions, such as the extent of the market, the price of a new product to be launched, the impact of a new advertising campaign, etc. In practice a majority of this information supply is accepted in a clearly defined range of tasks. This includes in particular the measurement of market volumes, market shares, ranges, distribution rates, publicity and memory values. Unacceptable questions like "Would you like to buy" and "Why-" are still prevailing. The perception, that innovation has to be comprehensively measured and managed, settles in hesitantly. Apart from this questions concerning the relevant competition dimensions are not being recognised as such in terms of positioning [5,6,12,13,39–42].

The advance of premium brands together with cheap products has been stated indeed, yet not explained and/or predicted. It is useful to know that markets are polarised. To know, whether the polarisation keeps up on increasing in the next years or decreases again – and why! – would be even more useful. The increasing environmental orientation of the German population is correctly recorded by the market research, but predictions about the future development of the environmental behaviour is pure trend extrapolation. It would be important to know the factors that prevent people from putting their environmental attitudes into practice.

10.6. Check list innovation market research (*)

- Is it preferred to lead or follow a technical product innovation?
- Is it preferred accepting a prolongation of the development process or meeting the deadline by means of a project billing increase instead?
- Innovation acceptance research: The success factors of product innovation. Customer orientation, interface marketing / R&D and marketing are not covered by classical market research.
- What-if-analyses: What-if-analysis using management-appropriate decision categories led from analysis to implementation. The strategic innovation market researcher must be part of the decision making process.
- "Paralysis by analysis": Innovation market research should not overlook strategic guidelines and management realities.
- Decision maker coaching: The innovation market researcher should help to overcome the narrow view of engineering and business management. It may support the management to view the customer in its true subjectivity.

10.7. Complexity control (*)

Innovations, which aim at the far future apart from the conventional market, are necessarily connected with rather complex decisions and unforeseeable results. People are incapable of systematically estimating complex effects of strategic decisions. Efforts to simulate the governing of small towns or states, that is pursuing objectives like health, supply or education and to decide on measures demonstrate the "logic of the failing".

Obviously we failed keeping an eye on cross-linked objective-tool-relations and calculating the side effects and long-distance effect. We suffer from one problem and through that cause additional problems of a different kind and range. Why are we unable to make complex decisions, why can we only think in linear, bivariate relationships, and not in causal networks? We are unable, because we do not have any idea of the complexity. Nobody supplies the decision-makers with network ideas about the system, which they manage.

This is a provoking task for the strategic market research. Today innovation decisions are horizontally, vertically and laterally cross-linked in a far more complex way than decades ago. However, cross-linked thinking in market research is absolutely possible. Approaches of the chaos research, the cross-linked thinking, the fuzzy logic, the causal structure analysis and the sensitivity analysis point at the right track.

At present market analysis for complex, future-oriented marketing-strategic decisions is poorly accepted: Fundamental decisions on product innovations, strategic competition positioning as well as those about internationalisation alternatives, diversity and acquisition are rather justified emotionally or at best based on management discussions. Here the market research shows considerable deficits.

10.8. Selection of tools (*) – (*"It is better to be roughly right than exactly wrong"*) –

Supporting future-oriented leading decisions in an informative way makes great demands on the strategic innovation market research. Although long-term prognoses of complex systems in traditional quantitative terms are impossible, the innovator must be envisaging on the long run (future analysis) and at the same time be sensitive on the short run (early solving). Both require qualitative approaches, which reflect complex contexts in an integrated way and which recognise the essentials with the "accuracy of the diffuseness". Tools like strategic early recognition, scenario technique, future simulations and also the behaviour of target customers and expert systems provide methodical support in this case. The market research faces special challenges when recording customer needs, which are existing, difficult to articulate, latent or just arising.

10.9. Conjoint Measurement (*)

An important procedure of the acceptance analysis for new products in the phase of realisation is the CONJOINT ANALYSIS (CA), a decomposition multivariate procedure for the quantification of benefit structures of target customers. The essential benefit of CA for the innovation marketing consists in that potentially new products, described according to their qualities, are not evaluated artificially elementaristic, but relatively realistic in an integrated way. The CA assumes, that the entire benefit of a product is additively composed of a number of partial benefit values. For innovations of a medium or low innovative level the CA supplies recommendations for the feature-specific product and price-fixing, f.e. the pharmaceutical industry supports a number of product innovations of medium level on CAs with physicians. However, the implementation of these recommendations into technical and commercial organisation requires further support.

10.10. Innovation business planning

Through high innovation costs, market risks and long payback periods the innovation financing becomes a serious barrier. The R&D costs have to be financed in advance – even in the middle-class enterprises – amounting to values of three-digit millions. Smaller technology enterprises, which very frequently bear interesting product ideas, lack the necessary capital.

Politics, proportional representation, contacts, past successes are frequent decision parameters. Internal decisions on the allocation of R&D-resources, which in the pharmaceutical industry become profit-effective earliest after 10 years of investing, are difficult to quantify. All the more important is justifying projects, which are not treated as first priority. Here an early market-, customer- and competition orientation may help in terms of innovation business planning.

11. Solution

The future of pharmaceutical marketing depends on the ability to achieve recognition and admiration from a much broader customer constituency that encompasses clinicians, patients, politicians, insurance companies, media, general public and all health care professionals. The increasing self-confidence of all customers in combination with the tightening ancillary conditions requires reconsidering the marketing of innovative substances. The major aspects of marketing, product, price, place, and promotion, which arose in the 1970s, need to be up-dated to fit the increasing complexity of sale. The traditional fields have to be extended by the following three Ps: Positioning, Politics and, last not least, Patients. The marketing is meeting new challenges, since the number of its potential target groups are continuously rising, which is due to the fact that more and more parts of the society are about to obtain impact on our health care system. Future chances can only be met successfully, when the changing environment is integrated into the marketing strategy as a comprehensive communication process. Equivalently, tasks to come up will only be solved by integration of the three additional fields of marketing. Since the implementation of the new concepts is not corresponding to the size of a company, it will rather be the faster displacing the slower, than the larger displacing the smaller.

References

[1] L.R. Basara, Practical considerations when evaluation DTC advertising as a marketing strategy for prescription medications, *Drug Inf. J.* **28** (1994), 461–470.
[2] BPI: Annual Report 1999/2000.
[3] BPI: Pharma innovative 1999.
[4] W.G. Castagnoli, Prospects for pharmaceutical promotion, *J Pharm Mark Manage* **10** (1996), 223–235.
[5] S.S. Cheng, Biopharmaceutical Sales and Forecasts to 2004, *Spectrum* (Dec. 1999), 16-1–16-16.
[6] S.S. Cheng, Worldwide Sales of Health Care Products to 2002, *Spectrum* (Feb. 1999), 2-1–2-10.
[7] P.M. DiBiaso, Providers, and Pharmaceutical Companies as Partners in the Development of Disease Management Programs, *Spectrum* (Nov. 1999), 4-1–4-10.
[8] Direct-to-consumer advertising of prescription drugs: Withdrawal of moratorium, *Federal Register* **50** (1985), 36677.

[9] Diversified 1998, Drug Trend Report. Edina, Minn: Diversified Pharmaceutical Services, 1998, pp. 2, 27.

[10] Draft guidance for the industry: Consumer-directed broadcast advertisements: Availability, *Federal Register* **62** (1997), 43171.

[11] F. Harms, Grosse-Wichtrup, Direct-to-Consumer (DTC) Nr. 1, PMJ 5/2000, pp. 150–154.

[12] F. Harms, Grosse-Wichtrup, Direct-to-Consumer (DTC) Nr. 2, PMJ 6/2000, pp. 204–206.

[13] E. Hefti, Advances in Drug Delivery Technologies, *Spectrum* (Oct. 1999), 10-1–10-12.

[14] M. Heise and V. Lessat, European Pharmaindustry, DG-Bank, 1999.

[15] R.H. Hill, Is Bigger Better? Addressing the Question of Scale in the Pharmaceutical Industry, *Spectrum* (May 1999), 6-1–6-12.

[16] M.F. Hollon, Direct-to-Consumer; Marketing of Prescription Drugs: Creating Consumer Demand, *J. of the American Med. Ass.* **4** (1999), 382–384.

[17] M. Hunt, Direct-to-consumer advertising of prescription drugs. Paper prepared for the National Health Policy Forum, Washington, DC, April 1998.

[18] IMS Health, 1998 US pharmaceutical market. What's on the horizon for the US pharmaceutical marketplace. Plymouth meeting 1998.

[19] B.G. James, Pharmaceutical Marketing and Selling in the 21st Century, *Spectrum* (Nov. 1998), 16-1–16-18.

[20] E.S. Jacobson, Trends in the US HMO Industry: 1998 Midjear Survey Results, *Spectrum* (June 1999), 3-1–3-11.

[21] P.C. Langley, Integrating Pharmacoeconomics into Clinical Trials, *Spectrum* (June 1999), 4-1–4-10.

[22] K.G. Krul, Pharmacogenomics: Key Technologies, Mayor Players, and Lingering Questions, *Spectrum* (Dec. 1999), 15-1–15-16.

[23] V. Lee, 1998 Update: Timelines to Commercialisation for Biomedical Products, *Spectrum* (Dec. 1998), 18-1–18-7.

[24] A. Lewis, Success Strategies for Disease Management Industry, *Spectrum* (April 1999), 9-1–9-8.

[25] M.S. Lipsky and C.A. Taylor, The opinions and experiences of family physicians regarding direct-to-consumer advertising, *J Fam Pract* **45** (1997), 495–499.

[26] P. Magyre, How Direct to Consumer Advertising Is Putting Squeeze on Physicians, *ACP/ASIM Observer* **1** (1999), 24–25.

[27] L.A. Morris, Prescription Drug Advertising to Consumers, National Technical Information Service, 1984.

[28] Navigation the Medication Marketplace: How Consumers Choose. Washington 1997: Prevention / American Pharmaceutical Association.

[29] T. Nordenberg, TV drug ads that make sense, *FDA Consumer Protection* **32** (1998), 7–10.

[30] N. Ostrove, Chief marketing Practices and Communication, FDA personal communication, 30 November 1999.

[31] Pharmaceutical Research and Manufacturers of America, *Industry Profile,* PRMA, Washington, DC, 1998, pp. 22.

[32] M. Peri and A.A. Nelson, An exploratory analysis of consumer recognition of direct-to-consumer advertising of prescription medications, *J. Health Care Mark* **7** (1987), 10–17.

[33] Prescription drug ads to consumer audience are producing dramatic effects. Scott-Levin Associates Inc., Jan 22, 1990.

[34] H.K. Shah, The Ascendance of Marketing in the New Pharmaceutical Era, *Spectrum* (March 1999), 3-1–3-14.

[35] T.A. Shimp and R.F. Dyer, The pain pill-pleasure model and illicit drug consumption, *J Consumer Res* **6** (1979), 36–46.

[36] R.K. Schwartz and S.B. Soumerai, Physician motivations for nonscientific prescribing, *Soc Sci Med* **28** (1989), 577–582.

[37] E. T'Hoen, Direct-to-Consumer Advertising: For Better Profits or for Better Health? *American Journal of Health-System Pharmacy* **55** (1998), 594–597.

[38] E. T'Hoen, Direct-to-Consumer Prescription Drug Advertising, *American Journal of Law and Medicine* **25** (1999), 149–169.

[39] R.J. Towsend, M.D. Dibner and T.L. Wright, Demonstrating the Value of Drugs in Development: The Key Role of Pharmacoeconomics, *Spectrum* (Aug 1999), 6-1–6-9.

[40] M.S. Wilkes, Direct-to-Consumer Prescription Drug Advertising: Trends, Impact and Implications, *Health Affairs* **19**(2) (1998), 110–128.

[41] M.S. Wilkes, Direct-to-Consumer Advertising of Prescription Drugs: An Idea Whose Time Should Not Come, *British Medical Journal* **318** (1999), 1301–1302.

[42] VFA, Innovation – Key to Success-, 1998.

5. Payment and demand

Pharmaceuticals Policy and Law 5 (2002) 153–165
IOS Press

How the reimbursement system may influence patients' decisions: Results from focus groups interviews on hypertension, hay-fever and hormone replacement therapy[1]

C. Huttin*
University of Paris, Thema, Nanterre, France and Groupe Image, French School of Public Health, St Maurice, France

This paper analyzes how patients' treatment choices are influenced by cost to the patient for three different diseases in France: mild hypertension, hay fever and hormone replacement therapy. Five focus groups of patients were conducted in May/June 1999. We found that cost conscious behaviors were very dependent on patients' health insurance status, mainly in relation with supplemental insurance. Major shifts of drug treatment decisions differ according to the type of conditions. For hypertensive patients, differences are mainly observed in relation with the timing of prescriptions, the number of packs and the payment method for drugs. For patients with hay fever, main decision shifts are observed in the choice among professionals and the more or less extensive search for different types of therapies. For HRT patients, main differences in decisions concern the number of packs purchased, how often prescriptions are renewed and which drug categories are prescribed. Overall, cost to the patient was a much more important issue for non-drug treatment costs such as the surveillance costs in the case of HRT patients or for costs of exams and referrals in the case of hypertensive patients. Cost minimization strategies in some ways are dependent on the type of anticipations in the long run that patients may have.

1. Introduction

For most health care products and services, reimbursement is a key condition to provide and secure access to markets. Especially, in European countries, where governments provide universal or extensive coverage, they also represent major purchasing powers for national populations.

This global picture tends to change though with a regular reduction of State's roles in the financing of baskets of health care goods and services. Major trends tend to show slow but regular reductions of the share reimbursed by public sick funds and increasing financing either from additional private insurers or patients. In France, the

[1]This research is part of a European project, within the BIOMED fourth program of the European Commission under contract n. BMH498-3576. The author is grateful to L. Amar for her help in the organization of the focus groups.
*Address for correspondence: Huttin C., PhD., BP 14, 92420 Vaucresson, France. E-mail: huttinc@aol.com

French Social Security reduced its share of health expenditure coverage by regularly increasing the share of the "Ticket modérateur": namely the cost sharing by the patient. For instance, French household's participation increased over the period from 21.05% to 25.1%, representing a 22% increase in cost sharing supported by the households [1].

The objective of this paper is to provide the results of focus groups' interviews, which aimed to explore how and if various reimbursement rates, various conditions of exemptions and different access to supplemental insurance affect patients' decision making process on different treatment choices. The focus groups' interviews occurred in France during the period of May–June 1999. Similar interviews took place in five other European countries at the same time. Therefore, this analysis presents the country findings within a larger international project, designed within the BIOMED program of the European Union. Patients have been interviewed on treatment choices concerning a selection of four diseases: mild hypertension, hay fever, dyspepsia and hormone replacement therapy. These four diseases have been selected for the project, in order to provide a broad picture of choices, and both in chronic and acute care. For instance, for patients, it means options for different drug choices, choices of prescription drugs versus OTC drugs, choices of non drug versus or in combination with drug treatment, choices among providers (specialists, generalists, pharmacists ...).

The paper presents first a brief description of the French context since the focus groups took place in France, then a presentation of the process of the focus groups and the analysis for each disease of the main findings resulting from group discussions.

2. The French context

France is a country with an individual price control system for pharmaceuticals and a universal coverage system, mandatory and employer based. The Ministry of Health defines the field of reimbursement. Once the price is fixed, the Ministry decides whether the product is on the reimbursement list (national formulary) and fixes the level of coverage rate paid by the Social Security. Two principles underline the reimbursement system in France: a reimbursement per drug and a reimbursement per disease. According to the first principle, coverage rate per medication is calculated as a percentage of its price. Three categories of medicines exist according to their rates of coverage: drugs covered at 100%, drugs reimbursed at 65% and drugs reimbursed at 35%. According to the second principle, conditions of exemptions exist for 31 diseases, which allow then a patient to be fully exempted for the treatment of these diseases. Different types of patient insurance profiles coexist: patients with or without social security coverage, patients with and without additional or supplemental insurance, exempted or not exempted patients.

The existence of a significant unemployed population, precarious situations and short-term labor contracts has in particular generated sources of inequalities to access the French health care system. One objective of the Law passed in July 1999 was therefore to provide a standard universal and supplemental coverage (CMU)[2] to address such an issue. However the resource threshold to get access to this comprehensive coverage is low (ex: 3500 FF for a single) and this research is still relevant to explore potential differences within the population and the impact on their decision making behaviors.

3. Methods

The exploratory nature of this study meant that a qualitative approach was most appropriate. Such methods provide a good insight into what people are thinking and believing, but may be less generalizable than extensive and rigorous quantitative work due to smaller numbers and localization of participants involved.

In this study, five focus groups of patients were conducted. Focus groups are 'group discussions organized to explore a specific set of issues' [2]. They are frequently used to learn about topics and groups of people that are poorly understood [3–5]: we think the ways cost or reimbursement systems influence patients' decision making process is still not very well explored and that this type of qualitative method will allow an in depth understanding of decisions' shifts that may occur when patients take into account cost into their decisions. The idea behind focus groups is that group processes can help people to explore and clarify their views in ways that would be less easily accessible in a one to one interview. The presence of patients within a group with partial health insurance coverage challenged other patients around the table, about their potential responses if they had to face such a situation. The group allowed to see other patients' reactions to different choices and to receive opinions whether they would tend to behave the same way in a similar situation. It was also useful to have in the group, patients of different generations, especially working population and elderly, since the increasing cost of premium of additional insurance for several elderly raised the degree of cost consciousness of the rest of the group.

The participants in these five focus groups were patients from Paris and various suburban areas around Paris. Patients were recruited essentially through their family practitioners and for hay fever through a recruitment agency. In another part of the same project, physicians had been recruited for a series of physician focus groups, and they have been very keen on recruiting some of their patients for patients' focus groups. A difficulty was the medical secret, which impeded physicians to provide patients' names. A consent procedure therefore was established with each individual physician in order to guarantee patients' privacy (for instance, the physician gave only the first name of the patient). The focus groups took place during the day or at the end of working hours. Table 1 shows the composition of the five groups.

[2]CMU: Couverture Medicale Universelle.

Table 1
Composition of the focus groups

	Group 1	Group 2	Group 3	Group 4	Group 5
Total	8	4	6	8	2
(number of men)	(3)	(1)	(1)	(0)	(2)
Age group	60–79	60–70	25–55	54–75	24–63
Without mutuelle	3	1	2	1	1
disease	Hypert1	Hypert2	Hay fever	HRT	Dyspepsia*

*In the case of dyspepsia, 14 patients were recruited, six were normally coming and only two patients effectively came to the meeting.

The five focus groups were held in neutral venues (rentals of a room in an office and in a hospital); they lasted around one hour. Patients were assured of confidentiality and were paid a 150 FF fee each for attending the meetings. The groups were conducted during the period May/June 1999. The focus groups were moderated by a social scientist, trained in focus group techniques. The focus groups went well. The flow of discussion was relatively easy to maintain. The topic guide was designed within a reinforced concerted action of the Biomed project, together with The University of Manchester, Department of Pharmacy. It needed adaptation to fit the French situation: specific probes, related to French cases, were essential to keep the discussion running. The focus groups were tape-recorded and transcribed at a later stage on the main topics. Data were analyzed using classifications by the main themes of the topic guide.

4. Results

4.1. General comments

The general view on the influence of cost on patient decision making resulting from the five focus groups is that French patients do not integrate these criteria in their decisions to purchase their prescriptions, except when they are not covered by an additional insurance ("Mutuelle"). There was a striking difference between the two categories of patients. The results from the focus groups also tend to confirm previous findings of the physicians focus groups [6]; namely that costs of exams or costs of visits to specialists are perceived more as a financial barrier than cost of drugs, even for the patients with a "Mutuelle", when they have to pay in advance for the cost of such services.

Majorities of the groups were generally not cost conscious. But, patients without "mutuelle" adopted a very cost conscious behavior. Contrary to physicians, who seemed to be more concerned about cost to the system than cost to the patients, patients clearly mentioned either drug prices or the cost they had to pay, and barely the cost to the system. We will now provide in the next sections our findings resulting from the focus group discussions with patients diagnosed with one of the three following diseases: hypertension, hay-fever and hormone replacement therapy (We have not analyzed dyspepsia since we had only two patients for this focus group).

4.2. *Cost to the patient in the case of mild hypertension and patients' decisions*

Mild hypertension is normally a case of an asymptomatic disease and the patient is not automatically aware of the need to be cured for such a disease, however a number of patients referred to some symptoms such as headache, vertigoes, migraines, heart palpitations.

The patients knew about theirs disease in various ways. Some patients discovered their hypertension during a medical visit on the job site; others had symptoms such as headache, others had other diseases and therefore had been checked by their doctors for the level of blood pressure. There was consensus in the groups that it was important to be treated, once hypertension had been discovered. The main factors which seemed to influence patients' decisions to be treated and to follow their physician's recommendation were the following: the willingness to be better, the willingness to have an efficient treatment, the perception of blood pressure as a barometer of good health, the feeling of being taking care, the trust in the physician, the feeling of threat or severity of disease (previous history of hemiplegia in the family), the environment, especially the family environment.

Influence of cost and copayment on drug purchasing behavior:

In the physician focus groups which took place in the first step of this project [6], cost did not seem to be an important cue to influence physicians' decisions, unless there was a patient demand, especially for the case of patients without an additional insurance (e.g. "mutuelle"). Because hypertension is a chronic disease and patients need to regularly purchase their medications, patients were well aware of the cost of prescriptions: around 300 FF to 500 FF. The general perception in patients' groups was that the treatment was expensive and required a good coverage (this mainly means, for a French patient, being able to have an additional insurance (e.g. a "Mutuelle"), being able to get a third party mechanism and not to have to pay cash). Under such conditions, the cost of a hypertensive drug treatment was not an issue.

The cost clearly became an issue for purchasing prescriptions, when there was no additional insurance ("mutuelle") and the patient had to pay in advance. However, the patients in the group, without "mutuelle", did not mention major shifts of decisions concerning the likelihood of purchasing or not purchasing medications. Such patients expressed that 'they had no choice', that it was an obligation and they felt they needed to do it (cf. previous section where they expressed the threat of more severe disease and the feeling that it is important for their health).

The perception of threat, the willingness to be in good health, the perception of lack of choice therefore seemed to reduce the likelihood that the financial cost was a barrier. As the recruitment of patients was mainly through physicians, patients were representative of a subpopulation of hypertensive patients who regularly visit their physicians. We did not access for instance patients who were once told that they had high blood pressure and did not regularly see a physician. We found through focus groups' discussions, three shifts of patients' decisions in relation with drug treatment and its cost to the patient. These shifts concerned the timing of the prescription, the number of packs and the payment method for drugs.

1. The timing:

A drug therapy for hypertension can be prescribed for one month or three months. The norm is usually that a French physician cannot prescribe for more than a month. However for chronic conditions, and therefore for hypertension in particular, some physicians tend systematically to prescribe for three months. Some patients, in the focus groups, did not want to pay for three months prescription in a row and preferred to spread expenses regularly every month. It was difficult tough, through these focus groups, to explore whether cost to the patient and patient demand influenced how a patient got a repeat prescription. It was hard to disentangle the impact of patient demand versus physician's demand for more visits. The great deal of variations in number of repeated visits can for instance not only depend on clinical factors and other patients' characteristics, but also on the level of competition among physicians in a geographical area and how that may affect their level of remuneration. [3]

2. The number of packs

Some patients "without mutuelle" were more cautious about purchasing only one pack a month although the pack usually only includes 28 tablets and therefore there is a need for more than one pack to cover exactly a month. Other patients would purchase more easily two packs and would go around the packaging problem.

3. The decision to purchase medications out of pocket or to buy a "mutuelle":

The trade-off described by some more cost-conscious patients was between paying the premium for the "mutuelle" or paying directly medications out of pocket. In fact the trade off was more cited between payment for regular visits to physicians and medications versus payment for the Mutuelle premium (One quote for instance was: "the cost of a physician visit is 100–155 FF and the cost of drugs is 100 FF, it is less than the monthly premium of my "mutuelle" which is 330 F/month"). These patients were more concerned about such a trade-off rather than choices to buy or not to buy or not to comply with treatments.

This trade-off does not integrate the risks of being sicker and the advantages of being better insured in order to cover most hospital expenses. One patient in the group, a former shopkeeper, complained that the premium of her mutuelle was 9000 FF and that she had to stop it. Some elderly in the group had to face substantial raise of insurance premiums and could not so easily pay the premium (one quote was for instance: "when you work, you can pay for the "mutuelle", it is not the same when you have a pension"). Clearly these quotes point out that factors such as the type of insurance linked to jobs (case of an independent retailer rather than an employee of a company), or age (with the shift of status between being a pensioner and being employed) are important characteristics which influence the choice between

[3]Most French physicians run an independent private practice and are mainly remunerated on a fee for service basis.

a direct payment of services and the payment of a premium. However, we could also identify through the focus group discussion, a more complex group of factors including attitudes towards risk, the role of the type of information and knowledge about the exact coverage of the social security system, health beliefs and beliefs about the reimbursement system (quote: it is a good protection),[4] the severity of illness, the expressed preferences, under tighter budget constraint, to spend relatively less on health and health care services than on other goods. We found during the focus group discussion with physicians that cost issues related to cardiologist referral and biologic tests seemed to raise bigger concerns than costs of medications or general practitioners'visits. Patients' focus groups also confirmed that when there is a cost issue, it is first on the cost of repeated visits to physicians, costs of exams or costs to see a cardiologist.

Cost to the patient and cardiologist referral:

A general answer in the group was that it is much less expensive to see the cardiologist in hospitals than in his practice. So, several patients in the group, and not only the patients without "mutuelles", expressed that when they had to consult a specialist they would come to see him in the hospital rather than in his private practice. This confirms previous findings on physicians' cost minimisation strategies. The main drawback then was that they might have to wait much longer in such a case.

Biologic tests and the role of cost to the patient in physician decision to order the tests:

There is a common belief that normally biologic tests are very well reimbursed and that nearly no one has any trouble with test payment in France. However, the group discussion revealed that patients found it was not very well reimbursed and it was expensive. This confirms that it probably depends on the type of agreement between biologic laboratories and "mutuelles". Some physicians said they would delay the use of tests in some cases. In the patient focus groups, the comments were to say that exams were not so frequent but patients again felt it was an obligation for them to do them. They would try again to go to hospital if possible for such exams in case of financial limitations.

The discussion on cost of exams revealed a potential interesting area for further research concerning types of "Mutuelles" contracts and payments of exam costs. As for drug treatment, the strong belief about the severity of disease seemed a determining factor to explain the decision to take the tests. As cost minimization strategies, patients mainly decided to opt for an alternative structure.

---

[4]"Some patients in the focus groups, believed that they were well covered and were surprised to learn, through the group discussion, that it was not the case for some hospital expenses.

4.3. Cost to the patient and patients' decisions in the case of hay fever:

Hay fever is quite different from hypertension since it usually happens once a year during the season of allergens. It was taken as an example of an acute condition. All patients in the focus group were willing to be treated (one patient even mentioned taking the treatment as a preventive treatment). Patients interacted with general practitioners or pharmacists directly; some of them were referred to allergologists.

The factors, mentioned during the focus group discussion, that influence patients to decide to be treated (mainly with drug treatment as a first choice) were the following: the lack of comfort and gene (it lasts more than three days, it can last ten days, some patients mentioned three months), a willingness for a rapid relief, the search for efficacy in a treatment, discomfort of others, pressure from work or family to do something (embarrassment vis a vis their family or work environment).

Concerning the role of cost and cost to the patient, clearly the general opinion in the group was that it did not affect the decision to search for a therapy. Spontaneously, patients expressed that, what is expensive, is the desensitization, not so much the cost of medications. This opinion confirms what the physicians also mentioned in the focus groups. So there is a shared view on the relative cost of desensitization versus medications between physicians and patients.

Influence of cost to the patient on drug purchasing behavior:

Within the group, there were patients with "mutuelle" and without "mutuelle" and the decision making process was clearly affected by this copayment status. The common behavior of patients with "mutuelle" was clearly to go directly and regularly to their general practitioner, each time they had to face a crisis. Several patients shared the opinion that if they had to go and see the doctor for hay fever, they would also take it as an opportunity for doing a "full visit" (namely to get prescriptions for other conditions at the same time). In the case of patients without additional insurance ("mutuelle"), the decision was to go directly to a pharmacist rather than to go to a physician. The patient would rather pay the medications out-of-pocket than pay the copayment associated with a physician visit and prescribed drugs. The main cost that such patients were aware of, when making such a decision seemed to be the cost of the physician visit only, rather than the cost of a visit and the copay for prescribed medications. So, once a physician has diagnosed a hay fever, patients without "mutuelle" would continue the drug treatment by going directly to the pharmacist. Some of these patients mentioned that they could directly receive from the pharmacist what was normally a prescribed medication for hay fever. Other patients in the focus group, who visited physicians, gave their opinion that they would do the same, in a similar situation. As a young patient described this behavior, some older patients in the group agreed that it was appropriate for young patients, especially, if they faced a financial barrier, to access health services.

This description of patients' behavior without "mutuelle" was also what was previously found when physicians were interviewed on the same condition [6]. There was a consensus among physicians that, once a diagnosis is given, patients do not need to come again for visits and that they can cure themselves. It also confirms physicians' beliefs that, when there is a financial problem for a hay-fever patient, the patient would rather not consult a physician. The physician therefore would not be aware of such situations.

Concerning different drugs choices, patients mainly mentioned that they cared about some potential side effects such as sleeping effects of antihistaminic or interaction problems. They never mentioned relative cost issues between different types of medications. When some physicians told them they were changing a prescription for more expensive medications, the patients did not see a problem, but were more concerned about the efficiency of a more expensive treatment. Several patients however mentioned in the group that their doctors never told them that they might prescribe a more expensive medication. Both types of patients, with "mutuelle" and "without mutuelle", did not pay attention to the different coverage rates of medications for this disease: 35% or 65%. Patients with "mutuelle" mentioned they trusted their doctors, and that, anyway, they were refunded by the "mutuelle". Moreover, even if they had to pay in advance for the share covered by the "mutuelle"; the range of payment for hay-fever medications remained limited, even for drugs reimbursed 35% since drug prices are low. Moreover, it did not represent a frequent purchase (hay fever happens once a year). Patients without "mutuelle" did not pay attention to coverage rates and did not compare with other prices; they would purchase mainly over the counter drugs or at least drugs directly to the pharmacist. Even the patient without "mutuelle" who bought directly a prescribed medication from a pharmacist did not discuss what could have been the reimbursement for these medications.

Therefore, the main influence of cost to the patient on drug purchasing behavior seemed to be on when and how the patient purchased the drugs (e.g. directly from a pharmacist or after a visit to a physician). The level of drug coverage or the drug prices was less an issue, mainly because of the relative low price of hayfever drugs.

Influence of cost to the patient on desensitization

The main treatment area where cost seemed to come into play to opt for the treatment was the cost of desensitization. The primary reason is that it represents a more expensive and usually less reimbursed type of care. The patients' focus group confirms previous findings of the physicians' focus group, namely that the desensitization did not look very efficient, for the patients who tried it several years. Patients were dissatisfied with the treatment. The decision to follow the desensitization seemed guided by physicians: all the patients, who tried it in the focus group, took first a physician's advice. Other patients expressed they did not want to try because they were afraid (they perceived a threat) or the treatment was too expensive (the cost to the patient clearly came into play in that case since it was not well reimbursed). The factors, mentioned during the focus group discussion, which therefore seemed to influence patients to opt for or against desensitization, are: the physician's advice, the willingness to try something new, the willingness to try something that "may work and cure for good, the willingness to pay for a relatively expensive treatment, the cost of the treatment, the perceived threat or the fear about the desensitization (for instance of receiving more allergens into the body), the time constraint (especially time constraint for people at work), the type of information through media (reputation of the treatment).

The discussion over the choice or not for a desensitization showed that patients were willing to try and pay quite a substantial amount of money, searching for a more efficient treatment, for something new that may work better. Other patients expressed similar willingness to experiment new treatment such as acupuncture for instance. Again, there was a clear cost issue in the decision making process for experimenting different treatments. The patients without "mutuelle" did not try different treatments, some patients with "mutuelle" tried even if it was not covered by the "mutuelle". This may rather reveal differences among patients with different disposable income and divergence in individual preferences to be either satisfied with the current treatment or to search for an improvement of current health status. The discussion revealed that the state of medical technologies on the market to cure hay fever was perceived by the groups as a half way technology. Clearly, patients expressed very different preferences and value judgements about different treatment options. For instance, some patients did not try to maximize a level of satisfaction but were rather satisfied with a median state ("we cannot cure the disease, so we live with it and use the current drugs"). Other patients were more willing to experiment various alternatives in order to improve their health status.

Patients, in the focus group generally, did not appear very concerned by the cost to the system. Two topics were discussed in relation with this issue: the use of generics and self-medication. Only two patients from the group expressed their concern to support some measures to reduce the cost to the system. On the use of generic drugs, only one patient mentioned the following quote: "if this can help to do some savings, I will be willing to try". The lack of awareness and knowledge of generics was shared by the majority of the group (most patients did not know what a generic was, never talked about generics before, and when questioned about it, they mentioned negative opinions such as: " they need a reference to something", "they had a feeling they would have a lower value treatment", "that it was introducing a medicine for rich and poor"). Only, one patient without a "mutuelle" mentioned the relation between self-medication and cost to the system, (the quote was: "it could lead to savings to the Social Security it costs only 30 FF to 40 FF to buy drugs direct from a pharmacy and it is much more costly to pay a physician visit and the copayment for drugs").

4.4. Cost to the patient and patients' decisions in the case of hormone replacement therapy:

Hormone replacement therapy is used for menopausal symptoms and as a preventive treatment for fractures (e.g. hip fractures). All women in the focus group experienced HRT, for a period ranging from 4 years to 20 years. Some women stopped the treatment, one for financial reason and one on her doctor's advice.

First, we explored in the focus group, what were the main factors that had lead this group of women to opt for a HRT treatment. The most cited factors were: prevention of troubles associated with the menopause, prevention of risks for fractures, prevention of aging problems (skin problem, handicaps . . .), trust in doctor's advice (most of the time the gynecologist), value/reputation of the doctor, previous history of cancer in the family, the knowledge about women aged 80's with hip fractures, the role of partners or husbands. The media also seemed to influence whether a woman opted for HRT. For example, some quotes were: "we feel obliged", "we must take hormones".

Clinical drawbacks or risks associated with HRT treatment were also clearly seen by patients. For instance, one patient mentioned headache associated with some drug treatment. It impeded her friend to take an HRT treatment. The risk of breast cancer was well perceived by the majority of the group, but the majority felt well protected since they had regular mammography.

Influence of cost to the patient and HRT treatment:

As for the chronic and acute cases described previously, the main differences of behaviors were found between patients with "mutuelles" and patients without a " mutuelle". The access to a "mutuelle" clearly determined the type of questions the woman was concerned about. One quote was for instance: "le jour où je n'aurai plus de mutuelle, je me poserai d'autres questions" (the day I will not have any more a Mutuelle, I will ask other questions). Some patients with "mutuelle" were also conscious that it might not be a permanent state and they may have to face some future without "mutuelle" (in case of job loss, increases of premium, especially for elderly).

The influence of the cost to the patient as a potential barrier to HRT treatment was always cited with the cost of visits to the physician, mainly the gynecologist, which prescribed or renewed the treatment. It was also associated with the series of exams (for examples, some quotes were "et tous les examens qui vont avec" (all the exams that go with it), "le traitement des médicaments et tous les examens qui s' en suivent") (drugs and all the exams that follow). So, on the cost issue, patients, as previously found in doctors' focus group, clearly referred to the whole treatment cost and not only to the cost of medicines

Cost to the patient and drug purchasing behaviour:

For patients with and without mutuelles, the cost of medicines was not perceived as a problem. The main reason was again, as for hayfever drugs, the low cost of the drug treatment. The cost of the copay was around 20 FF a month and no patient in the group said that such a level of cost represented a barrier to get the treatment or that it was a problem to pay in advance.

However, some aspects of the decision making process concerning medications for HRT were affected by the cost side or the payment form. It related to how many packs were purchased, how often the prescriptions were renewed (some physicians gave a prescription for six months, others for a month), which drug categories were prescribed, according to their reimbursement rates, 35% and 65% (only one woman mentioned that she asked her physician not to prescribe drugs reimbursed 35%).

Cost to the patient and physicians' visits and surveillance costs:

Concerning the visit to see a gynecologist, the cost issue was clearly raised. Even patients with "mutuelles" were concerned about the payment for private and good physicians who would ask for more than the fee negotiated with the Social Security. To minimize the cost of a visit, the range of choices differed between patients with and without mutuelles. Patients with "mutuelle" considered different types of private practices ("sector 1" versus "sector 2" (not usually fully covered)) or consulted a physician in hospital. Patients without "mutuelle" considered the hospital versus a private practice, and in one case, decided to stop the treatment (taking into account, in such a case, not only cost of visits but also cost of exams). One quote was for instance "when we have no "mutuelle", we can take medications, but for exams, it is another story, a test costs at least 300 FF"). This cost concern about tests was shared by physicians since several women mentioned that their physicians ask if they had a "mutuelle" before ordering exams.

Cost minimization strategies were partly driven by anticipation on the long-term costs when HRT was initialized (regular visits, exams and tests). However such anticipations were not shared in the group.[5]

Some women for instance did not know what an osteo-densitometry was, some had a mammography only once, despite several years of HRT treatment. These variations were partially due to a lack of knowledge or information, and women during the focus group discussion realized that their physicians were more or less willing to provide them with the relevant information. Since cost was an issue (as shown by the extended discussion on cost information), the exchanges however revealed that the level of information on price and cost to the patient, was very uneven among women. Some women did not know that they could get a mammography without a visit to a gynecologist or a physician, some were not aware of the cheapest structures available for exams (list of establishments "conventionnes", "or where to get a free osteo-densitometry").

The decisions whether to take exams and where to take the exams were therefore clearly cost driven. Cost or reimbursement level was however weighted with other

[5] A problem was discussed in relation with the cost of patches. They were quite expensive: 100 FF to 150 FF per month, three years ago when they were not reimbursed. Some patients were then ready to pay the price because they did not want the cream; some on the contrary were not willing to pay that price. For the last three years, patches have been reimbursed, their price is 51 FF and the copayment to the patient is around 30 FF, so in a similar range of copayment than any other types of drug treatment.

important factors such as the will to be checked or the anxiety to get exams, for the decision to take an exam; or proximity of the care center and the length of the delay, for the decision where to take the exam.

5. Conclusions

This paper provides the results of how cost is driving different aspects of a patient decision making process in cases of hypertension, hay fever and HRT. These three diseases provide a fair range of choices and diversity in types and prices of health care services. In the French reimbursement system, clearly the access or not to additional insurance induced different changes in the decision-making process. This relates, to a large extent, to whether, where and how often the patient is buying the services (e.g. private practice versus hospital, pharmacist versus general practitioner, initialization or not of a treatment). The level of price information on services, and therefore the net cost to the patient, seemed quite well known in the case of the chronic disease of hypertension (this is not surprising since patients need a regular treatment); in the case of the acute condition of hay-fever, it was mainly known by cost conscious patients without "mutuelles"; in the case of HRT, patients had a good knowledge of drug prices but many women lacked information on how to get access to cheaper services within the system, for the type of services where they were more concerned about costs (tests and exams for instance). Generally, patients appeared much more cost conscious with costs of visits and cost of exams than drug costs. However, the drug purchasing behaviors was, to a limited extent, influenced by cost to the patient, for patients without "mutuelle" (e.g. number of packs, different types of drug coverages, frequency of prescription renewal).

References

[1] J.P. Dumont, l'avenir de la protection sociale complémentaire en France, *Revue Française des Affaires Sociales* **48**(3) (1994), 31–48.
[2] J. Kitzinger, The methodology of focus groups, *Sociol Health Illness* **16** (1994), 103–121.
[3] D. Morgan, Future directions in focus group studies, in: *Successful focus groups,* D.L. Morgan, ed., Sage, London, 1998, pp. 225–244.
[4] K. Hassell and D. Hibbert, The use of focus groups in pharmacy research: processes and practicalities, *Soc. Admin Pharm* **13** (1996), 169–177.
[5] D.L. Morgan and R.A. Krueger, *The focus group kit,* (Vol. 1–6), Sage publication, 1998.
[6] C. Huttin and J. Andral, How the reimbursement system may influence physicians'decisions, results from focus groups interviews in France, (Forthcoming in Health Policy, 2000).

Pharmaceuticals Policy and Law 5 (2002) 167–183
IOS Press

Perceptions of biotechnology risks in the European Union: Trusting 'the public' for science policy making

Joan Costa[a,b,*] and Elias Mossialos[a]
[a]*LSE Health and Social Care, London School of Economics, London, UK*
[b]*Grup de Recerca EPS, Universitat de Barcelona, Barcelona, Spain*

Products obtained through techniques that genetically modify living organisms are widely extended in the medical, pharmaceutical and food industry. However, the usage of such techniques has led to widespread controversies in some European countries where it clashes with small public acceptance. Lack of knowledge also suggests that once people become aware of the possible effects on health or the environment that these risks pose this might cause conflicts in many countries. Moral concerns and lack of sufficient knowledge to understand both risks and benefits are typically the issues that policy makers fear. This paper empirically examines the acceptance of and perceptions of risks for biotech procedures using data from two public opinion surveys, developed in 1996 and 1999 respectively (Eurobarometer surveys 46.1 and 52.1). Additionally, we look at risk perception determinants.

Keywords: Biotechnology, public perceptions

1. Introduction

The extension of biotechnology products is currently a matter of concern in most occidental countries [1]. The lack of sufficient scientific evidence on the long run risks of genetic engineering applications is the largest cause of concern [2,3]. Individuals seldom have comprehensible scientific information on biotechnology, and existent information is largely ambiguous to allow choices in this area to be 'well informed' [4]. Information channels apparently are not neutral in influencing risk perceptions. Some channels do not seem to be trusted by the public according to recent Eurobaromter surveys (e.g, the industry and the government). Informed choices might even turn out to be 'idealistic', due to the regulators 'difficulties in providing information on the true risk' estimates. Furthermore, lack of information and ambiguity might give rise to sceptical beliefs on the future of biotechnology. Preliminary empirical evidence shows that individuals focus on small product characteristics rather than on the whole benefits of a specific technique [3–7]. Misrepresentation of biotechnology might, although restrictively, exaggerate moral concerns supported by

*Dr. Joan Costa i Font, LSE Health and Social Care, London School of Economics and Political Science, Houghton Street, London WC2A 2AE, UK. Tel.: +44 020 790 6840; Fax: +44 020 7955 6803; E-mail: Joan Costa i Font@lse.ac.uk.

particular reference groups (e.g., environmentalists and religious extremists) against biotechnology as a whole and/or some specific applications [8].

Expected policy responses to the lack of risk information in the European Union (EU) are the development of conservative risk regulations that flow from the application of the precautionary principle (PP)[1] as endorsed in EC Treaty. A non-extremist interpretation of this principle leads the regulator to anticipate potential harms from new technologies, although this principle implies an efficiency loss and a subsequent delay in innovation diffusion.

When risk policy implies (as it does in the area of biotechnology) providing information and regulating the industry on the basis of risks that can be identified and measured, policy makers can regulate on the basis of provisional observed risk estimates and/or, rely of public perceptions on risks and benefits (and in certain circumstances moral concerns posed by new technologies). Objective risks as estimated by 'experts' can be incomplete and may include substantial value judgements that the population might not accept. There are several additional reasons to support the need of examining perceptions of risk. First, whenever behavioural aspects are influential, individual perceptions are informative for policy making [10]. Second, if we assume that information on new science technology developments is a 'global public good', then risk perception estimates are a means for testing the efficacy of information provision. Third, from the developments of the subjective expected utility theories there is substantial agreement that 'risk' is rather as subjective a concept as utility benefits or moral concerns. Finally, even when regulation does not involve the individual, in a democratic setting, it must take into account the existence of heterogeneous cross-country perceptions [11].

Interventionism in risk policy is often regarded as following the hypothesis that individuals are not able to learn about risks alone, and thus the government must act paternalistically by communicating risks and enforcing labelling products. However, evidence from other risks (e.g, smoking risks) shows that individuals are capable to update their prior beliefs following a process that resembles the Bayes rule. From several studies [11] we also know that acceptance of risks is sensibly influenced by several identifiable qualitative characteristics such as knowledge, whether or not the substance is voluntary taken and controllability. Biotechnology risks are perceived as not being voluntary taken although they are sensibly unknown (i.e., the risks of harming or modifying an organism or the ecosystem) and enhance large information costs [12]. Thus, individuals might rationally decide to keep being ignorant [3] and adopt conservative non-reasoned risk attitudes. In this setting, regulators should identify the extent to which individuals perceive the risks and benefits of a specific

[1]The Precautionary Principle (PP) refers to the "foresight planning principle" proposed in the Conference of Rio in 1992, which states that 'where there are threats of serious or irreversible damage, lack of scientific certainty shall not be used as a reason for postponing cost – effective measures to prevent environmental degradation" (see Gollier [9]).

product and how they evaluate products in order to undertake communication policies that take into account attitude determinants [13,14].

Theoretically, when rational individuals decide whether particular risks are acceptable for society they apply a cost benefit rule, where acceptance means the benefits outweigh the risks. Furthermore, moral beliefs do play an important role because the extent to which a change is judged to be a harm depends on human values [16–18]. However, modelling how moral values influence is a rather complex issue. Moral attitudes might act as risk or benefit amplifiers or, might be simply cost and benefits if we consider morality as being an additional argument of factor in the individual utility function [19–21].[2]

In this paper we empirically examine risk perceptions of biotechnology products in different European countries and examine result to inform the design of science policy in the areas of health and food policy. From this analysis we test whether individuals are able to reason consistently on the area of biotech where information is small. Also, we test whether there is evidence of cross-country and product heterogeneity in the particular application of biotechnology techniques. We use a representative large survey (Eurobarometer, 1996 and 1999).

2. Public perceptions and prior empirical evidence

Public acceptance of biotechnology is the result of the interaction of several influences. These influences are summarised by Hoban [15] as education, culture, history, economic conditions and government response. However, identifying the impact of every specific variable is for the time being very ambitious. Education as a proxy of knowledge influences individual understanding of recent biotechnology advances. However, there is some evidence (Gaskell [8]) that shows that knowledge does not necessary increase public acceptance but just reduces the probability of having an opinion on biotechnology.[3] Cross-country heterogeneity expresses cultural differences, and specifically differences in societal values regarding modifying nature. As a result, different countries display different trade-off between efficiency and risk that comes out from the PP principle. The influence of reference groups depends on the role of religion and the influence of specific extreme political parties. Economic influences are especially relevant from both the demand and the supply side of the market. The more extended biotechnology is in one country, the larger the probability that consumers might have had some sort of experiences with consumption [19]. Similarly, the more developed the biotechnology industry is in one country, the more

[2] Although in this paper we undertake an explicit modelling of moral attitudes at the aggregate country, this is influential when perceptions are modelled at the individual level.

[3] Moreover, in Gaskell's study risk perceptions did not appear as good predictors of public acceptance of biotechnology. Public acceptance was positively influenced by usefulness and negatively influenced by moral acceptability.

likely some one will be occupied in the industry, and attitudes might then be reflecting self-interest.

Opinion pool studies already show some evidence. Two studies developed in New Zealand and Japan specifically study the public attitudes to genetic engineering, fertilisation and biotechnology. About 97% of the population in Japan and 57% in New Zealand have sometime heard of biotechnology. Another study revealed that the level of awareness on biotechnology was small in the EU [8].

About two thirds of the US consumers accept food produced by biotechnology techniques [14]. A more recent study takes into account three main components on consumer concerns for biotechnology products: awareness, willingness to buy and risk perceptions [15]. The study acknowledges that awareness of risks limits the individual willingness to purchase of biotechnology products. Table 1 shows, there are large differences in the awareness of risks across countries, and answers to the surveys reveal a 'lack of awareness'. Regarding the willingness to buy genetically modified products, the study showed that there is some opposition to buy these products in some countries such as Germany and Austria whereas in the US, the UK and the Netherlands we find that more than two thirds of the population would buy biotechnology products [6]. Germany and Austria show greater consumer concerns on the hazards of the products. This result suggest a double interaction term between the public and the research based industry. A study based on international perceptions and bioethical reasoning on gene therapy in 1993 showed that about 5–7% rejected gene therapy, considering it to be playing God, or unnatural [16]. There was very little concern about eugenics (0.5–2%), and more respondents gave supportive reasons like "improving genes", especially in Thailand and India. Support for specific applications was significantly smaller for "improving physical characters", "improving intelligence", or "making people more ethical" than for curing diseases like cancer or diabetes, but there was little difference between inheritable or non inheritable gene therapy.

Hoban and Kendall [13] show that certain applications were more acceptable than others, however, depending on the perceived value and potential effects. Using biotechnology to change plants was considered much more acceptable than using it to change animals. Transgenic applications of biotechnology, such as the insertion of animal genes into plants, were unacceptable to many participants. Environmental concerns were important to most people and many considered ethical issues important as well.

3. Methods

This study uses two Eurobarometer surveys 46.1 and 52.1 to examine people's attitudes and risk perceptions of biotechnology products. The two surveys were developed in 1996 and 1999 respectively. The surveys were carried out by INRA (EUROPE) interviewing around 16000 people in the 15 EU member states between

Table 1
Individual assessment on biotechnology products

	Awareness on the risks (%)	Willingness to buy genetically enhanced products (%)	Risk perception*
US	58	73	21
Germany	69	30	49
Austria	31	22	60
Denmark	79	55	44
Sweden	64	51	65
Netherlands	68	64	44
Italy	43	53	30
Greece	37	59	33
Spain	31	59	48
UK	52	63	39

*Obtained as a percentage rating as a 'serious risk'.
Source: [15].

October and November 1996 and November and December 1999 respectively. The aim of the survey was to elicit the individual support for genetically modified goods. This survey may be fitted in the context of other related studies about attitudes to consumer risks and may be a good instrument to examine the individual attitudes to risks derived from scientific progress. The term biotech is referred to as "modern biotechnology" in a broad sense, that includes genetic engineering as well. These surveys explore the acceptance of biotechnology at the EU level, although we focus on a set of risk perception issues. The question framed was the following:

> "To what extent do you agree or disagree that this application is risky? The application referred to six different biotechnology procedures (see Table 5)."

Questions for four biotechnology procedures were exactly the same whereas for two of them there were sensible variations that may have influenced risk perceptions.

Moreover, a additional question was used in this study to relate risk perceptions to public opinion respect to biotechnology procedures:

> "I am going to read out a list of areas in which new technologies are currently developing. For each of these areas, do you think it will improve our way of life in the next 20 years, it will have no effect, or it will make things worse?"

3.1. Measurement aspects

Quantitative questions may have the advantage in that they are easily to model in terms of subjective probability theory. However, there is strong concern on the capacity of respondents to answer perception questions when there is small information available. Therefore, qualitative questions may be a good alternative to capture using a scale as the ones used here " strongly agrees, agrees, disagrees, strongly disagrees and don't know".

There is no unique way of empirically analysing this data. Alternatives refer to ordered probit, logit models, multinomial logit models and other limited dependent

Table 2
Public opinion on new Technologies in the EU

	1999	1996
Solar Energy		
Improve	73.54	73.81
No effect	13.69	13.84
Worse	4.12	3.96
DK	8.58	8.30
Computers &Inform Tech		
Improve	78.22	76.56
No effect	9.62	8.25
Worse	5.22	7.97
DK	6.83	7.08
Biotech		
Improve	39.73	44.78
No effect	10.78	9.57
Worse	23.75	20.49
DK	25.58	24.92
Telecom		
Improve	80.69	80.85
No effect	10.81	9.43
Worse	2.95	3.47
DK	5.55	6.09
New Materials		
Improve	63.26	64.16
No effect	12.95	12.29
Worse	5.90	6.14
DK	17.75	17.22
Space exploration		
Improve	49.82	48.80
No effect	27.17	28.44
Worse	7.47	7.74
DK	15.40	14.83

Question: I am going to read out a list of areas in which new technologies are currently developing. For each of these areas, do you think it will improve our way of life in the next 20 years, it will have no effect, or it will make things worse?

variable models. However, a more comprehensive way to empirically estimate an overall risk perception measure is to transform these qualitative answers once they have been elicited in terms of a quantitative scale. Here we employ this procedure. We attach a value from 2 to -2 to answers according to risk perception and responses. This leads to a better understanding of results without loosing significant information.

The equation estimated for different biotechnology procedures has as a dependent variable a risk assessment measure. Let X_{ij} be a vector of variables characterising the sources of information that for every individual, and let β be the associated vector of coefficients. Then for each biotechnology procedure risk perceptions equitation can be represented as: $RISK_i = \beta_O + \beta_1 X_{1i} + \beta_2 X_{2i} + \beta_3 X_{2i} + u_i$ where u_i is the random error. The model was estimated by ordinary least squares.

The variables included refer to individual determinants X_1, individual attitudes

X_2 and knowledge X_3. The variables employed for each of this categories are the following:

a) Individual determinants

Covariates included were age, family members and gender to identify individual characteristics. Other risk perception studies [11] showed that gender appears as an explanatory of lung cancer risk perceptions. In particular, male showed a smaller risk perception than female [11]. Age is typically associated with information acquisition [18]. Older individuals are hypothesized to be more sensible to changes in the production of food, medicines and genetically procedures than young. Therefore, risks perceptions are expected to rise with age. Household size may influence the attitude towards possible risks as possible hazards are more likely to impact a family member if household size is large.

b) Individual attitudes

These refer to political ideology and religiosity as increasing individual risk perception [19–21]. We expect that those individuals that define themselves as more religious would be less likely to accept biotech procedures, and may are more likely to perceive higher risks from them [17,18]. Moreover, as left wing environmentalists in the EU are strongly opposed to some new biotech procedures we may expect that political ideology may have some positive influence in increasing risk perceptions.

c) Knowledge

Variables used to instrumentalize knowledge were education, income and concern with biotechnology. Education, income and the dummy variable concern with biotechnology should reduce risk perceptions as far as more information on objective risk of new procedures may reduce the risk perceived by the individual. Finally, a control variable was included to control for individual responses. This variable refers to the respondent co-operation when interviewed.

4. Results

Table 2 shows that the share of the EU population that perceives that Biotechnology will improve the Europeans way of living has decreased 11% from 1996 to 1999. In contrast, from perceptions on other new technologies it becomes clear that there was a small variation in public perceptions between 1996 and 1999. Looking at attitudes for each of the EU 15 countries we find that Europeans are more sceptical about biotechnology procedures. Except for Portugal and Finland, in all the other EU countries the share of the population that think biotech will improve has declined. This may be attributed to information on the hazards that biotechnology may pose to human health. Table 3, shows a global index for attitudes that weights responses by the differences in ignorance regarding biotechnology. Attitudes depend very much

Table 3
Attitudes towards biotechnology by EU countries 1996–1999 Question: 'I am going to read out a list of areas in which new technologies are currently developing. For each of these areas, do you think biotechnology will improve our way of life in the next 20 years, it will have no effect, or it will make things worse'

	Attitude index		% of DK answers		Adjusted attitude index	
	1999	1996	1999	1996	1999	1996
Belgium	21.9*	34.7	20.5	22.6	27.5	44.9
Denmark	−1.6*	13.9	15.1	15.5	−1.9	16.4
Germany	16.1	11.7	22.1	21.4	20.7	14.9
Greece	−18.4*	12.3	36.4*	46.9	−29.0	23.1
Spain	15.9*	41.8	24.5	24.4	21.1*	55.3
France	41.3	46.8	32.0	30.0	60.7	66.9
Ireland	18.7*	35.1	19.0	24.8	23.1*	46.6
Italy	9.5*	28.0	33.7	32.6	14.3*	41.5
Luxembourg	7.6*	41.1	33.4	35.4	11.5*	63.5
Netherlands	19.3	22.4	25.4	21.6	25.9	28.5
Portugal	30.7	27.6	16.3	16.6	36.7	33.1
UK	25.7*	47.5	50.0*	31.2	51.3	68.9
Austria	4.0*	22.9	33.7*	21.6	6.1*	29.2
Sweden	18.1	17.2	23.6	23.0	23.7	22.4
Finland	9.8	6.6	23.3	27.4	12.8	9.0

*Countries where there has been a very significant (> 50% change) increase or decrease between 1996–1996. Note: The index has been computed giving a value of 1 to improving answers, a value of −1 to pessimistic answers and a value of 0 to unchanged answers. The third column shows the index adjusted by the probability of a DK answer in order to ensure comparability.

on whether attitudes are the reasoned by individuals. To this extent, some countries show large variation between 1996 and 1999, specifically in Spain, Ireland, Austria ,Italy and Greece. The last country seems to be the most opposed to biotechnology, whereas France and the UK seem to be the countries where biotechnology was more accepted.

The definition of the variables of the model employed are reported in Tables 4 and 5. Table 6 shows risk perceptions estimates for all risk perceptions procedures included in the analysis. There is a larger share of people that perceive biotechnology procedures as being risky except for 'using genetic testing for inherited diseases'. From 1996 to 1999 there is a slight increase in risk perception, however, there is as well a large share of individuals that remain ignorant on this issue. As noted before, it is strongly difficult to summarise this data except if an index is established. Table 6 shows that whereas perceived risk increased for food biotech and gene transfer into crops and medicines, this was not the case of genetic engineering and genetic testing for inherited diseases. Looking at country data in Table 7 there were a large set of changes form 1996 to 1999. Food biotech and genetic transplants show a risk perception index higher than 0 for all EU countries during both periods. Regarding transferring genes into plants Sweden and Finland in 1999 appear to show negative

Table 4
Definition of variables

Explanatory variables	
Food Biotech	Risk perception index for use of modern biotechnology in the production of foods
Gene transfer into crops	Risk perception index for taking genes from plant species and transferring them into crop plants
Gene transfer for medicines	Risk perception index for introducing human genes into bacteria to produce medicines or vaccines
Genetically modify animals	Risk perception index for cloning animals which can be used to make medicines and vaccines
Genetic transplants	Risk perception index for cloning human cells or tissues to replace a patient's diseased cells that are not functioning properly
Genetic inherited diseases	Risk perception index for using genetic testing to detect diseases we might have inherited from our parents
Exogenous variables	
Gender	1 for males 0 for females, 0 otherwise
Age	Respondent current age
Fammem	Number of household members
Religious	1 for religious or very religious respondents, 0 otherwise
Income	Measured by dummy variables 1 = high income to 4 = low income
Educ	Age that respondent finished studying 1 = 15 or less, 2 = 16-19, 3 = 20 or more, and 4 = still studying.
Conern 1	Concerned with biotechnology measured form 1 to 3 where 1 refers to frequent discussions, 2 for occasional discussions and 3 for infrequent discussions
Cooper	Respondent cooperation 1 = Excellent to 4 = Bad.
Political	Political ideology measured using a 1 to 10 scale where 1 = Left and 10 is right.

risk perceptions meaning that more people disagree about the risk nature of this procedure than people agreeing with it. The same was found for these two countries and Germany when considering gene transfer for medicines in 1999.

Looking at specific procedure results for each biotechnology product examined show the following:

a) Food biotechnology

There was a sensible increase in perceived risk in France, Belgium, Ireland and Greece. A significant perceived risk reduction is identified in Portugal, Austria, Spain, UK and Finland. The last country is the one that displays the lowest risk perception for all EU countries. However, for a large set of countries, risk perceptions were quite stable as for Italy and Germany.

b) Gene transfer into crops

Risk perceptions were stable in France, Sweden, UK, Luxembourg and Austria. Finland and Sweden reduced their perceived risk and all the other countries increased their perceived risk from 1996 to 1999. The extreme case was Belgium which in 1996 had a risk perception index of −0.04 and in 1999 it increased to 0.4. In Greece it moved from 0.08 to 0.173.

Table 5
Content of the risk perceptions questions asked

Variable	1999	1996
Food Biotech	Use modern biotechnology in the production of foods, for example to make them higher in protein, keep longer or change the taste	Same
Gene transfer into crops	Taking genes from plant species and transferring them into crop plants, to make them more resistant to insect pests	Same
Gene transfer for medicines	Introducing human genes into bacteria to produce medicines or vaccines, for example to produce insulin for diabetics	Same
Genetic transplants	Cloning human cells or tissues to replace a patient's diseased cells that are not functioning properly	Introducing human genes into animals to produce organs for human transplants, such as into pigs for human heart transplants.
Genetic animals	Cloning animals such as sheep to get milk which can be used to make medicines and vaccines	Developing genetically modified animals for laboratory research studies, such a mouse which has genes which causes it to develop cancer.
Genetic inherited diseases	Using genetic testing to detect diseases we might have inherited from our parents such as cystic fibrosis, mucoviscidosis, and thalassaemia.	Same

c) Gene transfer for medicines

As before, Finland and Sweden are traditional exceptions of countries where individuals perceive lower risks from 1996 to 1999. This was the case for Austria, Germany, Portugal and the UK as well. Except for France, where risk perceptions were stable during the two periods considered, all the other countries showed a rise in risk perceptions of gene transfer to medicines.

d) Genetically modified animals

The rise in risk perceptions was even stronger than in all other cases. Except for France and Finland, which show a reduced risk perception, all other EU display higher risk perceptions.

e) Genetic transplants

Regarding gene transplants risk perceptions show the opposite pattern in most countries. They show a reduction of risk perceptions except for Germany, Greece and Denmark. The only exception is Austria that remains with similar risk perception estimates.

Table 6
Risk perceptions on six biotech procedures

	Food	Crops	medicines	Animals	Humans	Inherited
1996						
Strongly agrees	25.25	17.9	14.48	22.59	29.39	13.18
Agrees	33.68	29.94	30.1	29.11	28.91	25.4
Disagree	18.91	23.48	22.72	20.07	15.56	24.52
Strongly disagree	10.21	14.77	17.18	15.42	12.58	22.31
DK	11.95	13.9	15.51	12.82	13.57	14.59
1999						
Strongly agrees	28.32	21.6	22.11	16.62	25.72	14.31
Agrees	29.5	26.64	27.47	26.71	26.66	23.11
Disagree	15.02	18.12	15.62	18.83	14.9	20.89
Strongly disagree	6.76	9.23	8.74	10.19	8.21	16.45
DK	20.4	24.41	26.05	27.64	24.51	25.24

To what extent do you agree or disagree that this application is risky for society?

f) Genetic inherited diseases

Detecting genetic inherited diseases is not perceived as a risky procedure in may EU countries. Only in Belgium, Spain, Netherlands, Portugal and Italy is it perceived as risky. In those countries risk perceptions have increased from 1996 to 1999, however, the EU overall risk perception has not been significantly modified.

A common explanation of risk perception trends is a decline in 'acceptance'. Table 8 provides some evidence on this issue. From 1996 to 1999, there is a reduction in the acceptance of biotechnology products in the EU. The risk perception index is higher for those who believe biotechnology will worsen in the next 20 years. This was the case with all procedures except for detecting genetically inherited diseases. That is, individuals don't perceive this procedure as being risky. Acceptance for this last procedure may be explained by other factors [8].

Since results differ significantly from one procedure to another, we compute partial correlation coefficients of risk perceptions for different biotechnology procedures. Results from Table 9 show a small correlation coefficient. This may indicate that individuals were able to understand the meaning of every procedure and therefore to distinguish the risk component inherent in each of them. The only causality component found was a higher correlation coefficient between procedures that relate to food production and between procedures that relate to genetic engineering. This may be indicating that people do not have a general idea of "biotechnology" although they may be able to distinguish different single procedures.

Tables 10 and 11 report the empirical specification of biotechnology risk perception equations for 1996 and 1999. Regressions show a low explanatory power. For cross-country differences, which suggests that factors other than those accounted for biotechnology risk perceptions may be explanatory. However, the focus here is not to develop a predictive model for individual risk perceptions but to tests some hypotheses of their determinants. Regarding individual determinants, males have significantly lower risk perceptions on average for all procedures except for gene

Table 7
Risk perception index for biotechnology procedures*

	Food Biotech	Gene transfer into crops	Gene transfer for medicines	Genetically modified animals	Genetic transplants	Genetic inherited diseases
Biotechnology procedures (Eurobarometer survey 1996)						
Belgium	0.226	−0.041	−0.019	0.264	0.518	−0.107
Denmark	0.636	0.418	−0.264	−0.046	0.363	−0.364
Germany	0.578	0.082	0.046	0.240	0.379	−0.172
Greece	0.591	−0.080	−0.266	0.093	0.365	−0.973
Spain	0.498	0.014	0.064	0.390	0.668	−0.141
France	0.208	0.079	0.096	0.229	0.335	−0.071
Ireland	0.614	0.213	0.220	0.364	0.605	−0.149
Italy	0.365	0.140	0.102	0.220	0.517	0.041
Luxembourg	0.556	0.204	−0.157	0.389	0.438	−0.238
Netherlands	0.397	0.280	−0.234	−0.003	0.138	−0.262
Portugal	0.698	0.364	0.583	0.523	0.736	0.310
UK	0.523	0.151	0.327	0.468	0.729	0.211
Austria	0.542	0.228	0.218	0.499	0.760	−0.048
Sweden	0.261	−0.063	−0.200	0.105	0.274	−0.366
Finland	0.545	0.364	0.135	0.176	0.611	−0.022
Total	0.441	0.127	0.019	0.233	0.468	−0.173
Biotechnology procedures (Eurobarometer survey 1999)						
Belgium	0.611	0.401	0.459	0.583	0.449	0.324
Denmark	0.763	0.551	0.128	0.363	0.480	−0.139
Germany	0.578	0.173	−0.019	0.351	0.461	−0.163
Greece	0.986	0.430	0.274	0.498	0.727	−0.478
Spain	0.611	0.222	0.201	0.408	0.418	0.086
France	0.316	0.075	0.010	0.117	0.194	−0.107
Ireland	0.971	0.804	0.684	0.743	0.866	0.226
Italy	0.489	0.368	0.262	0.369	0.404	0.137
Luxembourg	0.417	0.207	0.188	0.248	0.303	−0.064
Netherlands	0.695	0.543	0.436	0.517	0.533	0.303
Portugal	0.635	0.587	0.455	0.704	0.699	0.151
UK	0.377	0.118	0.167	0.169	0.385	−0.024
Austria	0.442	0.282	0.127	0.253	0.293	−0.001
Sweden	0.368	−0.056	−0.183	0.146	0.314	−0.405
Finland	0.020	−0.144	−0.153	0.043	0.191	−0.464
Total	0.575	0.332	0.385	0.207	0.466	−0.020

*Index constructed from responses to the following question: To what extent do you agree or disagree that this application is risky for society? Definitely agree = 2,Tend to agree = 1, Tend to disagree = −1, Definitely disagree = −2 and DK = 0.

transfer into medicines and for detecting inherited diseases where no significant differences were found. This may reflect a gender divergence on attitudes toward risk, a finding consistent with other studies [11]. Age plays a significant effect on risk perceptions, increasing individual risk perceptions in food and medical biotechnology. This suggests that older individuals seem to be less comfortable with biotechnology procedures. Finally, the household size was only significant in 1996 for higher risk perceptions in detecting inherited diseases.

Table 8
Risk perception index and public opinion on biotechnology procedures

1999								
N	Improve		No effect		Worse		DK	
	6389		1733		3820		4144	
	39.73%		10.78%		23.75%		25.58%	
Variable	Mean	Std. Err.	Mean	Std. Err.	Mean	Std. Err.	Mean	Std. Err.
Food Biotech	0.456	0.016	0.443	0.030	0.927	0.020	0.489	0.017
Gene transfer into crops	0.254	0.016	0.160	0.030	0.625	0.021	0.254	0.017
Gene transfer for medicines	0.339	0.016	0.242	0.030	0.582	0.020	0.332	0.017
Genetically modify animals	0.138	0.016	0.089	0.029	0.391	0.020	0.193	0.016
Genetic transplants	0.373	0.016	0.368	0.030	0.720	0.021	0.420	0.017
Genetic inherited diseases	−0.038	0.017	−0.098	0.030	0.060	0.022	−0.035	0.018
1996								
N	Improve		No effect		Worse		DK	
	7708		1647		3527		4290	
	44.78%		9.57%		20.49%		24.92%	
Variable	Mean	Std. Err.	Mean	Std. Err.	Mean	Std. Err.	Mean	Std. Err.
Food Biotech	0.314	0.015	0.346	0.033	0.802	0.022	0.435	0.019
Gene transfer into crops	0.033	0.016	0.049	0.033	0.454	0.023	0.057	0.019
Gene transfer for medicines	−0.053	0.016	−0.035	0.032	0.204	0.023	0.020	0.019
Genetically modify animals	0.203	0.016	0.213	0.034	0.351	0.024	0.198	0.020
Genetic transplants	0.447	0.016	0.408	0.034	0.616	0.024	0.411	0.020
Genetic inherited diseases	−0.204	0.016	−0.152	0.033	−0.083	0.024	−0.203	0.020

Question: I am going to read out a list of areas in which new technologies are currently developing. For each of these areas, do you think it will improve our way of life in the next 20 years, it will have no effect, or it will make things worse?

Interestingly, when analysing individual attitudes we found that religiosity was only increasing risk perceptions for genetic engineering procedures. Being religious increases the perceived risk by a 10%. Furthermore, political ideology was significantly associated with a higher risk perception of food biotechnology. Left wing supporters overall tend to agree that food biotechnology or gene transfer into crops is more risky for society.

Finally, variables instrumenting knowledge (Tables 10 and 11) show that income does not explain differences in individual risk perception. However, education appears to be strongly significant. Education increased risk perception for all biotechnology procedures except for gene testing that reduces perceived risk. This was because the omitted dummy variable was those individuals still studying. Finally, the variable described as 'concern' 1 was significant and negatively associated with risk perceptions. Therefore, those individuals that tend to discuss biotechnology issues tend to assess a lower risk perception to biotechnology procedures. Co-operation with the interviewer was significant for food biotech and for detecting inherited diseases in both periods considered.

Table 9
Correlation coefficient for different biotech risk perceptions on biotechnology procedures (all significant at 1%)

	Food Biotech	Gene transfer into crops	Gene transfer for medicines	Genetically modify animals	Genetic transplants
1999					
Food Biotech	1				
Gene transfer into crops	0.501	1			
Gene transfer for medicines	0.340	0.369	1		
Genetically modify animals	0.331	0.407	0.494	1	
Genetic transplants	0.376	0.379	0.481	0.406	1
Genetic inherited diseases	0.209	0.296	0.371	0.419	0.296
1996					
Food Biotech	1				
Gene transfer into crops	0.468	1			
Gene transfer for medicines	0.280	0.352	1		
Genetically modify animals	0.246	0.268	0.360	1	
Genetic transplants	0.256	0.245	0.311	0.444	1
Genetic inherited diseases	0.196	0.278	0.422	0.294	0.255

5. Conclusions

Results from this study show that Biotechnology procedures enhance strong concerns that limit their acceptance even though shows large heterogeneity. They differ from other new technologies, where acceptance is higher and more stable. EU countries were quite similar with the exception of Finland and Portugal which seem to show an increase in public acceptance.

This study has examined the determinants of the individual risk perception of new biotechnology procedure. Specifically, how gender and education matter, risk communication campaigns should take into account a gender and low education bias often found when analysing risks perceptions of new technologies. Political attitudes and religiosity were not influential in all procedures which suggests that although the role of social reference groups is important, extreme risks attitudes affect specific procedures. We have shown that risk perceptions for food biotechnology seem to have increased for 1996 to 1999 on average, and for most countries with the exception of Finland. This may be due to several reasons, an important one being the uncertainty associated with the extension of the BSE and the dioxins scandals in France which not only affected perceptions but also stigmatised to some extent the use of new technologies in food production. An additional finding of the paper indicates that information acquisition by means of education and informal discussion explains reductions in risk perceptions of biotechnology procedures.

The main implications of this study can be summarised as follows. Risk perception of new products where information is small tends to be highly associated with traditional informational channels. Since biotechnology procedures are often negatively advertised in the media, individuals tend to show high-risk perceptions. Thus, science regulation and consumer policy have a large field to work together

Table 10
Regression results for Biotech risk perceptions (adjusted by country variation) 1996

	Food Biotech		Gene transfer into crops		Gene transfer for medicines	
	Coef.	t	Coef.	t	Coef.	t
Gender	−0.087	−4.198	−0.048	−2.274	−0.001	−0.045
Age	0.002	2.598	0.000	0.375	0.000	−0.347
Fammem	0.011	1.345	−0.001	−0.101	−0.008	−0.966
Religious	−0.016	−0.497	0.047	1.451	0.013	0.398
Income 1	0.004	0.132	−0.012	−0.365	−0.037	−1.182
Income 2	−0.052	−1.775	−0.064	−2.129	−0.003	−0.098
Income 3	0.039	1.371	−0.055	−1.851	−0.019	−0.658
Educ 1	0.112	2.473	0.092	1.978	0.149	3.244
Educ 2	0.132	3.368	0.136	3.369	0.098	2.47
Educ 3	0.058	1.406	0.107	2.53	0.128	3.075
Concern 1	−0.104	−3.374	−0.094	−2.963	0.007	0.238
Cooper	0.026	1.797	0.052	3.529	0.021	1.438
Political	−0.011	−3.109	−0.003	−0.977	−0.002	−0.713
Intercept	0.431	6.898	0.210	3.583	−0.107	−1.673
R−Squared	0.020		0.017		0.033	
F(27,16308)	12.46		9.86		19.26	

	Genetical modification of animals		Genetic modification for transaplats		Genetic testing for inherited diseases	
	Coef.	t	Coef.	t	Coef.	t
Gender	−0.070	−3.172	−0.084	−3.895	−0.012	−0.564
Age	−0.002	−2.376	−0.002	−2.145	−0.002	−3.087
Fammem	−0.009	−0.986	0.003	0.327	−0.025	−2.958
Religious	0.098	2.89	0.089	2.679	0.042	1.29
Income 1	0.015	0.452	0.009	0.285	−0.015	−0.463
Income 2	−0.040	−1.274	−0.010	−0.338	0.004	0.13
Income 3	0.006	0.195	0.039	1.297	0.042	1.43
Educ 1	0.018	0.377	0.059	1.252	0.161	3.45
Educ 2	0.057	1.373	0.077	1.872	0.091	2.27
Educ 3	0.094	2.141	0.088	2.052	0.070	1.657
Conern 1	−0.015	−0.458	−0.104	−3.229	0.019	0.615
Cooper	−0.016	−1.043	−0.024	−1.57	0.059	3.983
Political	−0.001	−0.354	−0.001	−0.28	−0.005	−1.547
Intercept	0.312	4.683	0.400	5.997	−0.089	−1.358
R-Squared	0.017		0.022		0.044	
F(27,16308)	9.75		12.72		25.86	

in the development of informational campaigns and the setting up of regulations to ensure safety. This implies offering the consumer the amount of information needed. Providing information on risks combined with individual lack of knowledge and experience with the biotechnology application might have influenced perceptions of risk.

This study is limited by the database used. In particular, it does not account for the impact of relevant variables that could be interesting to test e.g., the influence of information acquisition, the role of differences in knowledge and the dynamic effects

Table 11
Regression results for Biotech risk perceptions (adjusted by country variation) 1999

	Food Biotech		Gene transfer into crops		Gene transfer for medicines	
	Coef.	t	Coef.	t	Coef.	t
Gender	−0.110	−5.712	−0.060	−3.044	−0.027	−1.409
Age	0.014	1.913	0.022	3.055	0.013	1.894
Fammem	0.007	0.836	0.009	1.05	0.006	0.757
Religious	0.059	1.955	0.089	2.902	0.108	3.591
Income 1	−0.053	−1.781	0.021	0.683	0.040	1.358
Income 2	−0.030	−1.088	−0.023	−0.826	0.000	−0.015
Income 3	0.019	0.662	0.008	0.273	0.008	0.296
Educ 1	0.081	1.878	0.007	0.157	0.022	0.513
Educ 2	0.106	2.863	−0.009	−0.245	0.022	0.608
Educ 3	0.095	2.447	0.019	0.483	0.056	1.462
Conern 1	−0.078	−2.953	−0.098	−3.641	−0.076	−2.886
Cooper	−0.036	−2.742	−0.009	−0.691	0.031	2.347
Political	−0.005	−1.591	−0.006	−1.982	−0.004	−1.305
Intercept	0.726	10.706	0.573	8.312	0.346	5.145
R-Squared	0.044		0.046		0.039	
F(27,16308)	23.78		25.17		20.87	
	Genetical modification of animals		**Genetic modification for transaplats**		**Genetic testing for inherited diseases**	
	Coef.	t	Coef.	t	Coef.	t
Gender	−0.080	−4.051	−0.061	−3.149	0.002	0.106
Age	−0.001	−0.154	−0.020	−2.787	−0.013	−1.737
Fammem	0.005	0.628	0.010	1.259	0.012	1.412
Religious	0.069	2.229	0.104	3.418	0.093	2.923
Income 1	0.006	0.209	−0.012	−0.405	0.086	2.78
Income 2	−0.066	−2.353	−0.015	−0.533	0.021	0.714
Income 3	0.009	0.33	0.031	1.112	0.003	0.116
Educ 1	0.110	2.499	−0.012	−0.268	0.128	2.836
Educ 2	0.118	3.141	0.028	0.767	0.105	2.696
Educ 3	0.122	3.079	0.062	1.601	0.023	0.563
Conern 1	−0.131	−4.865	−0.058	−2.162	−0.044	−1.603
Cooper	0.010	0.714	0.016	1.168	0.033	2.4
Political	−0.005	−1.596	−0.005	−1.58	−0.007	−2.183
Intercept	0.594	8.579	0.492	7.239	0.164	2.298
R-Squared	0.026		0.03			0.04
F(27,16308)	13.99		16.1			23.66

that result from new information acquisition.

References

[1] C.M. Bruhn, Consumer concerns and educational strategies: focus on biotechnology, *Food Technol* **46**(3) (1992), 80–102.

[2] M. Cantley, T.H. Hoban and A. Sasson, Regulations and consumer attitudes toward biotechnology, *Nature biotechnology* **17** (1999), 3738.

[3] J. Costa and E. Mossialos, *Rational ignorance vs rational irrationality,* Perceptions of biotechnology products. LSE Health Social Care working paper (forthcoming), 2001.
[4] J. Costa and E. Mossialos, *Perceptions of biotechnology risks under an ambiguous environment,* Submitted for publication, 2002.
[5] P.K. Couchaman and K. Fink-Jensen, *Public Attitudes to Genetic Engineering in New Zeland,* DSIR Crop Research Report 138. Department of Scientific and Industrial Research, Chiristchurch, 1990.
[6] Food and Drug Administration, Statement of policy: foods derived from new plant varieties, *Federal Register* **57** (29 May 1992), 22984–23005.
[7] P. Frati, Theseus and the Labyrinth-Minotaur's syndrome, *Forum (Genova)* **9** (Jul–Dec 1999), 99–105.
[8] G. Gaskell, Europe ambivalent on biotechnology, *Nature* **387** (1997), 845–847.
[9] C.H. Gollier, Should we beware of the precautionary principle? *Economic Policy* (2001), 303–327.
[10] G. Gaskell, M. Bauer, J. Durant and N. Allum, Worlds Apart? The Reception of Genetically Modified Foods in Europe and the US, *Science* **285** (1999), 384387.
[11] P. Slovic, *The perception of Risk,* Earthscan, London, 2000.
[12] S. Harlander, Food biotechnology: yesterday, today, and tomorrow, *Food Technology* **43**(9) (1989), 196–206.
[13] T.J. Hoban and P.A. Kendall, Consumer Attitudes About Food Biotechnology. Project Report 1993, North Carolina State University and Colorado State University, Raleigh, NC, 1993, pp. 1–36.
[14] J. Hoban, Trends in consumer attitudes about biotechnology, *J. Food Distrib. Res* **27** (1996), 1–10.
[15] J. Hoban, Consumer acceptance of biotechnology: an international perspective, *Nature biotechnology* **15** (1997), 232–234.
[16] D.R. Macer, S. Akiyama, A.T. Alora, Y. Asada, J. Azariah, H. Azariah, M.V. Boost, P. Chatwachirawong, Y. Kato and V. Kaushik et al., International perceptions and approval of gene therapy, *Hum Gene Ther* **6**(6) (June 1995), 791–803.
[17] D. Macer, Perception of risks and benefits of *in vitro* fertilisation, genetic engineering and biotechnology, *Social Science and Medicine* **38** (1994), 23–33.
[18] D. Macer, Public acceptance and risks of biotechnology, in Quality of Risk Assessment in Biotechnology (International Centre for Human and Public Affairs, Tilburg, The Netherlands), 1996, pp. 227–246.
[19] J.C. Polkinghorne, Ethical issues in biotechnology, *Trends Biotechnol* **18**(1) (Jan 2000), 8–10.
[20] I. Rabino, Societal and commercial issues affecting the future of biotechnology in the United States: a survey of researchers' perceptions, *Naturwissenschaften* **85**(3) (March 1998), 109–116.
[21] M. Siegler, Ethical aspects of biotechnology applications, *Forum (Genova)* **93**(3) (Jul–Dec 1999), 106–112.
[22] S. Gottlieb, In vitro fertilisation is preferable to fertility drugs, *BMJ* **321** (2000), 134.

Pharmaceuticals Policy and Law 5 (2002) 185–190
IOS Press

Discussion and conclusions

This workshop occurred at a crucial time for the future of the pharmaceutical industry, when issues such as patent, intellectual property rights, compulsory licensing, generic competition and access to cheap medicines or other related sensitive topics moved more and more to the global scene. This has moved the dialogue from the traditional industry stakeholders and industrial/health national agencies to other key players, countries such as India, Brazil or China and other stakeholders such as NGO's and International Organizations (e.g. WTO, World Bank, WHO, PAHO, ASEAN). Access (or lack of it) to affordable good quality drug therapies for diseases such as HIV is a good example of the imbalance of access to medicines for individuals in rich and poor countries: "the availability of new antiretrovirals in the United States lead to a decrease of the age-adjusted death rate by 48% from 1996 to 1997", but 95% of individuals worldwide infected with HIV live in poor countries" (cited by Reich [4] from Fauci's findings [2]).

The objective of the workshop was to discuss a number of contributions related to globalization. Even if all papers presented did not directly address the impact of globalization, they brought better understanding of the high level of interdependence between the interests of different players. A major current topic in European circles concerned with pharmaceutical policy is to facilitate the access to cheaper medicines (increased generic competition) and to prioritize the solidarity principle (between Eastern and Western Europe and from well-insured populations to populations with poor health insurance systems). This priority setting can potentially damage the development of science in the field and innovation in Europe. According to the Italian report to the European Commission [3], European countries typically become licensees (developers) while "US firms act more frequently as licensors (originators)". However "strong success stories in some European countries exist in particular in the UK, Denmark, Sweden or Ireland". The relative decline of European competitiveness and the degradation of innovative performance is highly debated in high level groups; it raises a serious challenge for this business in Europe, with a global increase of highly competitive centers other than the US around the world, such as Taiwan, India and Canada.

The question of access to cheap medicines dominates the debate on drug policies in developed countries. On the contrary, in Europe as in the US, it is also the access to high-tech products and diagnostics and paying for quality of care in an equitable way between generations. Consumer voices however remain quite limited on the European scene, in contrast to the US scene; and therefore, there is a need to bring more evidence on the impact of pharmaceutical policies in the context of globalization, not only to traditional policy-makers and decision-makers, but also to different types of communities, for instance those exposed to different levels of risks from disease.

This workshop was a platform between academics but a few industry players, a representative from an NGO (Médecins Sans Frontières), a World Bank advisor and a trade policy-maker from the European Commission were also present. We will highlight here some of the major conclusions that can be drawn from the workshop in four areas: issues on the industry dynamics, on convergence, on pharmaceutical distribution, on payment and demand.

1. Emerging paradigms in the industry dynamics

Traditional industry analysis does not really suit the analysis of the pharmaceutical and biopharmaceutical sectors. In particular, the complexity of business models represents a big challenge for researchers trying to understand trends in research productivity, economic and financial performance and the sustainability of the current industry structure. The Finnish contributors (Brannback, Renko) and the Schweizer paper in particular confirmed the emergence of new paradigms to analyze the life-science industry, where pharmaceutical and biotech firms from Western countries are now increasingly challenged by newcomers. In particular, technological paradigm shifts were discussed such as the introduction of core products based on Monoclonal Antibody Technologies (MABS) by Drug Discovery Companies (DDC) that can be used to treat diseases from cancer to cardiovascular diseases or the new organizational forms of the drug supply, with the description of agile manufacturing systems. Moreover, capabilities required for establishing competitive advantage in the field need to combine very diverse scientific knowledge from chemistry, genomics, biotechnology and therefore may require cross-sectoral policies. Life-science was also described as an hybrid domain, whose future heavily depends on successful innovation not only from pharmacy or biosciences, but also from food science. Strategic moves towards functional food and the convergence of the pharmaceutical and the food industry were in particular discussed, based on the contribution from Brannback, De Heer and Wiklund. Functional food (nutraceuticals in the US terminology) are forecasted as "25% of all food products worldwide, in the coming decade, which means a total world market of at least US Dollars 300–700 billions", according to UBIC source (Sept. 2000).

Other forms of industry organization described during the workshop were the Pharmaclusters and virtual networks, whose locations are completely changing traditional geographical boundaries. Brannback et al.'s paper presented the strengths and weaknesses of the Finnish pharmacluster. In particular, it highlighted the strong links between university and business, but also some weaknesses such as control of financial support, size, business skills and educated labor force, and marketing know-how. The case study illustrated the strategic importance of organizations such as Contract Research Organizations (CROs); Drug Discovery Companies (DDCs) and business tools companies, in addition to university and established industrial players.

2. Convergence and political divergence

Two papers in the workshop discussed concepts of convergence and divergence. The Godet and Ferrand Nagel paper analysed the convergence of standards in the European scene with the completion of the single market. It mainly referred to technical harmonization (e.g. marketing approval, rational use, and patent), demonstrated the major divergence of political systems and discussed conceptual analysis of the convergence of medicine policies in Europe. The Cruz et de la Fuente Sabate paper provided a contribution proposing a new regulatory framework of transaction cost politics, based on the New Institutional Economics (from both public interest and capture theories). It compared the regulatory structure of Spain and the USA and concluded that despite the significant divergence of the two structures in term of flexibility, the increase of flexibility in the case of the USA lead to an increase of satisfaction of patients and pharmaceutical companies; however, the two countries showed many similarities in Spanish and US regulators' mode of action.

The convergence paradigm is a major research domain, in the context of the construction of European institutions and the debate about power redistribution between European, state or regional levels. This debate is very politically sensitive and dominated by major pressure groups.

Further research could in particular investigate how an increased role of science in the policymaking process might or might not, in the context of European countries, mediate some tensions, in particular to facilitate the distribution of power between different levels. Atik, working in the American scene seems to provide such an argument. However, in Europe, decisions are strongly influenced by lobbying groups and ideologies and shared values concerning health systems models. According to Atik: "Science-based discipline creates premises for the maintenance of national prerogatives" [1]. He argues that such premises can be particularly useful in balancing the globalization of regulatory power and that science can be a way to depoliticize international dispute.

In the pharmaceutical industry, the increased influence of science in decision making usually refers to an increasing role of evidence based medicine and economic evaluation (outcome research) in policy decision-making, especially in areas like pricing and reimbursement. However, if some European countries, such as the UK, Sweden or Holland, are already very driven by evidence-based medicine, other countries are still very reluctant to introduce scientific evidence in their political decision-making process.

Moreover, European markets, especially with the enlargement process, face increasing corruption, especially in critical areas such as the Balkans or certain PECO countries and this can largely limit the possible implementation of more scientifically driven policy-making decisions. The fight against corruption in the pharmaceutical sector has become, at the eve of the 21st century, a major priority of international agencies. During the workshop, a roundtable was organized and corruption was seen as a priority for a research agenda in Europe. For instance in the area of drug safety, corruption combined with globalization increase risks of unethical business practices or disruptions in drug supply chains (e.g. packaging).

3. Distribution and demand issues

Two papers presented during the workshop addressed pharmaceutical marketing issues. The Chansarkar paper discussed the interplay between prescription charge policy and pharmacists' role in the UK context. Even if the methodology did not provide clear scientific evidence, it presented some arguments on potential forms of collusion between the pharmacy profession and government for non-exempted patients. This lead in particular to changes in the respective roles of physicians and pharmacists, towards a transfer of responsibility from GPs to pharmacists, for a certain range of illnesses. The increase of the prescription charge facilitates the switch to OTC medications and this deregulation of the market can favor pharmacists interests.

The relevant shortage of physicians can explain in the UK the increased role of other providers such as pharmacists and nurses. However, if further research can confirm the preliminary findings from the paper presented during the workshop, it might lead to an increased fragmentation of health care providers and a reduced legitimacy of their representative bodies.

A second contribution from industry from Harms et al, provided an example of how innovation cost dramatically increased, in the case of some new drugs launched on reduced segments of the German market, with faster duplication of knowledge, very high marketing cost with traditional communication strategy towards physicians. These industry contributors present the start of the 21st century as a "time of upheaval for pharmaceutical marketing" with in particular, shifts of innovation locus towards innovative marketing. They introduce the New 3 P's of marketing and Direct to Consumer (DTC): Positioning, Politics, and Patients, to replace the traditional 4 P's used in marketing. During the workshop, it was emphasized that companies need to propose constructive solutions. If the first P, positioning is already well covered by traditional marketing management, the two other P's were largely discussed during the workshop. Companies' representatives, present at the workshop, agreed that they had to integrate the changing political scene and offer new product understanding, including social and political plans. The direct approach to patients was also discussed. Direct to consumer advertising is very controversial, especially in the area of health care and pharmaceuticals. However, most participants agreed that in different ways, patients and citizens need to be made more aware of limited resources and of reasonable use of health care services. This would also to ensure that the issue of health services is for the best patient interest (and not only for very influential pressure groups at a certain state of medical knowledge). The workshop also concentrated on the issue of how to implement 'three P's' marketing strategies. Companies made a number of proposals, which lead to a brainstorming exchange with academics during the workshop. The following ideas were then suggested: more innovation on market research, better management control of complexity, advanced forms of partnerships for problem-solving in different areas of health care, more education, more sophisticated communication strategies required by changing health care systems and a changing environment. The complexity control in particular raised serious concern, especially from industry stakeholders. For instance, in order to reduce and better control complexity, there is a trend towards more centralization (e.g. configuration of R&D centers and their relocation closer to headquarters). Innovation needs to be measured and managed. Such moves may limit productivity or efficiency of research and risk-taking behaviors from big players in the pharmaceutical industry. This may lead to a strong desire to reduce uncertainty. On the other hand, more and more major monopsonistic governmental agencies in Europe request value for money, but with stronger budget constraints, fostered by monetary union rules. Certain categories of patients are increasingly empowered with access to very reliable sources of information on the state of medical knowledge in the world, and they are challenging the power of health care professionals and traditional classifications of health care services.

4. Reimbursement systems and patients' perspective

The final research theme for the workshop concerned payment for medicines in Europe and patients' perspective. Pricing and reimbursement has always been a very sensitive topic for Western European countries and numerous regulations and cost containment measures exist to regulate drug systems. The two papers aimed to address some specific tools targeted at patients.

The first paper by Huttin was a preliminary report based on French findings from the European Biomed/ENDEP project on prescription charges and patient decision making. Cost shifting is a major cost containment strategy used in France. This strategy is not especially visible to French consumers, since supplementary voluntary or private insurers usually top up the proportion covered by the national sickness funds for drug coverage. Moreover, insurers are usually 'blind' payers and have so far mainly followed the policy orientations decided by the Ministry of Health. However, the gradual decrease of public sickness funding mainly in the coverage of some primary care services (such as physicians, some medicines and dental care) has increased the pressure on supplemental insurers. Some of them have responded by increases of premiums and some patient face affordability issues in this traditionally well-protected population. The paper presented the findings of patients' focus groups run in France. This method was used to explore whether and how cost of medicines, and especially copayment, influence patients' behaviors. It showed that drug choices were affected mainly with respect to timing of prescriptions, number of packs and ways to pay drugs (liquidity issues). However, the impact of cost on drug choices appears quite limited and mainly affects choice of providers in the case of an acute condition such as hay fever. In contrast to other European countries involved in the project, the key trade-off choices were more between regularly paying ‘out of pocket’ for medications versus paying additional insurance premiums. Price and drug coverage were quite well known by patients with chronic conditions such as hypertension but only known by cost conscious patients in the case of hay fever. Such focus groups findings were used to design patient surveys in six countries. The main findings of these surveys will be provided in the ENDEP book (under preparation, from IOS press).

Costa and Mossialos brought an important contribution, in their paper on the current changes affecting life science and public opinion’s risk perceptions of scientific progress. They identified a widening gap in Europe between science discovery and people’s knowledge. The paper is mainly based on the European barometer surveys conducted on 16000 people in 15 European Union Member States. The surveys mainly cover products artificially modified by science (such as GMO’s). The authors compare results from the 1996 and 1999 surveys to analyze potential shifts in risk perceptions. They showed a significant reduction in Europe in the public acceptance for biotechnology.

Such reduction could be taken as a warning against potential misuse of science, since the postwar period in Europe and the trauma from Eugenism have slowed down research and interest for genetically modified organisms. This is quite different from the North American scene, which is much more driven by science not only within the business, financial and academic communities but also within several consumer groups who are very informed about the development of sciences.

The series of appendices provided with this special issue also complements the inputs and discussions from this workshop, which was particularly important at a crucial time of reshuffling different powers on the global scene. In particular appendix 4 summarizes the main points from a roundtable, which took place for the first time during this series of workshops, in order to set priorities for a research agenda. Appendix 3 provides a summary of the contribution of the Trade department of the European Commission, updated with recent positions on major trade issues concerning the biopharmaceutical industry.

References

[1] J. Atik, Science and International regulatory convergence, *Northwestern Journal of International Law and Business* **17** (1996–1997), 736–758.

[2] A.S. Fauci, *N. Engl. J. Med.* **341** (1999), 1046.

[3] A. Gambardella, L. Orsenigo and F. Pammolli, Global competitiveness in pharmaceuticals, A European perspective. Report prepared for the Directorate General Enterprise of the European Commission, November 2000.

[4] M. Reich, The Global drug gap, *Science* **287** (17 March 2000), 1979–1981.

Appendices

Pharmaceuticals Policy and Law 5 (2002) 193–195
IOS Press

Appendix 1

Programme of the 5th workshop on challenges for pharmaceutical policies in the 21st century, Brussels, Belgium, 18–19 January, 2001

Thursday January 18 (a.m)

Introduction to the Workshop
Christine HUTTIN

Industry Dynamics

Technology, Market, Structure and Intellectual Property Rights: Evidence from the Pharmaceutical Industry
Manuel FERNANDEZ-BÄGUES
Moderator: Aart Jan DE HEER

Technology and Strategic Change in the Finnish Pharmaceutical Industry: the Emergence of a Cluster
Malin BRANNBACK & Maija RENKO

Competition & Regulation in the Pharmaceutical Industry: An Experimental Analysis of the Impact of Regulation on Competition Between Generic and Branded Drugs
Laura FERRARI BRAVO & Luigi LUINI
Moderator: Nicky SHAW

Thursday January 18 (p.m)

Political approaches

Product Piracy: the Sale of Counterfeit Pharmaceuticals in Developing Countries
Kristina LYBECKER
Moderator: Christine HUTTIN

Convergence of Pharmaceutical Policies Through heterogeneous social welfare ideologies.
A Political Positive Approach
Natalie MARTIN CRUZ & Juan Manuel DE LA FUENTE SABATE

Medicines in Europe: Scientific Convergence and Political Divergence.
Virginie GODET & Sabine FERRAND-NAGEL

Presentation of Commission's Experts: *Trade Policy Issues in Biopharmaceuticals*

Distribution and Demand

Pharmacists & Governmental Medicine Policy
Bhalchandra A.CHANSARKAR

Changes in the Pharmaceutical Marketing & Selling Direct to Consumer (DTC) or the New P's of Marketing
Fred HARMS, M. HEINRICH, S. ROHMANN, M. DRUENER & V. TROMMS-DORFF

Friday, January 19, (a.m)

Round-table/Panel Discussion

Globalization in Biopharmaceuticals
Joan ROVIRA, Kristina LYBECKER – Christine HUTTIN

Payment and Demand

Demand for Pharmaceuticals under co-payment Schemes: Evidence from Catalonia
Joan COSTA, Joan ROVIRA & Panos KANAVOS

BIOMED – Project on the impact of copayment on physician and patient decision making processes.
Christine HUTTIN

Acceptance of Biotechnology Products and Risk Perceptions in the European Union.
Joan COSTA & Elias MOSSIALOS

Friday, January 19 (p.m.)

Company Orientated Papers

The Key Success Factors for M&A and Post Merger Integration Activities in the Biotechnological and Pharmaceutical Industry
Lars SCHWEIZER

A Competing Edge for the Pharmaceutical Industry: Propagating Agile Processes Throughout the Supply Chain
Nicky SHAW & T. BURGESS

The Dynamics of Global and Local - Organizational Dilemmas and Struggles in a Pharmaceutical Company.
Stefan SVENINGSSON

The Convergence of the Pharmaceutical & the Food Industry Through Functional Food: Strategic Change and Business Opportunity or an Illusion ?
Malin BRANNBACK, Aart Jan DE HEER & Patricia WIKLUND

General Discussion and Closure of the Workshop

Pharmaceuticals Policy and Law 5 (2002) 197–209
IOS Press

Appendix 2 – Abstracts and short papers

Technology, market structure and intellectual property rights: Evidence from the pharmaceutical industry

Manuel Fernàndez-Bagüés
Universitat Ponpeu Fabra, Barcelona, Spain
E-mail: fernanma@upf.es

This paper looks at the role of intellectual property rights in determining the relationship between market structure and R&D intensity. Empirical evidence has for a long time provided mixed results about this relationship. Sutton's work in "Technology and Market Structure" (1998) presented a seminal contribution in the field. His theory suggests that whether concentration is high in R&D intensive industries essentially depends on the substitutability of products associated with different technologies. If substitutability is high then an increase in the effectiveness of R&D increases the lower bound to concentration; otherwise concentration may stay low.

We argue that in those industries where knowledge can be securely transferable this relationship is not robust. Furthermore we present empirical evidence from the pharmaceutical industry that supports our hypothesis.

Keywords: Market structure, technology, intellectual property rights, outsourcing, pharmaceutical industry

Introduction

The empirical evidence has for a long time provided mixed results about the relationship between R&D intensity and the degree of concentration of an industry. This is not surprising if some non-observable factor is affecting this relationship. Furthermore, if the true relationship is given by a bound approach, standard regressions may be misleading. John Sutton's work (1998) represents a seminal contribution in the field. His "lower bound" approach eschews detailed and sensitive game-theoretic results, but generates a few key robust and testable predictions from the theory of strategic behaviour, which exclude pathological cases but include a wide range of industry structures compatible with minimal assumptions about the rational behaviour of member firms.

This bound approach suggests that whether concentration is high in an R&D intensive industry essentially depends on the substitutability of products associated with different technologies. If substitutability is high, then R&D intensive industries must show high concentration.[1] Through a cross sectional study, Sutton obtained

[1]Because of the nature of the bound approach, if substitutability is low we cannot make any prediction

very robust results consistent with his theory [for some criticisms on Sutton's theory see Scherer (2000)].

Sutton's theoretical framework implicitly assumes that the different activities of the firm, such as research & development or marketing, can not be outsourced or cooperated. By relaxing this assumption[2] in Sutton's model, we show that the lower bound relationship between concentration and endogenous sunk cost is not robust. Consequently, our model predicts that a different relationship may be observed in those industries where property rights are strong, such that cooperating or outsourcing in R&D and marketing are possible.

For a series of manufacturing industries intensive in R&D, we show cross-industry evidence that supports our hypothesis. In those industries where property rights are strong, the lower bound relationship between concentration and R&D intensity is not robust.

By taking into account property right these results complement earlier cross-section econometric work on the relationship between market structure and concentration [Sutton (1991, 1998), Lyons and Matraves (1996), Robinson and Chiang (1996)].

While the results reported are consistent with our theory, it is natural to ask whether the patterns we find in the data might not perhaps be driven by some quite different mechanism than the one proposed. Little can be done to address this issue by means of further statistical analysis. A more helpful line of inquiry lies in asking whether there is any direct evidence for the operation of the mechanism that, according to our theory, drives this pattern in the data.

It is this idea that leads us to the examination of the pharmaceutical industry. By focusing in an individual industry we are able to better study how exogenous structural changes feed into the competitive process, and how this is affected by the possibility of cooperating or outsourcing. A second motivation for studying in detail this industry relates to the limitations of the Sutton's standard theory to explain its market structure.

Sutton pointed out the particular and fascinating characteristic of the competitive processes of the pharmaceutical industry, which although being highly intensive in R&D and marketing, still showed a relatively low concentration rate. He suggested that this peculiarity was due to the nature of pharmaceuticals R&D technology. In Sutton's original framework the R&D technology is represented by a series of different technologic trajectories, in which early innovators enjoy some advantage in introducing later products within the same family of products. This favours what he denominated the escalation mechanism, which, under certain circumstances, induced an increase in market concentration if a certain kind of exogenous shock (such as an increase in the R&D effectivity) disturbed the set of equilibrium configurations.

---

about the degree of concentration.

[2]Gruber (2000) studied a different variation of Sutton's theory by taking into account the role of product standards.

He argues that this is not the case in the pharmaceutical industry. Pharmaceutical firms focus on a wide range of technologies that moreover are weakly linked among them, both in the supply side and the demand side. Furthermore these technological paths do not constitute technological trajectories in its proper meaning. This is, early innovators along a certain technological path are not more likely to make the next successfully better product, or in other words, early innovators do not enjoy a significant first mover advantage. According to Sutton these characteristics of the R&D process made the payoff obtained by a firm that spent more that any of its rivals on R&D much lower, and therefore allowed concentration in the industry to remain low.[3]

In order to examine whether the pharmaceutical R&D paths, which Sutton identifies as the chemically related groups (CRG), could be interpreted R&D trajectories, Sutton studied the entries and exits in the group of the top 50 selling drugs for the years 1960, 1973 and 1986. Sutton finds that out of the 26 cases where there is a new bestseller drug in a chemical related group[4] only in 7 of cases the innovative firm had already a top 50 drug in that (chemically related) group in the preceding reference year. This is, only in 7 out of 26 cases the new entries can be classified as a follow-on discovery where the pioneer firm seems to have some lead in discovering a chemically related drug.

Other authors have also paid attention to the relationship between market structure and R&D intensity in the pharmaceutical industry. Particularly Matraves (1999) boards the topic and tests whether the industry changes in the late 80s and the early 90s were consistent with Sutton's predictions. Using aggregated concentration data, she finds that although the industry is becoming more consolidated, the leading firms still have a very little share of the market. Following Sutton's line, she argues that the cause of the industry's relative little fragmentation is in the nature of its R&D technology, which induces a proliferation mechanism rather than an escalation mechanism.

In contradiction with these previous studies [Matraves (1999), Sutton (1998)], we offer new evidence that points out that this description of the RAD process in the pharmaceutical industry is not valid anymore. Looking at the worldwide bestseller drugs in 1999 and comparing them to the 1986 top 50 bestseller drugs, we find that in those CRG where there is a change in the sales leadership, 8 out of 10 cases are follow-on discoveries by the pioneer firm.

In fact, this is not surprising given the dramatic changes, both qualitatively and quantitatively, that the pharmaceutical R&D technology went through in the 80s

[3] Still, he explains, two key features of the industry put smaller firms at a disadvantage. The first relates to the marketing side, where in order to exploit discoveries, a minimum scale of effort is needed. The second relates to the portfolio effect which makes small and medium-sized research-oriented companies vulnerable to takeover.

[4] Sutton only looks at entries for those groups where there was already a drug among the top 50 bestsellers.

and in the 90s. In qualitative terms, it switched from a chemical to a biological basis. The chemical approach hinged upon scale: discovery of new compounds stemmed from systematic assays of many molecules in laboratory and clinical tests to find a few promising candidates. The biological approach hinges upon rational understanding of the function of the human body and the action of drugs. Researchers can make more informed choices about the entities to be tested. While scale is still important for testing molecules and for clinical trials, drug research now requires solid understanding of molecular actions and pathologies. Therefore, according to Sutton's standard model, this technology change should have produced a great increase in concentration.

But on the other hand, all these changes also made it much easier to specify and communicate technological know-how. Patents have been always very important in the pharmaceutical industry. But further on, the rise of polymer chemistry, advances in chemical engineering and the advent of recombinant DNA technology have made it much easier to specify and communicate technological know-how in this industry than it used to be, or currently is in a number of other industries. Pharmaceutical patents can be made very strong. Moreover, since a slight change in the underlying gene sequence of a protein can result in very different functions, it is very difficult, for example, to invent around a patent on a drug. It is also possible to patent particular molecules, building blocks for innovations (such as enzymes, proteins, and hormones), and any delivery system.

Sutton had suggested that in response to an exogenous shock that raised the returns to innovation, an escalation process would follow on in which firms financed their increase in R&D expenditure through internal growth or through a process of mergers and acquisitions. However his model does not consider that whenever property rights are strong enough, firms may also obtain technology (or other assets) through joint ventures, alliances, co-marketing agreements or licensing.

To study the relationship between firms' growth and strategic alliances we use data on joint ventures and alliances from the Strategic Alliance database of the Securities Data Corporation (SDC), and data on m&a from the Mergers & Acquisitions SDC database. The sample universe for our analysis is all m&a and jv&a in the pharmaceutical industry worldwide between 1990 and 1997. SDC obtains information from publicly available sources, including SEC filing, trade publications and international counterparts, and news and wire sources. The data clearly do not track all the deals consummated over the period, due to inadequate corporate reporting requirements. However, since this database is probably the most comprehensive database on such deals, it is ideal for empirical analysis. On the other hand, for the firm financial data we use Standard & Poor's Compustat database and firms' annual reports.

By studying the joint ventures and alliances activities together with the mergers and acquisitions, our study complements previous empirical studies on acquisition activity in high technology industries and its relationship to the R&D process [Granstrand and Sjölander (1990), Hall (1990), Blonigen and Taylor (2000)] or on the relationship between joint venture activity and R&D [Friedman et al. (1979)].

Our empirical results suggest that the greater the involvement of firms in joint ventures and alliances activities, the lower their use of mergers and acquisitions in order to acquire innovation or technology, and therefore the lower the increase in market concentration.

Competition and regulation in the pharmaceutical industry: An experimental analysis of the impact of regulation on competition between generic and branded drugs

Laura Ferrari Bravo[a] and Luigi Luini[b]
[a] *University of Roma, Italy*
E-mail: lfbravo@ats.it
[b] *University of Siena, Italy*
E-mail: Luini@unisi.it

Abstract

Much of the public debate about pharmaceuticals over the past years has focused on prices. From a market intervention perspective, this has lead to the proliferation of a great variety of government regulations,[5] all of which aim at facing the conflicting policy targets of granting drug fruition to all citizens and containing/controlling public health expenditure.

However, policies designed to improve the efficiency of the pharmaceutical market have to take account of its features in terms of industry characteristics and rigidity of demand. Indeed, in the pharmaceutical market regulatory, contractual and financial mechanisms influence price formation and the information flow, while determining – at the same time – different relationships between economic agents along the chain consumer-decision-maker-payer. The paper aims at comparing within an experimental framework the impact of different government regulatory intervention over competition between generic and branded drugs.

[5] E.g. price control systems, profit caps, fixed price margins etc. For a review of regulations in the pharmaceutical industry see Jacobzone (2000).

Product piracy: The sale of counterfeit pharmaceuticals in developing countries

Kristina M. Lybecker
Department of Economics & International Business, Drexel University, 3141 Chestnut Street, Philadelphia, Pennsylvania 19104, USA

Abstract

Developing countries are awash in counterfeit pharmaceuticals and despite historically unprecedented protection for intellectual property rights, the problem is getting worse. The current ease of counterfeiting is unparalleled and enforcement officials describe pharmaceutical counterfeiting to be "... as lucrative as pushing heroin, ... about as hard as photocopying, ... (and) low on law enforcement's agenda".

Why are counterfeit pharmaceuticals more prevalent, when patent protection for ethical drugs is stronger than ever before? This paper presents an explanation by modelling a local pharmacist who responds to the intellectual property rights (IPR) regime governing the market for pharmaceuticals. The analysis explores the impact of the policy environment on the welfare of the consumer, the price of pharmaceuticals, and the composition of the market, and illustrates the importance of coordinating increases in both intellectual property rights and local enforcement. The model predicts that stronger intellectual property protection without increased enforcement (a common pattern in developing countries) will result in the elimination of the domestic generic industry (a producer of efficacious drugs) but will fail to root out the counterfeiters. The elimination of a secondary source for pharmaceuticals reduces competition and increases prices and profits, enhancing the temptations of counterfeiting.

Pharmaceutical counterfeiting is a problem that reaches beyond patent and trademark infringement to threaten both human lives and industry profits. Health concerns obviously motivate the discussion of counterfeit drugs. The consequences of the availability of spurious products in the market for pharmaceuticals can be death, [6] prolonged illness, a loss of confidence in the system of western medicine and drug resistant viruses. At the same time, companies risk losing sales and profits when consumers purchase infringing and counterfeit products. These firms also face the harmful reputational effects of counterfeit products.

[6] Medical experts have a difficult time agreeing "... on how many deaths are caused by fake drugs, although most acknowledge that World Health Organization statistics showing more than 500 fatalities caused by contaminated cough syrup over the past 15 years only scratch the surface of the problem" (Hajari 1998, p. 265).

At the national level, counterfeit drugs are only one aspect of the larger problem of intellectual property (IP) rights infringement. Given that intellectual property comprises a growing percentage of world output, IP protection has become an important element of international trade agreements, and many trade issues are linked to such protection. As a result, the problem of counterfeit drugs is primarily approached on the international stage, through multilateral trade negotiations. Facing the threat of trade sanctions, many developing countries adopt legislation guaranteeing stronger intellectual property laws. However, these countries often lack the resources or incentives to enforce the newly passed legislation. The result is an increase in IP protection without effective enforcement, a combination that may exacerbate, rather than solve, existing problems. Infringing generic pharmaceuticals are eliminated following the passage of strong IP legislation, but the production of counterfeit drugs increases without heightened enforcement.

This piece contributes to the body of work on intellectual property rights, as well as the sparse economic literature on counterfeiting. The existing literature on intellectual property protection has primarily focused upon the welfare consequences of increasing IP protection, examining the *ex ante* and *ex post* situations, and describing the potential effects of the introduction of patent protection for pharmaceuticals. While they may accurately describe the eventual outcomes, these papers fail to consider the process of transition, the gradual steps that nations must take to arrive at a regime of strong intellectual property rights protection. This work seeks to fill that gap, analysing an interim equilibrium by detailing the gradual process of conversion and the associated welfare effects.

This paper also contributes to the literature on counterfeit products. The two primary works in this area cover deceptive and non-deceptive counterfeiting. Grossman and Shapiro (1988b) analyse the positive and normative effects of non-deceptive counterfeiting, examining markets for status goods. Alternatively, Grossman and Shapiro (1988a) model a market in which domestic firms, which own trademarks and develop reputations for high-quality products, compete with foreign firms, which export legitimate low-quality goods and counterfeit copies of high-quality domestic products. These articles provide a complete treatment of the positive and normative effects of both deceptive and non-deceptive counterfeiting.

They do not, however, examine the changes that take place in the market for counterfeits as a country moves from a regime of weak intellectual property rights, to one of strong intellectual property rights protection. The interim equilibrium is considered here, examining the forces at work in the market for counterfeits, and the changes that occur in the market for pharmaceuticals as a developing nation adopts a strong IP regime.

The analysis begins with a familiar vertical differentiation model of two firms selling differentiated goods to consumers with differing tastes, and then introduces asymmetric information. The local pharmacist, the economic decision maker, carries either brand-name or generic drugs. Brand-name pharmacists possess private information about the quality mix of their drugs, carrying real drugs, produced by international pharmaceutical firms, worthless counterfeits, or some combination thereof. Consumers are sensitive to the brandedness of the pharmaceuticals they purchase, as well as price.

The model examines the quality mix and pricing decisions of pharmacists in response to changes in intellectual property legislation and enforcement on the sale of counterfeit drugs. Initially, the representative developing country lacks any protection for intellectual property rights and the market is composed of real drugs, worthless counterfeits and generic copies. With the signing of an international trade agreement, the developing country begins providing strong protection for intellectual property rights. The strengthened commitment to intellectual property rights makes it impossible for government officials to ignore the established domestic firms that have historically produced generic copies of on-patent pharmaceuticals. These firms and the generic copies disappear. The branded pharmacist, now a local monopolist, continues to sell both real and counterfeit drugs. Without a concurrent improvement in enforcement, counterfeiting worsens.

The tension between industrialized and developing countries escalates when the issue of intellectual property rights is raised. Positions are passionately defended when the subject of pharmaceutical patents arises. Masquerading as curative medicines, counterfeit pharmaceuticals are increasingly prevalent. At a time of unprecedented global IP protection, this prevalence is alarming and puzzling. This work examines the problems associated with increasing intellectual property rights in developing countries, focusing on the transition to effective levels of enforcement. The results indicate that the institution of stronger IP protection removes efficacious generics from the market, increasing profits and the temptations of counterfeiting. Without a concurrent commitment to enforcement, stronger IP protection can do more harm than good.

References

[1] G.M. Grossman and C. Shapiro, Counterfeit-Product Trade, *American Economic Review* **78**(1) (March 1988), 59–75.

[2] G.M. Grossman and C. Shapiro, Foreign Counterfeiting of Status Goods, *Quarterly Journal of Economics* **103**(1) (February 1988), 79–100.

[3] N. Hajari, Swallowing Bitter Pills, *TIME* **151**(30) (26 January 1998), 261–270.

[4] D. Stipp, Farewell, my logo, *Fortune* **133**(10) (27 May 1996), 128–138.

Demand for pharmaceuticals under co-payment schemes: Evidence from Catalonia

Joan Costa[a,b], Joan Rovira[b] and Panos Kanavos[a]

[a]*LSE Health, London School of Economics, London, UK*

[b]*Grup de Recerca en Economia de la Politico Social, Barcelona, Catalonia, Spain*

Objective: This paper estimates the demand for pharmaceuticals under different co-payment schemes. Currently in Spain pharmaceuticals have been reimbursed when consumed under doctor prescription at a 40% and 10% co-payment rate. This paper accounts for the role of co-payment rates in the consumption of pharmaceuticals in order to estimate the aggregate demand for pharmaceuticals in Catalonia using the 1994 Catalan Health survey. We describe the decision making scheme that leads to the pharmaceutical demand and consumption.

Methodology: We use statistical and microeconometric models to test the sensibility of the demand for drugs to characteristics influencing demand for health care. In particular we consider age, health care utilisation, the influence of chronic and acute diseases, and finally regional and price variations.

Policy goals:

Expected results: The demand for pharmaceuticals is highly sensible to acute diseases. There is evidence of regional and medical practice influence in acute diseases as well. Age is the major explanatory variable such as individual income. Health surveys show extreme limitations as they do not sufficiently account for heterogeneity in pharmaceutical products, results may shed additional evidence if cross-country comparisons were undertaken.

A competing edge for the pharmaceutical industry: Propagating agile processes throughout the supply chain

N. Shaw and T. Burgess
Leeds University Business School, Maurice Keyworth Building, Leeds University, Leeds, LS2 9JT

The pharmaceutical industry is undergoing substantial change and is experiencing a variety of new market factors. New technologies, global economies, emerging markets and the nature of drug development all provide simultaneous threats and opportunities [1,2]. Specific developments in biotechnology and genomics, and the uncertainty surrounding the size and scope of those markets increase the future complexity of this industry. The UK pharmaceutical industry presents interesting challenges for both manufacturers and researchers.

This paper draws upon UK government papers on the industry and the findings and methodologies generated from a three-year, multi-disciplinary research project called BRITEST (http://www.britest.co.uk/HomePage.asp), value £1.3M, which focussed upon improving new product and manufacturing process development. The aims were to reduce the time to market, levels of capital expenditure in new projects and overall asset responsiveness. The link with value chain performance is discussed in this paper and issues for future research set out.

References

[1] Keynote Hybrid Report on Prescribed Pharmaceuticals, http://hybrid.keynote.co.uk/keynotecd/HOME/dcrypt0.htm to http://hybrid.keynote.co.uk/keynotecd/HOME/dcrypt9.htm, 2000.
[2] S. Howitt, The Chemical Industry Keynote Report: 2000 Market Report, ISBN 1-84168-036-2, 2000.

The dynamics of global and local: Organisational dilemmas and struggles in a pharmaceutical company

Stefan Sveningsson
Department of Business Administration, Lund University, Box 7080, SE 220 07 Lund, Sweden
E-mail: Stefan.Sveningsson@fek.lu.se

Introduction

The empirical investigations of globalisation in organizations are often cast in general forms, focusing on some overall logic behind and effects of presumed global organizational forms and models. Much has been written about 'global webs', 'the borderless organization', 'the new organizations' and 'the lean networking organization' (Parker, 1999; Prud'homme van Reine, 1996). Part of the research has focused on the advantages of globalisation in order to sustain efficiency on account of the possibility to create 'lean' and 'efficient' organizations in which strategic resource allocation is made at central and thus global organizational levels. Another part of the research has focused upon the need to complement global strategies and universal organizational models with local initiatives and creativity, hence the talk of combining global and local into what is sometimes referred to as 'glocal'. All this research has been important since it has broadened the mainly conceptual understanding of globalism in organizations as well as the potential advantages and presumed problems of such efforts.

However, despite many contributions on a conceptual level, there are relatively few empirical studies addressing specific globalisation processes in organizations on a micro level. Consequently, our understanding of specific processes and situations of globalisation, its presumed advantages and problems, in, between, and around organizations is still somewhat poor. As some authors have pointed out, there is a lack of in-depth studies of specific acts, events and processes in organization studies in general. (Prud'homme van Reine, 1996). Analyses of globalisation in organizations is often caught in the traps of reification, and in mixing process and process outcomes in strategic and organizational analysis. Concepts such as 'global', 'local', 'glocal', 'global strategies' are treated as things or thing-like phenomena. In opposition to this dominating approach, the approach used here focuses on the specifics of globalisation in organizations, described in some detail. I attempt to contribute to a situational understanding of organizational phenomena, being more 'close' to empirical phenomena in organizations (everyday practice), focusing specific instances of globalisation and struggles within the global-local dynamics in an organizational context.

This is done through an investigation of globalisations practices in a pharmaceutical company, Pharma Inc. A pharmaceutical corporation constitute an especially interesting arena for investigations into and analyses of globalisation practices. This because of the emphasis regularly put on creativity and innovation in such corporations, an emphasis that partly challenges some of the main ideas in the global discourse. The tensions and challenges that emerge from the establishing of the global discourse thus presents managers and personnel at all levels in such organizations with fundamental dilemmas concerning the very future of the corporations.

The study

Pharma Inc., is a large research-intensive pharmaceutical corporation and the result of a merger between two corporations, of American and Swedish origin respectively. The empirical study here presented was largely conducted at a former subsidiary in the Swedish corporation. This company was founded in the forties and became international mainly during the seventies. The internationalisation was organized predominantly through the establishing of local independent subsidiaries in commercially viable markets, an organization that proved to be very successful. The corporation developed substantially during the eighties and became a world player in a few markets. However, in the middle of the nineties some of its products matured and corporate management searched for a merger candidate. The corporation subsequently merged with another pharmaceutical in the end of the nineties and Pharma was hence created.

Pharma Inc. is today quite traditionally horizontally differentiated into several global functions of which R&D is the largest in terms of both money and people. The R&D function is in its turn organized into local research cells scattered world wide and a variety of global sub-functions that are dispersed across the local cells, the consequence being that for every sub-function within R&D there is a global as well as local level. Since the merger the formerly local companies have been transformed from being independent subsidiaries to becoming substantially less independent local research cells.

Turning global

In the merger the concept of global was raised as a key topic by the upper echelons of management. While both the companies that entered the merger previously had been considered as being international the new corporation that emerged was to be seen as global. Since the merger, the corporation, the industry and the market has been reconceptualized in terms of global. In public statements the company is described as being "a corporation of impressive size and global scope" operating on a "global high-tech market" and the new organization as a "global restructuring of the pharmaceutical operations". Although global might refer to many things, "harmonization" among local cells (the former independent subsidiaries) is what most managers refer to, implying that drug development in some respects can be organized similar independent of local circumstances. To accomplish this corporate management have issued standardized operating models to be implemented throughout the corporation. This effort was also accompanied by efforts of centralization in decision-making areas where the former independent subsidiaries had a large scope of action, i.e. some investments, recruitments and project priorities. The logic behind this kind of globalisation concerns about allocating resources between local cells more efficiently by reducing overlapping activities within functions and/or projects. A global and homogenous organization is also supposedly more flexible when it comes to allocating resources because of easy comparisons among cells. Many of the decisions concerning larger investments have thus been centralized away from the local level, where the local cell manager now has minor coordinating tasks. The local functional managers are now responsible to the global heads rather than to the head of the cell. Both the implementation of the standardized operating models and the centralization efforts are putting a lot of pressure at the local level to exhibit both compliance to the corporate administrative demands and local creative initiatives in order to deliver commercially viable products.

These organizational practices are based on notions of global as "world wide homogenisation" (Levitt, 1983) and the talk of "global strategies" (Bartlett and Ghosal, 1989; Hastings, 1993). Prud'homme van Reine (1996) claims that the organization most referred to in this respect is the Swedish -Swiss merger Asea Brown Bovery. Wiseman (in Prud'homme van Reine, 1996:93) characterizes ABB "as a lean firm that employs communication effectively in thinking globally and acting locally". Pharma Inc. are using the same concepts in order to reduce tensions and this has resulted in talk of "glocalism", as one manager explained: "There's really no conflict between the global and local level, we combine them into what we describe as glocalism."

Local intricacies

However, the enthusiastic comments by global managers, usually referred to in a likewise enthusiastic business press, are rare at the local level. Local managers more often raise the problems of having global managers rarely present as one researcher expresses:

> "But in the old company (before the merger) I felt like: It was me, I had my department manager, I had my R&D manager and then I had the manager of the company. You met him sometimes. It wasn't that many steps. Since this new organization has come ... its like the company manager is sitting on the moon."

The extensive travelling by many managers as a result of scattering research facilities all over the world, have subsequently led to presumed problems of coordination of cell managers raising questions about the necessity of travelling as such. Several managers have raised the problems of having "global functions that are building their own castles irrespective of each other". The global discourse thus seems to lay a ground for fragmentation tendencies at the local level, hence raising further coordination demands on local cell managers. In sum then, the talk of global and the organizational changes following that seem to have created tendencies of both a higher degree of hierarchization and fragmentation between functions at the local level.

The development has, both at the local and global level raised questions about whether the globalisation practice hinders the possibility of delivering drugs on a creative and innovative basis. Parallel to the globalisation process there's a widespread belief in Pharma Inc. that effective drug development is partly based on creativity, small scale teams and mavericks working under principles of self governing rather than any universal principles of standardized and global operating models- In these situations, neither the mantra 'think global – act local' nor the more mundane operating models, issued from global levels, has been adopted and thereby become useful at the local level. Efforts of global managers to reduce tensions have proved difficult and the globalisation process has to some extent lost its momentum.

Purpose of the paper

Research on globalisation in organizations is meagre. To the extent that globalisation in practice, in spite of some conceptual claims, is followed by not only advantages of resource allocation but also extensive standardization and hierarchization, it obviously creates tensions and struggles at the local level. These tension and struggles concerns about what is considered to be of central importance in the pharmaceutical industry, namely creativity and innovation. Emerging out of this are organizational and managerial dilemmas that bears upon the long-term survival of the corporation. The paper takes seriously the advantages of globalism in the pharmaceutical industry, but also raises the need to investigate further the dilemmas of modern organizational notions of what constitute effective drug development. The paper does not purport to be normative in the sense of advising how to organise effective drug development. The purpose it to exhibits the inherent ambiguity, contradictions and dilemmas in advancing talk of global in pharmaceutical companies. Unless empirically rich and detailed studies of globalisation in organisations are done, much of what is said about it at an organizational level remains vague and mysterious for those targeted by it.

Pharmaceuticals Policy and Law 5 (2002) 211
IOS Press

Appendix 3

Main points of the Round-table "Globalization in Biopharmaceuticals"

For the first time, a round-table was organized in order to foster discussions between academics and industry players.

We summarize three main discussion points for future research:

1. Corruption.
   A dominant research question which emerged during the round-table, for the European scene, was corruption. It is not usually a research topic of great interest to academics (as contributions to this publication can show). However, most participants recognized that corruption spreads very fast in the pharmaceutical sector, and that there is especially a growing concern on the lack of effective enforcement powers.
2. Issues of enforcement.
   Most representative members in the audience recognized the limitation of regulations as an effective enforcement means. Police enforcement was also discussed as not sufficient. K. Lybecker's contribution on the Indonesian case suggested selecting a visible target as a point of entry for enforcement. Shifting competencies between different levels (local, regional, national and international) was also discussed as a way of establishing countervailing forces in corruption.
3. New visions on business models.
   Contributions during the workshop on agile manufacturing, nutraceuticals and the new P's in pharmaceutical marketing were good examples of needs for new visions for the biopharmaceutical industry and interesting areas for research applied to that sector.

Pharmaceuticals Policy and Law 5 (2002) 213–214
IOS Press

Appendix 4

The growing importance of trade and global issues

Christine Huttin

A representative from the EU trade division was invited to the workshop, and this provided an opportunity to enlarge the policy research questions from health and industrial issues to trade issues. It also shows the need to address health and trade policy questions simultaneously in the context of globalization.

The impact of globalization is very visible inside the European institutions, with substantial enlargement of competencies and powers to different directorates. For instance, in September 2000, the Development directorate and the Trade directorate of the European Commission decided to accelerate a set of actions on major communicable diseases (Malaria, TBC and HIV). So pharmaceutical issues became much more dependent on trade and development negotiations than on balanced arrangements reached by health and industry interests. This also shows the predominance of globalization issues over European interests. For instance, the priorities on the political agenda became access to affordable medicines and allocation of research to broader types of medicines and vaccines rather than developing drugs usually used for treating conditions prevalent in industrialized countries.

On the European political agenda, the two most advanced domains in 2002 concern intellectual property and pricing. The European Union adopted the special declaration at Doha concerning public health. By this, the EU agrees with compulsory licensing rights, rights of parallel importing and some extension of a transition period for an implementation of the TRIPS agreement till 2016. The compulsory licensing issue was especially discussed during the first post Doha TRIPS council (Geneva, March 2002). This issue is crucial for developing countries, but indirectly might affect strategic industrial interests of the USA, Japan and Europe. Countries without manufacturing capacities claim the right to import with a compulsory license from a third country with manufacturing facilities. The main points of current discussion concern territorial limits and types of restrictions on production volume. The USA supports the view that only a very limited percentage of a country's manufacturing capacity should be considered in this type of compulsory licensing. By contrast on this restriction issue the European Union is ready to consider what are called "constructive ambiguities". In particular, wide divergence of views exist on the definition of the "non-predominant part" of a third party country's manufacturing capacity.

The current proposals on trade issues are crucial for a redefinition of stakeholders' interests. In particular, in preparation of the second TRIPS Council of June 2002, it will be important to follow the modifications of article 31F, with potential withdrawal of restrictions and the proposals for revisions and interpretations of article 30. WTO members countries without production capacities could obtain a compulsory licensing, without prior authorization from the country with the patent. However, an alternative to a modification of compulsory licensing rules could be to negotiate voluntary licensing on an ad hoc basis or for certain categories of countries.

Pharmaceuticals Policy and Law 5 (2002) 215–216
IOS Press

Author Index Volume 5 (2002)